MONMOUTHSHIRE VILLAGES

Geoffrey Davies

© Geoffrey Davies, 2015

All Rights Reserved. No part of this publication may be reproduced, stored in a retrieval system, or transmitted in any form or by any means – electronic, mechanical, photocopying, recording, or otherwise – without prior written permission from the publisher or a licence permitting restricted copying issued by the Copyright Licensing Agency, 90 Tottenham Court Road, London W1P 0LA. This book may not be lent, resold, hired out or otherwise disposed of by trade in any form of binding or cover other than that in which it is published, without the prior consent of the publisher.

Moral Rights: The author has asserted his moral right to be identified as the Author of this Work.

Published by Sigma Leisure – an imprint of
Sigma Press, Stobart House, Pontyclerc, Penybanc Road, Ammanford, Carmarthenshire SA18 3HP.

British Library Cataloguing in Publication Data
A CIP record for this book is available from the British Library.

ISBN: 978-1-910758-15-1

Typesetting and Design by: Sigma Press, Ammanford.

Cover photograph: Cwmyoy © Geoffrey Davies

Drawings: © Geoffrey Davies

Printed by:Akcent Media Ltd

Disclaimer: The information in this book is given in good faith and is believed to be correct at the time of publication. No responsibility is accepted by either the author or publisher for errors or omissions.

Foreword

Geoff took his degree at Lampeter – the oldest University institution in Wales founded in 1822. Here he studied History under the distinguished Professor Douglas Chandaman. But like many of us who graduated through that Department, Geoff's interests went much wider than the university syllabus, and in recent years he has centred on the history and topography of the villages in the old counties of Wales. His splendid contributions are long overdue.

In the last few years Geoff has produced fine works on the villages of Glamorganshire, Pembrokeshire and Carmarthenshire, and now he brings us his valuable study on the villages of that most lovely and enigmatic border county of Monmouthshire. Just in living memory it was officially declared a part of Wales rather than just a fascinating 'bolt-on' to England. For instance, Arthur Mee's *Monmouthshire* sits coyly in the 'Kings England' series! And, 'enigmatic'? Certainly, for the old county of Monmouthshire takes so many contrasting influences from both east and west. It rubs shoulders with Gloucestershire and Herefordshire – and it nods to its near neighbour over the Wye, the magical 'island' of the Forest of Dean... and onwards over the Severn to the City and County of Bristol – and yet further on to Somerset.

Geoff has researched his subject thoroughly, and in this volume he takes account not only of what C.J.O. Evans has to say in the increasingly rare *History and Topography of Monmouthshire*, but also on much more recent works – amongst them the studies done on the Medieval Churches of Monmouthshire by Dr John Morgan-Guy, the influential works of Canon E.T. Davies, and the very recent works by Canon Arthur Edwards. But again, he has gone back to the classics on Monmouthshire, such as the valuable late 18th century studies of Archdeacon Coxe.

I commend this book most heartily. It deals with the smaller communities of Monmouthshire with a warm and human eye. It takes account of significant buildings including the churches and chapels. Again it often looks at the architects of the more modern buildings – and just like C.J.O. Evans, it examines the way in which areas have developed and changed as transport and communications responded to the Industrial Revolution. It also looks at more recent decline and then regeneration in the industrial Valley communities.

Truly this is a book for all seasons.

Richard Fenwick, Bishop of St Helena
Bishopsholme
St Helena
July 2015

(Dean of Monmouth and Vicar of Newport 1997-2011)

Contents

Introduction 7

Villages of the Monmouthshire 13
(in alphabetical order)

Bibliography 240

Introduction

For the purposes of this book, villages that were within the boundaries of the old county prior to 1972 are included, meaning that the administrative areas of Monmouthshire, Newport, Blaenau Gwent, Torfaen and Caerphilly, east of the River Rhymney are covered. This area is roughly equivalent to the old Kingdom of Gwent. The definition of a village is difficult as some towns are smaller than some of the villages in the book. Many villages have been swallowed up by the expansion of Newport. The old part of Caerleon is included as this has the atmosphere of a village and expansion has taken place outside the former boundaries.

Geography

The old county was in the main bordered by the Rivers Rhymney, Monnow and Wye, though around Monmouth the county extends beyond the Monnow and Wye. The Severn Estuary provides the southern boundary. The Usk flows from the border near Crickhowell past Abergavenny to Caerleon and on to Newport. The area between the Usk and the Wye is relatively well wooded, but the forests today are much smaller than at the time of the Norman Conquest. Parts of the mountainous north-western area are within the boundaries of the Brecon Beacons National Park. The western valleys were heavily industrialized, which directly led to the expansion of Newport from a small town with a population of under 1,100 in 1801 into a major port with a population of 67,000 in 1901. Iron and later coal and steel were the major products, though the iron industry was also to be found around Tintern in the beautiful Wye Valley. The valleys of the Rhymney, Ebbw, Sirhowy and Lwyd (Welsh Rhymni, Sirhywi, Ebwy and Lwyd) lie in the west of the old county. Much of the area south of the M4 between Chepstow and Newport and Newport and Cardiff is flat land, reclaimed from the sea and lying below the high tide levels, protected by sea walls and drainage ditches. The mountainous region to the north and west of Abergavenny, including the Blorenge, Sugar Loaf, Skirrid and Black Mountains are part of the Brecon Beacons National Park.

Both the Usk and Wye were navigable and provided an early form of transportation, the Wye as far as Monmouth and the Usk to Caerleon.

Roads were poor and in evidence to the House of Commons in the 1750s Valentine Morris said there were no roads in Monmouthshire. When asked how people travelled he replied "We travel in ditches". As industry developed a canal was constructed connecting Brecon with Newport. Tramways connected the iron and coal industries to the canal. Later the railways provided the major transportation infrastructure, though this has in turn given way to roads, often built on the old rail tracks.

History

This was the land of the Silures, who fought the Romans for some 30 years from 48 AD before Rome prevailed. The Roman fort of Isca (Caerleon) was established on the River Usk and Venta Siluram (Caerwent) became the administrative centre.

According to legend, after the Romans left, Caerleon became the centre of King Arthur's kingdom and there are many stories of battles with the Anglo Saxons. During the Dark Ages Wales was rarely united, but divided into a number of small kingdoms of which Gwent was one. An early king of the area around Newport was St Gwynllyw the Bearded, to whom, under the English version of his name, St Woolos Cathedral at Newport is dedicated. He was the father of St Catwg and the area was Christianized from the 5th century.

Prior to the Norman Conquest the Kingdom of Morgannwg stretched from the Towy to Gloucester Bridge and included parts of Herefordshire, Breconshire, Gloucestershire and Carmarthenshire. The name referred to King Morgan the Old, a 10th century monarch who had briefly united the kingdoms of Gwent and Glywysing (roughly equivalent to Glamorgan). Previously the Kingdom of Gwent had emerged after the Romans left Britain and derived its name from Venta Siluram. The area largely corresponded with the Iron Age tribal area of the Silures. Gwent and Glywysing were again united in 1055 under Gruffydd ap Llywelyn who died in 1063. In the 8th century the Mercian King Offa constructed a dyke defining the border between Wales and Mercia from Chepstow to the estuary of the River Dee in the north. There is some dispute over the attribution of the whole dyke to Offa, but the long distance Offa's Dyke Footpath borders a number of the villages covered in this book.

The Normans arrived in the area shortly after 1066 and the whole of Morgannwg came under the Marcher lords, with lordships established at

Abergavenny, Caerleon, Monmouth, Striguil (later Chepstow) and Usk. This was a time of castle and church building with the Celtic wooden churches replaced by more permanent stone structures. It was also a period when the monasteries of Llantarnum, Llanthony and Tintern were established.

Under Edward I the Principality of Wales was established, covering Anglesey, Caernarvonshire, Merionethshire, Cardiganshire, Carmarthenshire and Flintshire. The rest of Wales, including parts of Gloucestershire, Worcestershire, Herefordshire and Shropshire remained under the Marcher Lords until 1536.

Wales and Monmouthshire

Under Henry VIII there were two Acts of Parliament, the first in 1535-6 was "An Acte for Laws & Justice to be ministred in Wales in like fourme as it is in this Realme" the second in 1542 was "An Acte for certaine Ordinaunces in the Kinges Majesties Domynion and Principalitie of Wales". The Acts are known as Laws in Wales Acts 1535-42. The intention of Henry VIII was to unify his kingdom into a single sovereign state with a single judicial system and to end the privileges of the Marcher Lords coupled with the lawlessness of the Marches. Five new counties were created in total, Monmouthshire, Brecknockshire, Radnorshire, Montgomeryshire and Denbighshire. Twelve of the counties were divided into four circuits for judges, while Monmouthshire for this purpose was joined with English counties. This gave rise to the notion that Monmouthshire was no longer part of Wales and in the 19th century books, such as Samuel Lewis's *Topographical Dictionary of Wales*, excluded the county. This was not the intention of the Tudors, as Shakespeare showed in his play, *Henry V*, written in 1599 where Henry, who was born in Monmouth, proclaims to Fluellen "For I am Welsh, you know, good countryman". And Fluellen replies "All the water in Wye cannot wash your majesty's Welsh plood out of your pody".

Parliament added to the confusion by including Monmouthshire in certain Acts related to Wales but not others. The Sunday Closing (Wales) Act 1881 did not apply to Monmouthshire though it was extended to the county by legislation in 1921. The Disestablishment of the Anglican Church in Wales Act of 1920 included churches in Monmouthshire (other than those that elected to join Hereford) but not those around Oswestry.

The issue was finally settled by the Local Government Act 1972, which provided that "in every act passed on or after 1 April 1974, and in every instrument made on or after that date under any enactment (whether before, on or after that date) 'Wales', subject to any alterations of boundaries..." included "the administrative county of Monmouthshire and the county borough of Newport".

The 1535-6 Act provided parliamentary representation in Wales for the first time and introduced the system of Justices of the Peace, Sheriffs and Lords Lieutenant. It also ended the system of Gavelkind or Cyfran, whereby a man's estate passed equally among his sons and replaced it with the system of Primogeniture where the first born inherited.

The Welsh Language

There has been controversy over the effects of the 1535-6 Acts on the language with the banning of Welsh from the Law Courts and an insistence that "from henceforth no Person or Persons that use the Welch Speech or Language, shall have or enjoy any manner Office or Fees within this Realm of England, Wales, or other the King's Dominion". The immediate effect was actually to increase the use of the Welsh language in towns. Prior to the Act the language of the towns was almost exclusively English, but by the time of Queen Elizabeth more Welsh was used than English even in a border town like Abergavenny. The Welsh or British language was the dominant tongue in Monmouthshire well into the 19th century. As the South Wales Argus reported as late as 1890, employers in Newport demanded bilingual ability in their apprentices. The Welsh language and culture were encouraged in the county in the 19th century by prominent figures such as Lady Llanover.

Gwenhwyseg or Gwentian Welsh, derived from the Silures, was the language of South East Wales and indeed was the language of the North Walian princes' courts and bards prior to 1300. Pronunciation differs from that of Mid and North Wales and despite the lack of Welsh speakers is still reflected in the local English dialects and the pronunciation of place names. Perhaps the best known example is the Cardiff accent where the city's name becomes 'Cairdiff', with the long 'A' sound pronounced as in fair or care, while the diphthong 'OE' in Pencoed is pronounced as 'O' as in code. In many cases the anglicized spelling reflects the original Gwentian pronunciation, as in the River Monnow, where pronunciation of the final 'Y' in the Welsh form of Mynwy is dropped. Little true Gwentian Welsh is now spoken in the county, while the language taught in schools tends to be the Irish tainted North Walian pronunciation. Some spellings also change. For example St Cadog as he is known in West Wales is more usually St Catwg or Cattwg in the churches of Monmouthshire. As is normal in Welsh, the first letter of a word mutates depending on the word that precedes it, so Catwg becomes Llangatwg and 'Melin' and 'Bach' becomes 'Y felin fach' (The little mill).

Religion

Religion played an important part in the history of the county. The early kings of Gwent were converted to Christianity and many of the local saints were of the local royal families. The early history of the church is not always clear as the written record in the *Liber Landavensis* was compiled in 1125 when the Normans were intent on establishing the importance of the cathedral at Llandaff. However it contains details of 149 charters gifting land to the church and is therefore an important record of the history of Wales and the county. Caerleon was the ancient seat of the bishops which was moved by St David to Minevia (St David's), away from the Anglo-Saxon invaders. The diocese of Llandaff included Monmouthshire although the town of Monmouth was in the diocese of Hereford, while the parishes of Cwmyoy and Llanthony were in the diocese of St David's. Llandaff's Bishop's Palace was at Mathern with possibly another at Bishton. The Diocese of Monmouth was created in 1921. The Newport Cathedral of St. Woolos, King & Confessor was designated the pro cathedral of the Diocese in 1922 but only granted full cathedral status in 1949.

A number of the landed families continued their allegiance to the Roman Catholic Church after the break with Rome which, in some cases, continues to this day. Prior to the English Civil War the county exhibited little of the dissent seen across the Severn in Bristol. The county was loyal to the King. A non-conformist chapel was established by William Wroth in 1639 at Llanvaches where he had been rector but had been ejected for refusing to adhere to the *Book of Common Prayer*. Wroth was a relatively mild non-conformist and had not envisaged breaking with the established church. During the time of Cromwell there was a concerted effort to bring the Puritan message to the county. The Act for the Propagation of the

Gospel in Wales, 1650, led to a missionary campaign in the Welsh language by Walter Cradock and Henry Walter. Churches were damaged during this period with rood screens removed and preaching crosses destroyed. After the restoration of the monarchy, the non-conformist movement continued with chapels being built and rebuilt through the following centuries. The latter part of the 20th century saw a marked decline in attendance at religious services with many chapels and churches closing. Some have been demolished, others have been adapted for community use or as dwellings. A few have been adopted by the Friends of Friendless Churches and preserved.

Where older texts are quoted the original spellings are used.

Villages of the Monmouthshire

Aberbeeg (Welsh: Aber-bîg)

Aberbeeg is a former mining village a mile and a half south of Abertillery. It takes its name from the Nant Big which flows into the River Ebbw here. The first colliery in the village was sunk around 1860 by the Aberbeeg Colliery Company. It changed hands on a number of occasions before being purchased by Budd and Co in 1902. Known locally as Budd's it employed up to 334 men before closing in 1926. It was sited between Cwm Road and the railway beneath the modern flyover. By 1880 the village had its own malthouse and brewery as well as the Ivorites Inn and the Hanbury Arms, a school and reading room.

The large Aberbeeg Primitive Methodist Chapel on Aberbeeg Road was built in 1889 and rebuilt in 1905. Now known as Aberbeeg Methodist Church it remains in use. The large, Grade II Listed Christ Church was built in 1909 to plans by Edwin Arthur Johnson of Abergavenny. Enjoying an elevated position, it has a nave, north and south transepts, a chapter and vestry as well as a tower. The architect also made provision for an extension to the nave to the west. Situated on Pantddu Road, the church was deconsecrated in 2012 due to structural faults and a falling congregation. The congregation has now joined St Mark's at Llanhilleth.

Near the church is the Abertillery Cottage Hospital, built in 1920 and funded by the miners of the Abertillery area. The gates form a war memorial with a plaque which reads "The Abertillery Municipal Officers as a tribute to their colleagues who served in the Great War 1914-1918".

There has been little development in the village which is relatively small and scattered. There is a modern medical centre. The railway passes through the village but the nearest station is at Llanhilleth.

The ghost of a cloaked, tall-hatted man is said to haunt the road between Aberbeeg and Cwm. Some believe it to be PC Hosea Pope who died as a result of a heart attack during a scuffle with a local man in 1911.

Aberffrwd

Aberffrwd is a hamlet five miles south-east of Abergavenny at the confluence of the Ffrwd Brook and the River Usk.

Aberffrwd corn mill was operational until 1921 and fed by a 600 yard leat part of which was destroyed by the A40.

To the north, beyond the A40 is Llansantffraed Court. Now a hotel the Court was built in 1912 as a mansion more typical of Surrey, constructed of decorated red brick beneath a tiled roof. Nearby is St Bridget's Church, a Norman church retaining many original features though it was restored in 1856-7 by John Prichard and John Pollard Seddon. The restoration saw the porch moved to the west and a new wagon roof. Aerial views indicate that the chancel is what is known as a weeping chancel, out of line with the nave. It used to be said that this was symbolic of Christ's head leaning to one side on the cross, but modern scholarship suggests that nave and chancel were built at different times and the builders used sunrise on Easter day to determine east and of course the date of Easter changes from year to year. There is a nave and chancel with a bellcote added prior to the Victorian restoration. In the churchyard is the four stepped base of a medieval cross with part of the original shaft, though the upper part and crosshead are modern.

Abertysswg   Mouth of the Tysswg

Abertysswg is a former mining village in the Rhymney Valley a mile and a quarter north-west of New Tredegar. Originally in Monmouthshire, the village developed after the opening of the Mclaren Colliery in 1897. The Colliery was named after Sir Charles Mclaren, a director of the Tredegar Iron and Coal Co. Ltd.

The Colliery employed 1,833 men in 1913. It closed in 1959 but the shaft continued in use for access to the Ogilvie Colliery a mile and a half south west, which eventually closed in 1975. Seventeen miners were killed in an explosion at the Mclaren in 1902.

The village only developed after the opening of the colliery and churches and chapels followed. Jerusalem Calvinistic Methodist Chapel in Alexander Street was built in 1903 but is no longer in use. Elim Tabernacle Pentecostal Chapel on Warn Terrace is a corrugated tin structure. Bethania Welsh Independent Chapel on Walter Street was built in 1902 but has since been demolished. Ainon Welsh Baptist Chapel on

Walter Street was built in 1906 but has since been demolished with a sign in the garden marking the site. St Paul's Mission Church next to the school is a large church built in 1903. It has recently been refurbished and has a hall beneath the church.

There is a modern community centre facing the Green, a small park and play area and the Abertysswg Working Men's Club on Walter Street, but no pub in the village. There are a number of village shops and takeaway restaurants. The Tredegar and Rhymney Golf Club course sits above the village and there are playing fields on the site of the old colliery. There is a village primary school although this is under threat. There has been some new building in the village, but most of the housing dates from the early 20th century.

Aberystruth

This was a parish also known as Blaenau Gwent (The extremity of Gwentland) which covered a large area that included Nant-y-glo and Blaina, though there was never a village of this name. The parish church was St Peter's, first built in around 1500, in what is now the town of Blaina. The present church is the fourth to bear the dedication. The original church was visited by Archdeacon Coxe in 1801 who described it as a handsome gothic building with a square tower. There was a nave and north aisle but no chancel. Coxe also comments on the 1779 book by Edmund Jones, a Congregationalist minister, *A Geographical, Historical and Religious Account of the Parish of Aberystruth* which contained a section on the ""apparition of fairies and other spirits of hell" like a company of children, with music and dancing. He asserts, that they frequented the parish of Aberystruth, as much or more than any parish of Wales, and were particularly fond of Havodavel and Kevenbach, because they were dry, lightsome, and pleasant places, where they were often seen leaping, and making a waving path in the air. He seriously warns his countrymen not to think them happy spirits, because they delight in music and dancing, or because they are called in Monmouthfhire, "Mothers' blessing, and Fair folks of the wood". He narrates several childish stories of people who heard them sing, but could never learn the tune; who heard them talk, but could seldom distinguish the words; of many who were tormented and wounded by them, and of others who were transported through the air. He also gives an instance of their apparition from his own experience... This whimsical publication would have been unworthy of notice, did it not shew the tendency of the people in these mountainous and sequestered regions, to credit superstitious tales".

Argoed The Trees

Argoed is today a quiet rural village in the Sirhowy valley, a mile and a half north of Blackwood. Coal mining came early to the village with the Cwm Crach pits producing house coal prior to 1840. In 1842 the pit was owned by the Tredegar Colliery Company employing 141 men but numbers steadily declined and in 1923 only two men were working there. The Llanover colliery was sunk in 1912 to the north-east of the village and closed in the 1930s. It employed up to 434 men. New Road by-passes the village which was once served by the Sirhowy branch of the London and North Western Railway, closed in 1960.

There was a corn mill and a woollen mill in the valley with a mill race providing power. The village had two inns in 1879, the Argoed Arms and the Castle Inn. The Welfare Hall and Institute was converted from two houses during the First World War, but later became the Sirhowy Arms Hotel which has now closed and used to provide bed and breakfast accommodation. In 2014 it was the scene of the murder of Ceris Yemm in what was alleged to have been a cannibalistic attack. The only licensed premise remaining is the Reform Club.

The attractive Argoed Baptist Chapel set above the High Street was built in 1817, renovated in 1851 and again in 1890. Argoed Methodist Chapel, constructed of corrugated iron was built in 1900 but has now been demolished. On a hillside a quarter of a mile to the south-east of the village stood the Penmaen parish church of St Philip and St James. The church was built in 1855 to the design of the London architect John Norton. It was a Gothic stone structure comprised of a nave, chancel, south porch, spire, and one bell. It was deconsecrated in 1969 and has now been demolished though the graveyard remains under the parish of St David Penmaen (Oakdale).

Ashvale (Welsh: Dyffryn Onnen)

Ashvale is a largely modern development a mile north-west of Tredegar. In 1880 there was Ashvale House and Ashvale Cottages to the south of the railway with the Crown Inn, a smithy, school and brickworks to the north. There were also the Quick Pit and Bryn Bach coal mines but these, like the brickworks, had closed by 1901. Over the following 20 years more houses were built along Birch Grove, now known as Merthyr Road and Ashvale. The major development was post World War II in the form of a housing estate with development continuing.

The village has a primary school, village store and the Ashvale Supper Bar. There are a number of factories and a football ground. The area around the old Bryn Bach colliery is now a park with a lake.

Bassaleg (Welsh: Basaleg)

Bassaleg today is a suburb of Newport, two miles west of the city centre and a little over a mile north west of Tredegar House, home of the Morgan family. The local pronunciation is Baizelig.

There are a number of explanations of the name. The generally accepted version is that it derives from the Latin 'basilica', meaning a religious building constructed on the site of a saint's or martyr's shrine. There was a Celtic church here dedicated to St Gwladys, wife of Gwynlliw (St Woolos) and mother of Catwg. According to legend she was persuaded to live apart from Gwynlliw and moved to Bassaleg which became the mother church of the cantref of Gwynlliog, more important for a time than St Woolos'. A priory of black monks of the Benedictine Order was founded by Robert de Haye, and his wife, Gundreda, in 1101 which became a cell to Glastonbury Abbey though this was abandoned in 1235. By the middle of the 19th century the only remains of the priory, was a ruin situated in a dense wood, about a mile from the church, which is supposed to have been part of the structure. In 1079 the church was completed on its present site, it was re-built between 1101-1126 and together with six daughter churches, was made over to the Abbey of St Mary at Glastonbury. The Black Monks of the Benedictine Order were given fishing, pasture and wood rights on the de Haye lands free of charge until the Priory Church was leased to the Bishop of Llandaff

In the 19th century a number of antiquarians put forward other explanations for the name Bassaleg, including the Revd. W. Gunn who, in his translation of *Historia Brittonum* by Nennius, argues that Bassaleg was the birthplace of Merlin. "Nennius says, Merlin was born, in regione quae vocatur Glevising. It is in the hundred of Gwaunllwg. In campo Electi, that is, in the field of battle, or camp of Electus. Now, the Welsh for campus Electi would be Maes Elect; and not far from Caerleon there is a village called in Welsh Maesaleg, and commonly at present Bassaleg." "On a comparison of these names; the true reading of Nennius would be 'In campo Allecti', that is, in the camp or field of Alectus, the Roman general; and this being the birth-place of Merlin, according to Nennius, the city of the ten thousand must necessarily have been Caerleon, in this instance." A field to the south of Bassaleg still bears the name Maes Arthur, while nearby is Craig y Saeson, held by many to have been a Saxon encampment.

The church at Bassaleg is dedicated to St Basil and from the start of the 19th century it became the site of the family mausoleum of the Morgan family of Tredegar House and there are a large number of monuments to the Morgans. The tower dates from the Tudor period with some 14-15th century features of the chancel intact, but the church was extensively remodelled in the 19th and early 20th centuries. In 1878-9 the Morgan family architects, Habershon Fawckner & Co reconstructed the medieval nave arcade. In 1902 C.B. Fowler restored the chancel, while in 1916 W.D. Caröe converted the Morgan mausoleum into a chapel. This large church occupies a prominent position above the River Ebbw. The Tredegar Arms adjoins the churchyard.

In 1819 Dudgale recorded in his book *The New British Traveller* that "In the year 1811, the largest oak tree ever cut down in this kingdom, was felled at Bassaleg, near the canal. Of this tree, which was purchased by Mr. Harrison, the dimensions were as follow: The trunk, (10 foot in girth) measured 473 feet; twelve limbs altogether 2302 feet of sound timber; dead limbs 120 feet timber: and it required the labour of four men, for twenty days, to fell the tree and strip the bark!"

Beaufort (Welsh: Y Cendl)

Beaufort is a village a mile north of Ebbw Vale.

In 1779 Edward, Jonathan, Henry and Jonathan Kendall leased land from the Duke of Beaufort to build an ironworks. The Kendalls had extensive interests in the charcoal fired iron industry in the Midlands and the Lake District. The resulting village was initially known as Y Cendl but adopted the name Beaufort after the ironworks. In 1796 1,660 tons of iron was produced from a single furnace and three further furnaces were added by 1824, raising production to 7,276 tons in 1830. In 1833 the

Beaufort Ironworks was bought for £45,000 by Joseph and Crawshay Bailey to supply pig iron to the puddling furnaces and rolling mills of their Nantyglo Ironworks. A tramroad and incline connected the two works. The Bailey brothers operated seven furnaces at Beaufort. In 1871 ownership was transferred to the Blaina Iron & Steel Co. and the Beaufort works closed in 1873. The site of the ironworks has been covered with modern housing to the east of Beaufort Terrace. The southern block of Beaufort Terrace was formerly known as Shop Row. The Kendalls built a mansion known as Beaufort House which by 1920 was the Isolation Hospital, now the site of Plas-y-coed residential care home.

The old Parish Church of St. John was built by Crawshay Bailey in 1843, at a cost of £1,560, but was not consecrated until 1873. The Church was poor in design and workmanship, with a nave, north porch, and embattled tower with one bell. Minerals had been worked in close proximity, and it was condemned in 1890 as unfit for worship. It has been demolished and the site of the church and cemetery is behind houses on Newchurch Road. St David's church was built in 1892 to a design by George Eley Halliday. Consisting of a nave, chancel, vestry, north porch and a curious cube shaped bellcote, the church is built of yellow brick outside but with a red brick interior. Barham English Congregational Chapel on Rassau Road was built in 1859 and rebuilt in 1886. It has been demolished with new houses built on the site. Nearby Carmel English Independent Chapel was built in 1821and rebuilt in 1829 and 1865. It gave its name to the area of Carmeltown. A Baptist Chapel was built in the latter part of the 19th century on Beaufort Rise but has been demolished. Bethel English Wesleyan Methodist Church was built in 1832 and rebuilt in 1851 on Park View. It is still in use. Ebenezer Primitive Methodist Chapel on Primitive Place was built in 1825 and rebuilt in 1836, 1861 and 1906-12. It has now been demolished. Bethesda Calvinistic Methodist Chapel on Beaufort Rise was built in 1829, rebuilt in 1865 and demolished in 1980. Soar Welsh Baptist Chapel on Beaufort Rise was built in 1851 and rebuilt in 1861. It has now been converted to a guest house. Sardis Welsh Wesleyan Methodist Church was built before 1880 at the bottom of Beaufort Hill but has been demolished. Siloam Baptist Chapel on Heol Siloam was built in 1868 and closed in 1989, being demolished in 1991. Zion Wesleyan Methodist Chapel off South Street was built in 1849, rebuilt in 1903. Bethel English Presbyterian Chapel on Beaufort Hill was built in 1851, and rebuilt in 1865 and 1903. St Andrew's Church on Beaufort Hill was built in 1893-4 as a corrugated iron church. It was extended in 1902 and remains as a red corrugated iron building with western porch.

Beaufort has a theatre, housed in the former cinema, a welfare hall, two schools as well as a range of shops, takeaways and pubs. It is well served by parks and recreation areas and is proving a popular commuting centre with good road communication along the Heads of the Valleys Road.

St John's churchyard is said to be haunted by the ghost of a young woman who drowned in the river with her young baby. She had been abandoned by her supposed husband who married the daughter of a wealthy shipping family, who, ironically later drowned at sea.

Bedwas

Bedwas is a large village two miles north-east of Caerphilly. Its name is difficult. Borrow referred to it as Pentref Bettws. Betws in Welsh means oratory, but is thought to derive from the Anglo Saxon 'bedehus', a form of almshouse where the poor were given shelter in return for praying for their benefactor. Sabine Baring-Gould however offers St Bedwas, one of the twelve sons of Helig ab Glannog as a solution but also quotes the *Liber Landavensis* where a brook called Betguos or Betgues is mentioned as forming the boundary of, apparently, Llangoven, Monmouthshire, on the far side of the county. Betgues would later yield Bedwes, which also occurs in an early form for Bedwas. Others suggest a 'Place of Abundant Birch Trees'.

In 1876 Bedwas was a rural village of a single street stretching from the church alongside the Brecon and Merthyr Railway down the hill to Bedwas Bridge over the River Rhymney. The Bridge End Inn and Post office were at the bottom of the hill, while Church House Station and Hephzibah Chapel stood to the north with a boys' school and Felin Fach corn mill across the railway. Along the road which is now Church Street there were some dozen dwellings, a pub and the Wesleyan Methodist Chapel, all on the western side, with farmland to the east.

Bryngwyn Colliery was started in 1866 by W.S. Cartwright of Newport, half a mile west of the church on what is now Dol-y-pandy. The mine suffered from excess water after the closure of Energlyn, Cwmyglo and Rhos Llantwit Collieries and closed in1893 with the loss of 200 jobs. Attempts were made to revive the pit a year later and up to ten men were employed but it was finally abandoned in 1903. The scheduled ruins of the tall colliery engine house remain in woodland off Dol-y-pandy. Cwmyglo Colliery opened in 1873 and closed in 1893. It was situated at what is now Trethomas. The Energlyn Colliery was situated a mile and a half south-west of Bedwas on the outskirts of Caerphilly and was opened in 1858-59 by Thomas Thomas. Production ceased in 1889 but the colliery remained open for pumping until the Rhos Llantwit pit closed in 1892. The Rhos Llantwit Colliery opened in 1862 and was situated alongside what is now Bedwas Road, Caerphilly.

The sinking of Bedwas Navigation pit in 1909 led to an expansion of the village with a number of terraced streets including St Mary Street built around this time. Coal production started in 1912 and by 1923 employed 2,578 men. The colliery was situated half a mile to the east of the church. It was the subject of a number of accidents over the years, with three men dying as a result of an explosion in 1912, two in a roof fall in 1914 while a deputy was killed in an explosion in 1952. The colliery failed to re-open after the miners' strike in 1985.

The area between Hillside Terrace and Glebe Street was developed in the 1920s, while that to the east of the church came post 1945. Developments to the west are more recent.

There were three major farms in the village. Bedwas Fawr Farmhouse was on the site of what is now Peter's Food Service Ltd. Porset Farm was just to the north, while Glebe Farm was just north of the river, south-east of the Bridge End Inn. Next to the inn is Bridge House, dating from the 18th century, which was the old post Office. Pont Bedwas over the River Rhymney is attributed to William Edwards, son of the builder of the Old Bridge at Pontypridd.

Hephzibah Welsh Baptist Chapel on Church Street was built in 1851 and rebuilt in 1875. It remains in use but notices are in English. Bethel English Baptist Chapel on Church Street was originally built in 1901 but has been replaced by a modern building. The Wesleyan Methodist Chapel, again on Church Street, was built in 1874 and rebuilt in 1897. It is still in use. Saron Congregational Chapel on Pandy Road was built in 1891 and is still in use. Bedwas Pentecostal Church on the Crescent is a modern building.

St Barrwg's Church was first recorded in 1102, but the present church is 13th century with alterations by John Prichard in 1875-78, when new windows and general repairs, including the rebuilding of the north chapel were carried out. There was an infestation of Death Watch Beetle in 2013 and the church received a grant from the Heritage Lottery Fund to aid the repairs.

St Barrwg (otherwise spelt as Barroc or Barruc) was a disciple of St Cadoc in the 6th century. According to legend "It happened that the blessed Cadoc on a certain day sailed with two of his disciples, namely Barruc and Gualehes, from the island of Echni which is now called Holme, to another island named Barry. When, therefore, he prosperously landed in the harbour, he asked his said disciples for his Enchiridion, that is to say, his manual book; and they confessed that they had lost it through forgetfulness, in the aforesaid island. On hearing this, he at once commanded them to go aboard a ship, and row back to recover the codex, and blazing with fury broke into the following invective, saying, "Go, and never return!" Then the disciples, making no delay, at the command of their master quickly entered the boat, and rowed out to the aforementioned island. When, having recovered the volume, they were on their way back about midcourse, and were seen in midsea by the man of God sitting on top of a hill in Barry, the boat unexpectedly upset, and they were drowned. The body of Barruc being cast by the tide on the shore of Barry, was there found, and was buried in that island, which bears his name", (Vita St Cadoci). The Enchiridion was later found in the stomach of a salmon. St Barrwg's is the only church in Wales dedicated to the saint.

The church occupies a prominent position with its integrated saddleback tower. The nave has a panelled wagon roof while the chancel has an arched brace roof with a decorated ceiling above the altar. The round Norman font has cable moulding around the base. The north chapel has been converted to a vestry. In the churchyard is the octagonal socket stone of a churchyard cross though the shaft is not thought to be original.

Bedwas Navigation Workmen's Hall and Institute on Newport Road was opened on 8th December 1923 by Sir Samuel Instone, owner of the colliery. It contained a 1,000 seat cinema and hall as well as a library, reading rooms, billiards hall, and committee rooms. The building remains in use today as the Bedwas Adult Education Centre. The modern library is nearby as is Bedwas Leisure Centre together with sports pitches and a bowling green.

The village still has the Royal Oak, White Hart and the Bridge End Inn. There is a range of shops including a Cooperative supermarket and takeaways. There are junior and comprehensive schools and an extensive industrial park to the south-west of the village.

Bedwellty (Welsh: Bedwellte)

Bedwellty is a small village, situated on a ridge between the Rhymney and Sirhowy valleys, which was once at the heart of a large parish.

The Revd. W. Fothergill in his pamphlet of 1859 titled *The Legend of Bedwellty* gives the story of the founding of the church and the origin of the village name. According to the legend Gomer ap Llyder who lived in the village had been hunting wolves without success and fell asleep to be awakened by the morning sun. Returning to his home he found his family dead with their bodies blackened. All the animals had suffered the same fate and when he visited his neighbours they too had died. Not a thing was living in the area. He searched for three days and then, gazing at the sky a strong white form appeared which took on the appearance of the holy cross and then of the Angel of Death. The angel laid his sword on Gomer and said "Byd gwell i ti" meaning "A better World to thee". Gomer, formerly a pagan set off for Caerleon where the priest baptized him and sent him back to his home with seven monks. There they buried the dead and built a church on the spot where the angel had appeared to Gomer. It was consecrated by the bishop on the anniversary of the angel's visit and Gomer decreed that the church should be known throughout Christendom as the Church of Bedwellty. In the 19th century the remains of a large number of skeletons were found beneath the church, giving credence to the story of the plague. The churchyard is large, extending to five acres. A more prosaic explanation of the name is 'Dwelling of Mellte'

The parish of Bedwellty stretched as far as Tredegar, Rhymney and Ebbw Vale. The church, which is dedicated to St Sannan, is a large whitewashed building dating from the 13th century with a 14th century tower containing a ring of six bells, with a chancel, nave, north aisle separated by an arcade and south porch. It was restored in 1858 by the architects William Gilbee and Edward Habershon with the chancel reconstructed in 1903-05 by G.E. Halliday, and the vestry added in 1909-10 by E.P. Warren. A restoration of the arch braced timber roofing was undertaken recently. There are some good early 20th century stained glass windows. Mounted on the south wall is a 1770 iron gravestone originally on the grave of Mary Rowlands of the village of Merthyr. St

Bedwellty Inn

Sannan was a 6th century Irish bishop and a friend of St David. On Pen Heol Shenkyn is the holy well, Ffynnon St Sannan, set in a recently refurbished walled enclosure at the side of the road.

Although there is just the church and a few houses, Bedwellty boasts two pubs, the Church Inn and the New Inn and even more surprisingly a greyhound race track. The track dates from the 1920s and was the last to be used in Wales when the last race was staged in 2007.

Fothergill gives a vivid description of the Nant Cevy which drains from Bedwellty to the River Rhymney in the west. It 'flows in perfect beauty down one of the most romantic valleys in the wilds of Monmouthshire. The rocks through which it forces its way have their crevices filled with a profusion of the wild strawberry, and hence its name, for in the Welsh language 'cevy' means strawberry. It is a not a large stream, but simply a wild, dashing, reckless, headlong, mountain brook; yet it never, even in the hottest summer, fails to maintain its dignity".

Another story about Bedwellty was told by the dissenting minister of Tranch near Pontypool, Revd. Edward Jones, otherwise known as Prophet

Jones. He relates that at a wake following the death of the four year old son of Meredith Thomas, two 'profane men' were playing cards and swearing when a dismal groaning noise was heard at the window. The card players ignored the noise but eventually stopped as did the noise. They however resumed the game and at "once the groaning set up in most lamentable tones, so that people shuddered". The card players claimed that it was someone outside playing tricks but when one man offered to go out with the dogs, the dogs refused and hid under stools. Jones continues: "This at last convinced the profane men, and they left off playing, for fear the devil should come among them. For it was told in other places that people had played cards till his sulphurous majesty appeared in person".

Bettws (Welsh: Betws) Chapel

Bettws is an old parish two miles north-west of Newport, today dominated by the 1960s housing estate, one of the largest in Wales.

In 1901 Kelly's Directory listed just nine families, eight farmers and a miller. Bettws is named after the chapel of ease to St Woolo's, now the church of St. David. Originally it consisted solely of the chancel, which was built in the Early English Style using local sandstone. The nave is a later addition as is the western bellcote containing one bell above the porch. There was a refurbishment in 1858 while the vestry was added in the 1970s. The graveyard contains the tomb of Pte Samuel Pitt, one of the defenders of Rorke's Drift.

St David Lewis Roman Catholic Church is a modern building, dedicated to the 17th century Abergavenny born Jesuit. Lewis' father, Morgan Lewis, was headmaster of the Royal Grammar School at Abergavenny. Lewis eventually returned to Wales in 1648 after being ordained as a Roman Catholic priest in 1642. He was arrested at St Michael's church Llantarnam in 1678 and was hanged at Usk on 27 August 1679. He was among the Forty Martyrs of England and Wales canonized by Pope Paul VI in 1970.

The Bettws Free Church or United Reformed Church was built in the late 20th century, but is now disused.

The village has a shopping centre, schools including Newport High School and the Nightingale pub, though the Merry Miller closed in 2010.

Bettws Newydd (Welsh: Betws Newydd) New Chapel
Bettws Newydd is a small, delightful, rural village some three and a half mile north-west of Usk on the old road to Abergavenny.

The little church dedicated to St Aeddan has a stunning interior. The rood screen with its loft above and tympanum together with the decorated panelling between the screen and the ceiling is described as being the most complete surviving example in England and Wales. Only the cross with its figures of Christ, Mary and John is missing, removed during the English Civil War. St Aeddan or St Aidan was a disciple of St David and founded Llawhaden church in Pembrokeshire. He later became Bishop of Ferns in Ireland. The church is reached up a narrow lane, passing Bettws Lodge, an early Victorian three storey country house. The single cell church with its western porch is mainly 15th century though some of the original 12th century original remains. The wagon roof stretches the length of the church with the section above the chancel infilled with plaster. The font is Norman. In the churchyard is a three step cross base with a modern shaft and cross head.

At the northern end of the village is a fountain erected in memory of William Richard Stretton, a former High Sheriff of Brecknockshire who resided at Bryn Derwen overlooking the River Usk and died in 1868. An inscription from Isaiah reads "Draw water out of the wells of salvation".

The village, which has seen some individual development, has a pub, the Black Bear Inn, a village hall and a golf course at Court Windermere. A mound to the west of the Black Bear was thought to be a tumulus, but is now considered to be a former motte, known as Castell Crov. Half a mile north-east of the village is Coed y Bwnydd camp, dating from the Iron Age. Archaeologists have found evidence a long house and a number of round houses.

Bishton (Welsh: Llangadwaldr Trefesgob)
Bishton is an attractive small village five miles east of Newport city centre and sandwiched between the main London to South Wales railway and the M4.

The church is dedicated to St Cadwaladr, according to Geoffrey of Monmouth, the last King of the Britons. The earliest record is in the 12th century *Liber Landavensis* which records that in 570 AD Guidnerth was pardoned for killing his brother, Merchion, three years earlier and granted the land, woods and sea coast of Llangadwaladr to the church. The date is somewhat dubious as Cadwaladr did not die until around 664 and the charter is witnessed by Bishop Berthguinus, the successor to St Oudoceus who died circa 700. The circular outline of the Celtic llan is clear but the church which dates from the Early English period with a later tower was largely rebuilt in the Victorian Gothic style in 1887 by John Prichard. The font is 14th century while the five sided stoup is 15th century. The tower has a single bell.

The Presbyterian Hall, now a private house, first appears on Ordnance Survey maps in 1921. The village pump and pound have disappeared.

To the north of the village, between the road and Castle Farm is a piece of raised ground, said to have been the site of Bishton Castle. Owain Glyndŵr destroyed Bishton's Bishop's Palace which is thought to have been the derivation of the village name.

Bryngwyn White Hill

Bryngwyn is a rural village two miles west of Raglan.

St Peter's Church is said to have been founded in 1188 following the visit of Archbishop Baldwin on his tour to recruit for the Third Crusade. Architecturally the church dates from the 13th century. There was a restoration in 1871 by John Prichard when the north aisle was added. There is a tower and a weeping chancel which contains a trefoiled piscina together with Early English and Perpendicular windows. The family of Richard Crawley, the 19th century writer and translator of Thucydides's History of the Peloponnesian War, who was born in the village, gifted the oak reredos. The Oak braced porch is particularly attractive. Outside is the base and socket stone of a medieval churchyard cross though the shaft and head are modern. There is a mounting block at the entrance. The village once had its own school near the church and once boasted the smallest post office in Britain.

At Wern-y-cwrt, south of the A40 is what is believed to be a motte, some 14 feet in height though others believe it is a burial site for casualties of the English Civil War.

Bryngwyn Manor was held by Llantarnam Abbey but in 1560 Queen Elizabeth I granted it to William, Earl of Pembroke who, in 1561, sold it to William Morgan of Llantarnam. The house was rebuilt in 1690 and substantially modified in 1901 after its purchase by Reginald Herbert of Clytha. The walls are covered in a red limestone wash.

Buckholt

Buckholt is a rural village stretching along the Hereford Road two miles north of Monmouth. The Mally Brook which runs alongside of the road to the east forms the boundary with England. The name derives from the Norse Bøk Holt meaning Beech Wood and the surrounding area is still well wooded.

Charles Heath described the road in the late 18th century from the turnpike to the end of Buckholt Wood as "one continued Holloway, ten feet deep near the whole of that distance; while above the road, was a rough stone causeway half a mile long, for the accommodation of foot passengers". A holloway was a sunken path.

The area around Buckholt has been occupied from the earliest times with a prehistoric enclosure at the highest point of Buckholt Wood to the west of the village. After the Conquest the area was in the possession of the Benedictine monks of Monmouth Priory founded in 1075. In the early 13th century Lord John of Monmouth granted the monks his 'new' corn mill at Buckholt, subsequently attached to Old Mill Farm it was in use until the late 19th century. It was fed by a pond and leat. There are two further probable mill sites, but the main activities were quarrying and charcoal burning. The red sandstone was used in many of the cottages locally as well as in Monmouth School and the Hereford town walls.

The church of St John was built in 1889, a single cell structure with gable end entry through a small porch with a bell beneath the extended eaves. The octagonal font is dated 1663 and is reputed to have originated at Dixton church. In April 1841 the *British Magazine* reported that Mormonites at Buckholt "were treated in an unpleasant manner, and much as we dislike everything like violence, it is greatly to be regretted that persons should, by their absurdities, not to say impieties, actually invite such treatment".

The village had a school opposite the church which later became the parish room. The Plough Inn to the north-west of Buckholt Farm is now a private dwelling.

Caerleon (Welsh: Caerllion)

Caerleon lies two and a half miles north-east of Newport city centre. Formerly a market town it has in recent years seen considerable expansion with the University and hospital to the north-west though the old part of Caerleon retains its village atmosphere. The area south of the Usk is known as The Village.

The name is thought to derive from the Welsh, meaning Fortress (Caer) of the Legion, indeed Bishop Godwin referred to it as 'Caerlegion', although others have suggested Fortress of the Waters. This was the site of the important Roman legionary fortress of Isca Augusta, headquarters of the 2nd Legion between 75 and 300AD. It was also known as Isca Silurum and Isca Colonia, Isca being the Latin for Usk. There is evidence of Roman occupation as late as 380, but between that date and 1086 Caerleon enters the realm of legend with Geoffrey of Monmouth making it King Arthur's capital. (The name Camelot appears later in the works of Chrétien de Troyes.)

There is a legend that the martyrs St Julius and St Aaron were put to death at Caerleon in the 3rd century. Chapels were erected in their honour at St Julian's across the Usk and at Penrhos. St Dubricius was said to have made it the principal see (place in which a cathedral church stands) in Britain, superior to Canterbury and York before St David moved it to St David's.

A pre-conquest Welsh fortress was taken in 1086 by Turstin Fitzrolf but he fell from favour and in 1088 it was held by Wynebald de Ballon. A town had developed by 1171 when castle and town were destroyed by Iorwerth ab Owain. In 1217 William Marshall took possession of Caerleon and built the stone castle. It would appear that much of the Roman town had survived into the 12th century. Geoffrey of Monmouth recorded that "Many remains of its former magnificence are still visible; splendid palaces which once emulated with their gilded roofs the grandeur of Rome, for it was originally built by the Roman princes, and adorned with stately edifices a gigantic tower, numerous baths, ruins of temples, and a theatre, the walls of which are partly standing. Here we still see, both within and without the walls, subterraneous buildings, aqueducts, and vaulted caverns; and what appeared to me most remarkable, stoves so excellently contrived, as to diffuse their heat through secret and imperceptible pores'" Many of the structures were raided for building material for the new town.

Caerleon Castle was captured by the forces of Owain Glyndŵr in 1402, but the castle stood until the walls collapsed in 1739 following a severe frost. Before the development of Newport docks, Caerleon was for many years the major port on the Usk, with masted ships able to sail up the river. Iron from Pontypool was shipped from Caerleon in 1698. The wooden bridge across the Usk collapsed in 1779 and the stone bridge was built as a turnpike 1806-12. The iron and concrete footbridge was added in 1974.

Caerleon is celebrated for its Roman remains. The fortress covered an area of 50 acres and housed over 5,000 men. It is the home of the National Roman Legion Museum established in 1850 which exhibits finds from the site, preserving and displaying half a million objects. The Museum includes a Roman garden. The amphitheatre is the most complete in Britain while there are also the Fortress Baths and the only remains of a Roman Legionary barracks on view anywhere in Europe. There is a Military Spectacular held annually in August. The motte of Caerleon Castle stands on Castle Street but is part of a garden. The size of the castle bailey can be appreciated with the Round Tower next to the Hanbury Arms.

St Cadoc's church dates from the 12th century with two arches of the south aisle arcade surviving from this time. The church was rebuilt in the 15th century with a west tower, a broad nave with north and south aisles and a chancel. The church was restored and rebuilt in 1867 by J.P. Seddon except for the chancel which had been rebuilt in 1857 by J. Prichard and J.P. Seddon. Chapel and vestries were added in 1932-5 by W.D. Caroe. The furnishings are Victorian and the tower has a clock and a peal of six bells. The lych gate is a memorial to the fallen of the First World War by W.D. Caröe, erected in 1919.

The little Roman Catholic church of Ss Julius, Aaron and David on High Street was built in 1884-5 by Graham Son & Hitchcox. Gothic in style it has a single bellcote and is sited on land donated by Robert Wollett of The Mynde. The castle like wall along parts of High Street and Castle Street was built in 1839 by the then owner of The Mynde, John Jenkins the owner of Ponthir tinplate works. Jenkins was concerned that Chartist rioters would damage his property. The Mynde is now 14 High Street, while a house in Castle Lane is now known as The Mynde and its grounds include the castle mound.

A market hall once stood on the square. Built in 1622 it was demolished in 1848 and the materials used in the construction of the museum. The building consisted of a loft or chamber mounted on four Roman columns with the room used for meetings and as a court room. Market stalls filled the area beneath the chamber. Also on the square was the War Memorial in the form of a drinking fountain, erected in 1920 but removed to its present position in the small park at the top end of High Street in 1960. The area around the square as Cross Street meets High Street presents a most attractive aspect with its range of 16th and 17th century properties.

Caerleon Wesleyan Methodist Chapel on Church Street was built in 1814 and rebuilt in 1851.

The Hanbury Arms is thought to date from 1565, with the rear wing reconstructed in the early 18th century. Originally a house, Ty Glyndŵr, built by the Morgan family, it became an inn on the Caerleon Quay in the

Caerleon Round Tower and Hanbury Arms by Sir Richard Colt Hoare

17th century. One room was used as a Magistrate's Court with a lock-up in the adjacent Tower. Alfred, Lord Tennyson wrote a part of the *Idylls of the King* during his stay at the inn in 1856. The timber bridge was located upstream of the Hanbury Arms so the quay here was the limit for shipping. Despite the new bridge Caerleon saw shipping until 1896.

The Olde Bull Inn on High Street was built in the early 16th century but the mock timber framing dates from 1925. The Red Lion is a late 17th century house. The Priory Hotel is said to have been built on the site of a 12th century Cistercian priory. It was a private house belonging to the Morgan family from 1450 to 1835 and has been a hotel since the mid 20th century. The Malt House Hotel on New Road was actually the maltster's house and dates from 1830, after the new bridge was built. Along with the adjoining coach house it was converted to a hotel in 1970. The Ship Inn, formerly the Ship Hotel is another 19th century inn, situated opposite the Old Toll House which was built in 1825. Tolls were charged until 1879. The Bell Inn on Bulmore Road in the area known as The Village dates from the late 17th century.

Opposite the Museum is the Endowed School built in 1724 at a cost of £500. According to legend Charles Williams had fled the country after killing his cousin, Edmund Morgan of Penrhos, in a duel in 1670. He made a fortune in Turkey and returned home and received a pardon from Queen Anne. He left £4,000 for the upkeep of schools for 'the poorer sort' and a further £3,000 for the interior of St Cadoc's church. The balance of money from the school bequest was invested in land and continues to support the school which became part of the state system in 1948.

Coxe relates the story of a Mrs Edward Williams who on the 29th October 1772 was crossing the bridge from The Village at 11 o'clock at night when the current caused four piers and a considerable part of the bridge to collapse, carrying the pregnant Mrs Williams downstream. Her cries were heard on the bank but the current was too fast and she was taken downstream on a substantial part of the bridge. At Newport however it was smashed against the piers of the bridge and she was left on a single beam. Despite the lights of Newport and her cries for help she was carried for about a mile out to sea before being rescued by a boatman and returned to Caerleon unharmed.

Caerwent Gwent Fortress

Caerwent, five miles west of Chepstow was built on the ruins of the Roman town of Venta Silurum, founded in 75 AD a the market town for the Silures tribe. The remains of the Roman town, especially the walls, are some of the best preserved in Britain, with the town walls on the southern side 12 foot high. Venta Silurum was oblong shaped with walls measuring 505 yards in length on the north and south sides, and 395 on the east and west. Villas and baths covered an area of upwards of 50 acres. Most Roman towns went on to become modern towns and cities and have been obliterated by later building. Venta Silurum simply decayed. There is no museum and entry is free with car parking at the barns near the west gate. Information boards are provided. Originally there was an earth bank with stone walls built in the 2nd century. Polygonal towers were added to the north and south walls in the 4th century. The south-east corner was converted into a motte around 1150. There were gates in each wall and streets were built on a grid pattern with a Forum and Basilica at the centre. An amphitheatre has been identified at the north-east corner of the site. A temple was built on the main east west street and as with the Forum and Basilica the remains are on display. Most buildings within the Roman walls pre-date the major archaeological excavations of 1901, with new development in the village taking place to the east where there are playing fields and a village hall.

The church is dedicated to St Stephen and St Tathan. There are a number of versions concerning Tathan's origins and even sex. Baring-Gould gives a number of alternatives. Tathan was alleged to be Irish and "was directed by an angel in a dream to cross over to Britain. Taking with him eight disciples, he put to sea in 'a sorry boat without tackling,' and so sailed without a rower or sail or any oar, as the wind directed them, until they landed on the coast of Gwent, probably at Portskewett". Caradog was then king of Gwent and, hearing of the arrival of Tathan and his monks, sent him an invitation to come and see him. This Tathan declined, but the king, accompanied by his twenty-four knights, went to him in person. Caradog besought him to come and found a monastic school at Caerwent. Tathan founded a collegiate church in honour of the Holy and Undivided Trinity and placed therein twelve canons. The present church is 13th century in origin and may not occupy the original site of St Tathan's foundation. There was a rebuilding in the 15th-16th century when the tower and vestry were added. At some time the south aisle was demolished, to be restored by G.E. Halliday in 1910-12. Before this Revd. George Cornwall enlarged the church and built a gallery in 1829. The 1828 plans show a west door and a two storey 'porch or vestry' where the porch now stands, presumably the first floor being used as the vestry. There was a further restoration in 1851 when the chancel arch and north wall were replaced and in the 1890s by Halliday. The oak pulpit which was given to the church by Sir Charles Williams of Llangibby is from 1632 and stands on a panelled Victorian stone base. The organ and north nave window glass are memorials to the First World War although the window by Lavers and Baraud dates from 1865 and was brought to the church from Angersleigh in Somerset. The west tower window is a memorial to Word War II and dates from 1948. It was designed by A.W. Robinson for the studio of Joseph Bell & Son. The three bay nave arcade is medieval and reopened when the south aisle was rebuilt. There are two fonts, both Norman in origin but the second was originally in the now destroyed church at Dinham. The altar, communion rail, candlesticks and hanging cross date from 1965, designed by George Pace. In the porch are a number of Roman items including an 152 AD altar, dedicated to Mars. The chancel weeps to the north. The tower contains a single bell and has a clock in the north face, a memorial to The Rev W Coleman Williams (Vicar of Caerwent 1910-33).

Caer-Went Baptist Chapel was built in 1815 and is now the Caerwent Evangelist Chapel. A National School was built in 1856 and enlarged in 1893 but has now closed.

The village has two pubs, The Northgate Inn on the A48 and the Coach and Horses near the old east gate. The Old Ship Inn is now a private house. Just outside the east wall is a group of twelve almshouses, built in 1913 in memory of Colonel H Burton MD of Slough Farm by his wife. They were designated for twelve 'old and decrepit' women.

North of the A48 is the Royal Navy Propellant Factory, established in 1939. Between 1967 and 1993 it became a United States Army storage base after General de Gaulle expelled the US military from France. It is now used by the British army for staff training and has been used as a film and television set for productions such as *Torchwood* and *Captain America: The First Avenger*.

Castleton (Welsh: Cas-bach)

Castleton lies four and a half miles south-west of Newport on the A48. It takes its name from Wentloog Castle which stood to the north of the trunk road, with only the motte remaining in the garden of Wentloog House. Wentloog was a hundred, an old form of administrative area between Cardiff and Newport, the name being a corruption of Gwynllŵg, the title of the Welsh cantref named after ruler of Gwent in the 5th-6th centuries known today as St Woolos.

While the old village was along the A48, modern development is mainly to the south along Marshfield Road and the Craig yr Haul and Tynewydd development with a few executive homes to the north on Mill Lane. Craig yr Haul Court is a block of flats built on the site of the 17th century house which in the 19th century was the home of Col. Frederick John Justice, agent to Lord Tredegar. Bryn-Ivor Hall was a large mansion to the east of the Coach and Horses. It was the home of Thomas Beynon Esq. D.L., J.P. the owner of the coal mining and shipping company T. Beynon & Co. The house was demolished in the late 1950s.

Castleton today is a popular commuter village offering good road links to Cardiff and Newport.

Castleton Particular Baptist Chapel with its tower and prominent wheel window in the centre of the village was built in 1859 but sold by the congregation in 2001. The graveyard lies across the Marshfield Road. Castleton Masonic Hall was built in 1854 as the Wesleyan Methodist Chapel. Seion Calvinistic Methodist Chapel on Mill Lane was built in 1836 but has been demolished and the burial ground cleared.

Mill Lane is named after the corn mill which was closed by 1901. In 1883 there were two inns in the village. One at the entrance to Mill Lane has been demolished along with a terrace of cottages to allow for road widening, but the 18th century Coach and Horses remains.

Catbrook (Welsh: Catffrwd)

Catbrook is a rural community six miles south of Monmouth. The name is thought to be derived from the Welsh Cad meaning Battle. Set in rich agricultural land there has been considerable development of mainly large individual properties but well separated allowing the village to retain its rural feel. A tin chapel was demolished in 2005 and the only amenity is the Village Memorial Hall.

Cefn Fforest Forest Ridge

Cefn Fforest is a 20th century development, now forming a suburb of the town of Blackwood. In 1900 there was just a saw mill set amongst fields in an area that is today home to over 3,500 people. The oldest part of the village was built by 1920 and is the area to the north of Waun Borfa Road.

The village has infant, primary and secondary schools, a sports and leisure centre and plenty of open space and playing fields. There are some shops, mainly off Central Avenue together with the Central Club and Institute. The Miners Welfare Hall and Institute on Twynyffald Road was built between the wars and is now used as the local rugby club.

Church and chapels are 20th century.

Christchurch (Welsh: Eglwys y Drindod)

Christchurch is a small village perched on a hill overlooking the River Usk, two and a half miles north-east of Newport city centre.

The church of the Holy Trinity has had a difficult history. Norman in origin, possibly on the site of an earlier church, the massive tower was started in the 13th century. The walling of the nave is late medieval Perpendicular. The chancel, which is earlier, is weeping, angled to the south relative to the nave. By 1291 the church, belonged to the neighbouring priory of Goldcliff, which was granted to the abbey of Tewkesbury in 1442 and, in 1451, to Eton College. The stained glass was largely destroyed by Cromwell's troops who were camped nearby prior to their attack on Newport in 1648. A fire in 1877 led to a rebuilding by John Pollard Seddon while a further fire in 1949 led to the church being gutted though the tower remained unaffected. George Gaze Pace was the architect responsible for the further refurbishment including the fittings. The east window is by Harry J. Stammer and was installed in 1958. Revd. William Coxe in 1802 described the 1376 tomb of John and Isabella Colmer: "It contains a sepulchral stone, on which are carved two whole length figures of a man and woman, with their arms folded, standing on each side of a cross. The lower class of people superstitiously believe that sick children, who touch this stone on the eve of the ascension, are miraculously cured, provided they remain all night in contact with some part of it. It is related, that in 1770, not less than sixteen were laid on it, but the custom is gradually declining." In the graveyard is the tomb of William Howe, Captain of the packet *Welsh Prince*, the image of which is on the headstone.

Church House to the south of the church is late medieval in origin, but remodelled around 1600. Coxe in 1801 noted "Near the church is a public house, built with oblong pieces of hewn stone, which were not improbably the facings of Roman edifices. It bears the appearance of a religious house, and was undoubtedly the ancient manse; for even now the vicar has a right to a room, to which there was an entry through a gothic arched doorway from the church yard". Opposite is the church room. The War Memorial in the form of a cross stands at the entrance to the churchyard.

The village has a pub, The Greyhound, though the building is not that referred to by Coxe in 1801. The municipal cemetery lies off Christchurch Road. There has been some mid 20th century building of mainly detached properties on Old Hill Crescent giving extensive views across the Usk valley.

Clydach

Clydach lies between Brynmawr and Gilwern in the Clydach Gorge and is situated within the boundaries of the Brecon Beacons National Park. There are a number of Clydach rivers in South Wales and the name is considered to have the same derivation as the Clyde in Scotland, meaning a river flowing through a place of shelter. Today the village is divided by the Heads of the Valleys road and the western part of the village is known as Cheltenham. There is a Bath Row in the eastern part of the village.

Clydach Gorge was a secluded spot famed for the natural beauty of its waterfalls as the river falls 1,000 feet in the course of three and a half miles. It was reputed to be the haunt of pwccas, mischievous goblins and it is thought that Shakespeare, who visited the area in 1595, based his character Puck in *A Midsummer Night's Dream* on the pwcca.

In 1693 the Llanelly Furnace was established on a site north of the river, taking advantage of the local supplies of lime, coal and iron ore. Clydach House was built by Edward Lewis, clerk to the ironworks, also in 1693. By 1802 it was the home of Edward Frere, owner and manager. His son was Sir Henry Bartle Edward Frere, born at Clydach in 1815, who was to become the Governor of Bombay and subsequently High Commissioner for South Africa, where his policies led to the Zulu War of 1879 and the First Boer War the following year. Edward Frere was the son of John Frere, MP for Norwich and a noted antiquarian.

The Clydach ironworks began with two square blast furnaces in operation by 1797 with a third circular furnace added in 1826 and a fourth in 1841. Water power drove the bellows for the first two furnaces, while steam was in use for the later pair. In addition to the blast furnaces there were two forges in operation by 1805, converting the pig iron into bars. In 1805 there were 400 men employed with wages ranging from £40 to £100 a year. After Edward Frere the ironworks were purchased by Sir John and Lancelot Powell of Brecon who continued to run and expand the ironworks which by 1841 along with associated coal and limestone workings employed 1,350 men. Financial difficulties led to the sale of the works to a Mr Jayne who worked them for a short period before closure and dismantling in 1861. The site is freely accessible and there are the partially restored remains of three blast furnaces, a charging house and the pit of the waterwheel. Nearby is the 1824 Smart's Bridge, built to provide a tramroad to the works. Initially pig iron was transported by horse to Newport but the completion of the Monmouthshire and Brecon Canal enabled greater loads to be carried, first by tram and then by canal. There were a series of inclined planes and tramroads bringing raw materials to the works. The ironworks had closed before the opening of the Merthyr, Tredegar and Abergavenny Railway which ran to the east of the village though this was used by the limeworks and quarries which provided limestone for the building of bridges on the line. The railway closed in 1958 and much of the trackway is now a cycle route.

The limeworks above the village to the east were built in 1877 to provide lime for the railway viaduct and continued working into the 20th century. There are extensive buildings associated with the works, including three limekilns. Limestone to supply the kilns came from Gilwern Hill Quarry by means of an inclined plane tramroad. Quarrying has affected the sites of two possible Iron Age hillforts, Craig y Gaer to the west and Trwyn y Ddinas Camp to the east.

There was a woollen factory around the year 1900, on land now occupied by the council estate

The village of Clydach grew quickly on both sides of the gorge with terraced cottages climbing up the sides of the valley. The Wesleyan Chapel on Main Road, Cheltenham was built in 1829 and rebuilt in 1901-2 with the addition of a Sunday School. Ebenezer Welsh Calvinistic Methodist Chapel further down Main Road was built in 1828 and rebuilt in 1845. It has now been converted into two houses. Siloam Independent Chapel below Main Road was built in 1829 but has now been demolished. Nazareth Baptist Chapel was built on Rhiwr Road in 1851 and is now a private home.

Public houses included the Cambrian, the New Clydach Inn, the Railway, the Firemen's Arms, the Clydach Inn and the Rock and Fountain Hotel. Only the Cambrian remains.

The area around Clydach has a number of footpaths, both in and above the valley. At the northern entrance to the village is a car park and picnic site with a footpath leading to the ironworks site, Smart's Bridge and the river.

Clytha (Welsh: Cleidda)

Clytha is a hamlet west of Raglan, straddling the A40, south of Llanarth. There is no centre but a collection of interesting houses and a folly. The name is thought to derive from the now unnamed stream which flows past Llanarth Court.

Clytha House was built in the early Georgian era by John Berkeley, second son of Thomas Berkeley of Spetchley in Worcestershire and Mary Davies, heiress of the Clytha estate. John's son Robert succeeded him but on inheriting Spetchley, sold Clytha to his father-in-law Richard Lee who in turn sold it to his brother-in-law William Jones, third son of John Jones of Llanarth.

In 1788 William Jones built Clytha Castle, designed by John Davenport. Charles Heath offered this description in 1829: "The building occupies a gentle rise, and is built on a Gothic model, with circular towers at the north-west and south-west angles, the principal front extending nearly an hundred feet in length. In the centre is placed a neat marble tablet, which announces the domestic affliction that induced Mr. Jones to the undertaking: "This building was erected in the year 1788, by William Jones, of Clytha House, Esq. Fourth Son of John Jones, of Lanarth Court, Monmouthshire, Esq. and Husband to Elizabeth, the last surviving Child of Sir William Morgan, of Tredegar K.B. and grand-daughter of the most noble William, Second Duke of Devonshire. It was undertaken for the purpose of relieving a Mind sincerely afflicted, by the loss of a most excellent Wife, whose remains were deposited in Lanarth Church Yard, A. D. 1787, and to the Memory of whose Virtues this Tablet is dedicated"."

Clytha House before rebuilding

Clytha House after rebuilding

Regarded as one of the great follies of Wales, Clytha Castle stands 750 yards to the south of Clytha House.

William was succeeded by his great-nephew William Jones, later known as William Herbert. Between 1821 and 1828 the house was rebuilt by Edward Haycock of Shrewsbury in Neo-classical style. Grade I Listed it is one of the finest houses in Wales and is now in the care of the National Trust. It is not open to the public, but the park is freely accessible. The entrance gates date from the time of the elder William Jones while the lodge is 19th century. The Park was the site of the first polo ground in Wales.

There are a number of 16th and 17th century houses in the vicinity including the Great House and Pit House.

The Clytha Arms is a former dower house.

Coedkernew Cernyw's Wood

Coedkernew is a former parish four miles south-west of Newport.

The church was founded by Glywys Cernyw, according to Baring-Gould, a brother of St Catwg. The church of All Saints, which stands on a Celtic llan, was rebuilt in 1853-4 by Edward and William Gilbee Habershon. It was a simple country church with nave, chancel, northern porch and western bellcote. Grade II Listed, it has been converted to a private house.

A mainly agricultural area, Parc Golf Club was established in 1988 with its 18 hole course, driving range and restaurant. To the north-east is the massive factory built for the LG Electronics Company and north of the A48 some modern housing.

Within the boundary of the modern community of Coedkernew is Tredegar House and Park. Tredegar House was the seat of the Morgan family, descended from Cadivor Fawr, Lord of Cil-sant who died in 1089 and whose grandson, Llywelyn ab Ifor, lord of St Clears and Gwynfe, married Angharad, the daughter and sole heir of Sir Morgan ap Maredydd and so acquired the estates of Tredegar and Cyfoeth Feredydd. In the 15th century Sir John Morgan journeyed to Jerusalem, where he was created a Knight of the Holy Sepulchre. A strong supporter of the Lancastrian cause, he gave military support to Henry VII in 1485 and was subsequently knighted and made steward of Machen, sheriff of Gwynllŵg and Newport and constable of Newport. The family maintained a prominent position with Sir William Morgan (1560-1653) entertaining

Charles I at Tredegar House in 1645, though he was arrested on the orders of the King later that year. Various members of the family represented Monmouthshire in Parliament through the 17th, 18th and into the 19th century. In 1859 Sir Charles Morgan who had been MP for Brecknock was created Baron Tredegar. He was succeeded by his second son, Godfrey who at 22 was a Captain in the 17th Lancers and took part in the Charge of the Light Brigade. Both Godfrey and his horse, Sir Briggs, survived and the horse was eventually buried with full military honours in the Cedar Garden at Tredegar House. Godfrey was created Viscount Tredegar, of Tredegar in the County of Monmouth in 1905, but he died unmarried and the title died with him in 1913. He was succeeded by his nephew, Courtenay, the third Baron who was created Viscount Tredegar in 1926. He was succeeded by his son Evan Frederick Morgan in 1934. Evan was an eccentric, who served as chamberlain to Pope Pius XI while practising the Black Arts. He entertained guests at Tredegar House by dancing with his kangaroo, was a lover of King Paul of Greece, a favourite of Queen Mary and worked for British Intelligence. After disclosing secrets to a party of girl guides he was sent to the tower of London but released by MI5 and returned to Wales as Colonel of Third Monmouthshire Battalion of the Home Guard. Aldous Huxley, one of his guests at Tredegar House commented "Why even bother trying to make up characters for one's books when real people like Evan Morgan already exist". Evan died in 1949, unmarried and with him died the title of Viscount. He was succeeded as Baron Tredegar by his uncle Frederick George Morgan and in 1954 the sixth and last Baron Tredegar was Frederick Charles John Morgan, known as John who died without issue in 1962.

In addition to their real estate (at the end of the 18th century they owned more than 40,000 acres in Monmouthshire, Breconshire and Glamorgan), the Morgan family benefited from the fortune of John Morgan, High Sheriff of Monmouthshire in 1697 and Member of Parliament for Monmouth, who had amassed great wealth as a London merchant.

The original house was built in the late 15th or early 16th century and part survives in the south-west wing of the house built by Sir William Morgan in the 1660s. A square two storey house with a central courtyard, it was brick built and apart from a lowering of the roof and a 19th century north-east porch, remains as built in the 17th century. In 1951 it was sold to the Sisters of St Joseph for use as a Catholic girls' boarding school and in 1974 house and grounds were purchased by Newport Borough Council. The House, gardens and park extending to 90 acres are now in the care of the National Trust and open to the public.

Lying within the parish to the north of the M4 is the site of the Gwern-y-Cleppa long barrow, marked by the fallen megaliths including a capstone leaning against a tree.

Coed Morgan Morgan's Wood
Coed Morgan is a scattered farming hamlet a mile and a quarter west of Llanarth. There are a number of farms but little modern development.

Coed-y-caerau Wood of the forts
Coed-y-caerau is a tiny hamlet a mile north of Langstone. Of interest are the three earthworks along Coed-y-caerau Lane overlooking the Usk valley. The north-eastern enclosure is rectangular and is conjectured as having been a Roman fortlet, though it is likely to have Iron Age origins.

Coed-y-Paen Payne's Wood
Coed-y-paen is a small, compact village three miles south-west of Usk and just 600 yards from Llandegfedd Reservoir. The early 17th century Coed-y-Paen farm lies to the south. The name possibly refers to Payne's Wood, Payne being a Norman name, or could be a corruption of the Welsh 'Paun', meaning 'peacock'.

The village is relatively modern with a number of bungalows. At the centre is Christchurch, built as a chapel of ease to Llangybi in 1861 to an 1848 design by Sir Matthew Digby-Wyatt. The interior is relatively plain, reflecting the date of its design prior to the impact of the high church Oxford Movement on church architecture. The interior is lime-washed. The chancel is relatively small and entry is through the dominant west tower. Nearby are the old school and the Carpenters' Arms which pre-dates the church and incorporates the former smithy.

Crick (Welsh: Crug)
Crick is on the A48 a mile east of Caerwent, described by J.T. Barber in 1803 as "a genteel village". The name has the same derivation as Carrick

in Ireland and Craig meaning a rock, but in this case possibly referring to a round barrow.

There was a chapel in the village and Baring-Gould reported that "The remains of the old chapel of S. Nuvien, Nyveyn, or Nyfain, are still to be seen, converted into a barn, in the yard of the old manor- house of Crick". St Nuvien was an early Monmouthshire male saint. The barn, now St Nyvern's Chapel House, together with the 16th century manor, later Old Manor Farm, is part of the cul-de-sac to the north of the A48 although Old Manor Farm backs on to the main road. On July 22nd 1645, Charles I met Prince Rupert at Crick Manor following the King's defeat in Somerset. In the grounds of the Monmouthshire County Council depot is a moated platform, which is thought to have been the site of the 13th century Manor House of Sir William Derneford, Lord of Crick. Crick House on the southern side of the A48 dates from the 18th century. In the mid 19th century it was the home of John Lawrence JP, Lord of Langstone and High Sheriff of the county in 1869. It is now a care home.

There has been some modern housing development north and south of the A48, which is now a relatively quiet road.

To the west of the village are the remains of a mid Bronze Age round barrow, just five feet high. Excavations in 1940, uncovered funerary fragments along with evidence of Roman building on the site.

On Ballan Moor, 600 yards south of the village, beyond the M48 and to the west of the railway line is the motte of a Norman castle dating from the late 11th century. Further south on Mount Ballan is the David Broome Equestrian Events Centre.

Croesyceiliog The Cock's Cross

Now a suburb of Cwmbran, the hamlet of Croesyceiliog, in the parish of Llanfrechfa Lower, was named after a medieval stone cross. There were two inns, Upper Cock which is still open and Lower Cock which had closed by 1920. In 1839 a contingent of Chartists marching from Blaenavon to Newport passed through Croesyceiliog stopping at the Upper Cock Inn to dry their gunpowder.

Pontrhydyrun Baptist chapel was first built in 1815 on land given by William Conway, the owner of the local tin-plate works and whose family burial ground is here. The chapel was rebuilt in 1837 and remains in use. On Newport Road is the modern Church of Latter Day Saints (Mormon).

A school was built prior to 1882 and enlarged in 1993. The modern suburb covers a much larger area than the original hamlet.

Cross Ash (Welsh: Croes Onnen)

Cross Ash is a hamlet on the old Ross to Abergavenny road, four miles north-east of Abergavenny. Situated in rich agricultural countryside, the valley running south is known as Golden Valley, Cross Ash is an extensive scattered community centred on Cross Ash Green. Apart from the village hall and school to the north of the Green, little has changed at the heart of this estate village over the last 150 years. The house south of the green was the post office while one of the two cottages on the road to Abergavenny was the police station. Graig Hall, dating from the 16th century, lies a quarter of a mile to the north of the green and was the home of Thomas Wakeman, a noted antiquarian who died in 1868. Thomas traced his ancestry to John Le Wake who was living at the time of the Conquest. The Wakeman family initially settled in Ripon in Yorkshire, but by the 16th century had moved to the Gloucester area. John Wakeman was the last Abbot of Tewkesbury, while in the 17th century another John married the daughter of Lord Abergavenny. It is thought that Thomas Wakeman designed Cross Ash Farm House in the 19th century when it formed part of the estate. The estate was sold off in 1954.

There has been some development in the area around Graig Hall while further north, opposite the former New Inn is a restored well house which supplied the inn with water until 1960. Half a mile to the south-west of the Green is '1861', a restaurant housed in a public house built in that year and called the Three Salmon Inn.

Crosskeys

Crosskeys lies seven miles north-west of Newport at the confluence of the Sirhowy and Ebwy rivers. It was part of Monmouthshire but is now within the Caerphilly County Borough. The village takes its name from the Cross Keys Hotel.

Coal was the impetus for the growth of Crosskeys. In 1840 John Russell, a Worcestershire born businessman opened the Black Vein Colliery. It was situated south of the village across the A467 from Waunfawr Park. The colliery suffered from the gaseous nature of the coal with explosions causing the deaths of 35 men in 1846, three in 1849 and ten in 1853. In

1858 a new ventilation system was installed but in 1860 a naked flame caused a further explosion resulting in the worst mining disaster in Wales to that date, with 146 men and boys dying. John Russell sold his home, Piercefield House near Chepstow, which he had acquired in 1850, to provide a trust fund for the dead workers' families. The colliery passed through a number of companies before its closure in 1921.

The New Risca Colliery also known as the North Risca, Crosskeys not being regarded as a village at the time, was sunk in 1876 with the first coal brought to the surface in 1878. It was owned by the London and South Wales Colliery Company and sited where the Islwyn Road industrial estate stands today. In 1880 there was an explosion killing 120 men and boys while in 1882 four men and 68 horses died in another explosion and two died in a roof fall caused by an explosion in 1886. By 1892 the colliery was supplying 100,000 tons of coal a year to Egyptian Railways. Up to 1,700 men worked at this colliery which eventually closed in 1967. Nearby was the Rock Vein Colliery, adjacent to the Monmouthshire Railway, now the site of the waste transfer depot. This colliery closed in 1876.

The Workmen's Hall and Institute was built at the end of Gladstone Road in the early 1900s. A block of flats now occupies the site. St Catherine of Alexandria's mission church was also built in the early years of the 20th century and is still in use. Originally a single cell building with porch, there have been some additions to the north-west side of the church.

Adjacent to the church on Gladstone Street was the Primitive Methodist Chapel, dating from before 1900, together with a later Sunday School. Both have been demolished and a car park now occupies the site. Gladstone Street Pentecostal Chapel was built before 1900 as a Calvinistic Methodist Chapel. It is still in use. Hope English Baptist Chapel on High Street was built in 1880 and remains in use. Crosskeys Wesleyan Methodist Chapel was built in 1835 though the present chapel is later and now known as Crosskeys Methodist Church. It remains in use.

Crosskeys was at one time served by the Ebbw Vale and Sirhowy branch lines of the Monmouthshire Railway and Canal Company, and the Monmouth and Brecon Canal. The canal is still a feature of the village and the Ebbw Valley line reopened to passengers in 2008 with a station at Crosskeys. The Sirhowy branch line closed and part of the A467 runs along its route.

There is a range of factories manufacturing products from pickles to coloured steel and the village is home to a campus of Coleg Gwent. There are some shops, and takeaways together with the Cross Keys Hotel and The Eagle. There is a range of recreational facilities and the Welsh Premiership Rugby club of Crosskeys ground at Pandy Park, the park name signifying that there was once a woollen mill in the village. With the two rivers converging, the valley floor is relatively broad with mainly wooded slopes. Traffic has been taken away from the village by the by-pass built on the line of the old Monmouthshire Railway.

Crossway

Crossway or Crossways is a hamlet a little under a mile south-west of Skenfrith in the north of the county.

The hamlet itself consists of six houses around the crossroads, including the old smithy. In 1882 a hospital is shown on the Ordnance Survey map on the Skenfrith road, but by 1924 this had changed to Hospital Cottage.

The main interest lies a quarter of a mile to the west at Hilston Park. Hilston House was the home of the Needham family in the 17th and 18th centuries. The house then changed hands several times over a relatively short period, first in 1803, to Sir William Pilkington who sold it to James Jones of the Graig. It was then purchased by Gen. Sir Robert Brownrigg, Bart., GCB, colonel of the 9th Regt. of Foot, and sometime Governor of the island of Ceylon who died there in 1833 and is commemorated in St Maugham's church. The next owner was a Lancastrian, Thomas Coates but the house was destroyed by fire and was purchased around 1838 by the Bristol banker George Cave who set about building Hilton Park, a Palladian mansion. The Cave family had owned slave plantations in the West Indies before setting up the Cave Bank. They were also investors in the Great Western Railway and George Cave was a director of the Coleford Monmouth Usk and Pontypool Railway along with Thomas Powell and Crawshay Bailey. Cave sold the house to Alfred Crawshay who in turn sold it to John Hamilton who completed the rebuilding. After several more owners, in the 1950s the house was converted to a Special School for the County Council and in 1971 became a residential outdoor education centre run by Gwent Outdoor Centres for the various local authorities in the old county of Monmouthshire. Associated with the house are a lake and boathouse, a pond, and several streams, several gardens and areas of woodland, and a late 18th-century red sandstone folly in the form of Hilston Tower.

Cwm Valley

Cwm is a former mining village in the Ebbw valley two and a half miles south of Ebbw Vale.

There was some small scale mining at Cwm by 1880, when the village had a single terrace of cottages, the Baptist Chapel a station and the Castle Inn. Expansion took place with the sinking of the Marine Colliery by the Ebbw Vale Iron & Steel Company in 1889. Production began in 1893 and employment peaked in 1913 when there were over 2,400 men employed. An explosion in 1927 killed 52 miners. The colliery continued in production, linking with Six Bells Colliery in the Ebwy Fach valley in the 1970s, until 1989 when it was the last deep mine in the valley to close. The Marine Colliery was sited to the south of the village.

Thirzah Welsh Baptist Chapel was built in 1859 but destroyed by fire in 1917 to be rebuilt as Thirzah Baptist Church in 1921 and remains in use. It stands on Station Terrace with a Sunday School to the rear on Falcon Terrace. Cwm Wesleyan Methodist Chapel was established in 1873 and rebuilt on Crosscombe Terrace in 1908 but was demolished at the end of 2011. Cwm Calvinistic Methodist Chapel on River Road was built in the early years of the 20th century but was converted to an old people's home in the 1990s though by 2011 it had closed and was boarded up.

St Paul's Church on School Terrace was built as a mission chapel in 1882 on land donated by Crawshay Bailey II. It was enlarged in 1908-0 to plans by E.M. Bruce Vaughan which included an arcaded north aisle and porch and a chancel. Refurbished in 2011 the church remains in use.

A number of buildings have disappeared over the years, including the Coliseum Cinema, Public Hall and Institute. There are a number of shops and takeaway restaurants, the Victoria Arms Hotel, clubs and Joe's Fish Shop. (The actor Victor Spinetti was raised above a fish and chip shop in Cwm.)

The village has a primary school. The Monmouthshire Railway and Canal Company opened a station at Cwm on 19 April 1852. It closed in 1962 and while the rail line has reopened to Ebbw Vale there is currently no station at Cwm.

Cwmavon (Welsh: Cwmafon) Valley of the River (Lwyd)

Cwmavon is a former industrial village lying in a steep sided valley two miles north of Abersychan. It was designated a conservation area in 1984.

A tramroad running through the valley from Blaenavon to Pontnewydd was engineered by Thomas Dadford in 1796. This is now the route of Cwmavon Road. With coal, iron ore, fire clay and limestone all easily accessible in the vicinity, a forge linked to Blaenavon Ironworks was established in the village in 1800. The forge bellows and hammers were powered by water and remains of the sluices are still visible. Forge Row was built 1804-6 to accommodate the workers. Originally a terrace of twelve houses set high above the road they were converted to six houses in 1987-8 by Ferguson Mann, architects for British Historic Buildings Trust. Forge Row, which is Grade II* Listed, is considered to be the finest surviving in-situ terrace of industrial housing in the South Wales valleys.

The forge was initially short lived but in the 1820s was linked with the Varteg Ironworks on the western side of the valley. It was then that Cwmavon House was built for Mr Partridge, owner of the forge. By 1843 this late Georgian house was owned by the Varteg Iron Company which operated a forge and engineering works on the site opposite the house. The works were capable of boring steam engine cylinders and the beam engine now displayed at the University of Glamorgan was built there in 1840. The Eastern Valley Section of the Monmouthshire Railway passed through Cwmavon in 1854 and the LNWR Blaenavon-Brynmawr Branch line opened in 1868 giving the village two stations. These lines closed in 1962 and 1953 respectively.

The forge is shown as closed in 1880 but industry survived in the form of a small file factory and 1900 saw the building of the Westlake Brewery. This five storey tower brewery was built by the Bristol firm of George Adlam & Sons for Charles Westlake, replacing his Blaenavon Brewery built in the 1880s which suffered poor water supplies. Beer was produced until 1928, but the brewery complex survives and is now a plastics factory, with the manager's house used as offices. On Cwmavon Road the Railway Inn was renamed the Westlake Arms but this has now closed.

The area is wooded and scattered with cottages and small terraces. There are forest walks and a village hall.

Cwmcarn Carn Valley

Cwmcarn is a former mining village in the valley of the River Ebwy, situated between Crosskeys and Abercarn.

The first shaft in the village was the Abercarn No 6 shaft started in 1836 by the Monmouthshire Iron & Coal Company, but the Cwmcarn Colliery was not sunk until 1876 and then it only operated as a downcast shaft for the Prince of Wales Colliery at Abercarn. In 1912 it was owned by the Ebbw Vale Co. and began operating in its own right with a second shaft sunk in 1914. The colliery employed up to 1,056 men at its peak in 1923 and continued to operate until 1968. It was sited to the east of the village in the Nant Carn valley near the lake on the Cwmcarn Forest Drive.

The oldest part of the village is at the southern end with the feeder for the canal giving Feeder Row its name. There were two flannel factories in the village in 1880. Chapel Farm owes its name to an ancient chapel which once stood on the site, while Chapel Bridge replaced Pont Mynachlog or Monastery Bridge. The main part of the village was built in the late 19th century. The Cwmcarn Hotel with its double bay windows over the arched front door gives an idea of the prosperity of the village. The primary school dates from this period, while the Cwmcarn Library and Institute which now also serves as village hall was built in 1923.

The church of St John the Evangelist on Park Street was built in 1925 designed by the Blackwood architect A.F. Webb. It replaced an earlier mission church and was built in the Gothic style with small north and south transepts, it is unusually coloured blue with white surrounds to the porch and windows. The Roman Catholic Church in Caradoc Street has been replaced by a bungalow. Nazareth Primitive Methodist Chapel (later Calvinistic) on Newport Road was built in 1841 and rebuilt in 1878 and 1891. The chapel has been demolished and the graveyard is overgrown. The Arts and Crafts style English Baptist Chapel on Caradoc Street was built in 1912 but now appears to have been converted to a private dwelling.

Possibly because of its late development, Cwmcarn was well laid out with recreation fields and a central park. It retains a number of shops as well as the Cwmcarn Hotel. In addition to the primary schools there is a high school and there are a number of factory units on the Chapel Farm Industrial Estate.

The village is developing as a tourist centre with the Cwmcarn Forest Drive, a seven mile route giving views of the valleys and across the Bristol

Channel. There is a campsite, visitor centre, a ten mile mountain bike trail and fishing from the lake.

Cwmcarvan (Welsh: Cwmcarfan) Carfan Valley

Cwmcarvan is a small rural village four miles south-west of Monmouth. The name of Cwmcarvan or Cwmcarfan has the same root as Llancarfan in the Vale of Glamorgan, Cwm meaning valley and Carfan is derived from Catwg in its Latinized form of Carhani Vallis. This would fit with the dedication of the church to St Catwg, which is given by the Royal Commission on Ancient Monuments and used locally by the priest in charge, but the Church in Wales gives the dedication to St Clement, while Ordnance Survey maps up to 1920 gave the dedication as St Michael's, though this may be because the church was under St Michael's Mitchel Troy.

The church at the centre of this tiny community dates from the 13th century with an early 16th century west tower containing a peel of six bells. It has a north and south porch, the former now forming the vestry. Local tradition has it that the reason for the two porches was so the neighbouring squires of Cwmbychan and Trevildu did not have to enter the same door. The interior walls are plain stone and the nave has a blue painted, medieval, ribbed barrel-vaulted roof. The church was extended at the time of the building of the tower and restored by John Prichard in the 1870s, with a further restoration in 1962. In the graveyard is the medieval five step base and socket stone of a cross, topped with a modern shaft and crosshead.

North of the church is the former school, now a hall with the old school house attached. Cwmcarvan Court is an 1820s Regency house built for James Richards, steward to the Duke of Beaufort. In the 1920s it was the home of Capt. W.P. Jeffcook, a noted breeder of hunters. Church Farm dates from the 17th century. East of the church is evidence of a corn mill and leat on the Cwmcarvan Brook. It was disused by 1880. 630 yards to the west of the church is a probable Roman fort, with its western perimeter delineated by field boundaries with curved corners. A mile to the north-east of the village is Craig y Dorth, the site of the 1404 battle between the English and the forces of Owain Glyndŵr, in which the English were defeated and pursued to the gates of Monmouth.

Cwmfelinfach Small Mill Valley

Cwmfelinfach lies in the Sirhowy valley between Ynysddu and Wattsville. As late as 1901 this was a scattered community with its flannel mill, Babell Chapel, a few farms and cottages. In 1902 however Burnyeat and Brown began the Nine Mile Point Colliery, initially designated the Coronation Colliery. The name of the colliery is derived from the fact that it was located nine miles along a tram road from Newport Docks. A relatively large pit it employed up to 2,105 men. A collapsed roof during sinking in 1904 killed seven miners while in 1935 the colliery hit the headlines with a 177 hour 'sit in' in protest against the employment of non-members of the South Wales Miners' Federation. A further shaft was opened to the Rock seam in 1908. The colliery which was sited to the east of the village, on what is now an industrial estate, closed in 1964.

The village was established by 1920 with its terraces, shops, chapels and Workmen's Institute. Capel y Babel, Welsh Calvinistic Methodist Chapel was built in 1827 and retains its original tub pulpit. In the graveyard is the tomb of William Thomas, a poet with the Bardic name of Islwyn. Thomas wrote in both Welsh and English and died in 1876. Bethany English Calvinistic Methodist Chapel on Commercial Road was built in 1912 but is now a private residence. Noddfa Chapel on New Road has been demolished as has the attached former Sunday School which was used for services for a while. There is a modern Community Church on Maindee Road.

The village has a primary school but the Workmen's Institute on New Road has been demolished with two large bungalows occupying the site. The large Pioneer Hotel is closed. There is the Ynys Hywel Activity Centre to the east of the village together with the Sirhowy Valley Country Park. There are plenty of green spaces in the village while the hill to the south is cloaked in trees.

Cwmtillery (Welsh: Cwmtyleri) Valley of the Tyleri

Cwmtillery lies less than a mile to the north of Abertillery. In 1802 Coxe described the local scenery: "At the extremity of this moor we approached the descent leading to Cwm Tylery, and I was surprised with the view of an extensive district well peopled, richly wooded, and highly cultivated almost rivalling the fertile counties of England. Slowly descending from the dreary heath, we looked down with delight upon numerous vallies which abound with romantic scenery, and passed several rills bubbling from the sides of the hill, and swelling the Tylery".

In 1843 the owner of Blaina Iron Works, Thomas Brown, sank a shaft at Tir Nicolas Farm, establishing the Tir Nicholas Colliery. In 1852 it was taken over by John Russell. He described Tir Nicholas Farm as: "A typical Welsh valley farm with massive gables and a stone-tiled roof, situated low in the valley for shelter. The front garden was surrounded by hedges of Holly and Beech and its stone-flagged pathways were lined with dwarf bunders of clipped box bushes. Near the house was a watermill. Inside the house sat two women working at spinning wheel, making wool for knitting or weaving. Large sides of bacon hung from the rafters and simple food, including milk, butter and cheese made from ewe's milk, and instead of wheaten bread, crisp fresh oatcakes was the diet". In 1864 the South Wales Colliery Company was formed to take over Tir Nicholas which became known as the South Wales Colliery. In 1872 the company opened the Rose Heyworth Colliery across the mountain in the valley of the Ebwy Fach. The two collieries employed up to 2,760 men and continued in operation until 1985. There were a number of accidents with 13 men killed in 1857, 3 killed in 1866, 6 in 1873 and 18 in 1876, all from explosions. A smaller colliery working the Red Ash Seam was opened further up the valley in 1888, but had a chequered history, eventually closing in 1949.

The village grew rapidly with the usual terraces of houses, churches and chapels. Cwmtillery Primitive Methodist Chapel on Ty-Dan-y-Wal Road was built in 1872 but demolished by a landslide and rebuilt on another site on the same road in the early 20th century. The chapel has since been demolished. Zion Baptist Chapel was built in 1902 on Tillery Road and is now the Mynydd Lodge Guest House. East Side Wesleyan Methodist Chapel near the school on East Bank was built in 1887 but has now been demolished. Cwmtillery Bible Christian Chapel also on East Bank was built in 1855, rebuilt in 1871 and has now been demolished. St Paul's Church was built in 1891 as a chapel of ease to St Michael's in Abertillery. Initial designs were by the Staffordshire architect W.A. Keates but completed by E.M. Bruce Vaughan. St Paul's was created a parish in 1923 but is now part of the Tillery Churches Group. The church which occupies an elevated position overlooking the lake at the northern end of the village has a nave, chancel, western bellcote, northern porch and vestry. Services are held every Sunday.

The recreation field now occupies the site of the South Wales Colliery and the reservoir which once supplied the coal washing works is now a tranquil lake with car parking and walks. Gone are the workmen's hall and the South Wales Inn. There has been new building taking advantage of the local scenery, now reflecting more of Coxe's 1800 description, but there is an industrial estate to the south of the village. Above the village is the Cwmtillery Reservoir built by the Abertillery Urban District Council in 1906 and now frequented by fly fishermen.

Cwmyoy (Welsh: Cwm-iou) Valley of the Yoke

Cwmyoy lies five and a half miles north of Abergavenny in the valley of the Afon Honddu, within the Brecon Beacons National Park. A small, remote village, Cwmyoy parish covered a large area, which included Llanthony with its abbey. The hill, described in 1840 by Nicholson in *The Cambrian Traveller's Guide* as a 'frowning hill', on which it stands is described as 'yoke-shaped', hence the village name.

The fascinating church of St Martin enjoys an elevated position on the northern side of the valley but on unstable ground. A large block of sandstone, split after the Ice Age, slipped down the hillside causing the church to move and twist, making it the 'most crooked church in Great Britain'. The north wall and roof of the nave have a marked curve while the weeping chancel is far from rectangular and leans. Repairs in 1887 by James Spencer included heavy buttressing to the medieval walls. In addition to the nave and chancel there is a south porch and a medieval, heavily leaning, castellated, west tower. In the graveyard are a number of painted tombstones. On a windowsill in the church is an unusual carved cross depicting Christ being crucified, dating from the 11th-12th century. The cross has had an eventful history. Buried at the time of the Reformation for protection, it was placed in the church only to be stolen and found in a London antique shop. The four step base with broached socket stone and cross shaft of a medieval churchyard cross is to the south of the church, while a modern cross stands above the grave of Arthur Gill, a gentleman racing driver of the early 1950s who travelled to races with his butler. Gill farmed locally.

The graveyard once contained the grave of Heinrich Harrcatta, a German prisoner of war, interned at the outbreak of war when his ship was docked at Newport. He worked on farms in the area and was popular locally. Towards the end of the war he was killed when he was caught in the belt

St Martin's Church, Cwmyoy

of a saw at Tredunnow Mill. He was buried at Cwmyoy and a fund was set up locally to maintain his grave and provide flowers. His parents also sent money on his birthday. After 1945 it was decreed that all deceased prisoners of war should be buried at Cannock Chase and despite local protests, the remains were removed and the headstone smashed and buried. In the late 1940s Heinrich's parents arrived to visit the grave but the young man working at the church had no knowledge of the removal and the parents went away. Subsequent efforts to contact them with the whereabouts of Heinrich's remains were unsuccessful.

The village used to have two pubs, the Black Lion above the church and the Queen's Head a mile to the south-east. The Queen's Head remains.

The churchwarden at Cwmyoy was the subject of a court case in 1841 concerning two paupers who were then residing in Llanelly in the county of Brecknockshire. Thomas Williams was ordered to pay the sum of £109.19s.3d. to William Williams of Llanelly for the care of John Price and his wife Jane who had been ordered to be transferred to Cwmyoy. The transfer was delayed because of illness. It appears however that as the Prices had been resident in Llanelly for more than five years, the original order was invalid. The case continued to the Court of Chancery but was eventually dismissed in 1852 by which time the two paupers were dead.

Devauden (Welsh: Y Dyfawden)

Devauden lies four and a half miles north-west of Chepstow. The name is thought to derive from the Welsh Ty'r Ffawydden, meaning Beech Tree House. The village used to be known as The Devauden.

The Anglo Saxon Chronicle records that in 743 the combined forces of Ethelbald of Mercia and Cuthred of Wessex defeated the Welsh. The site of the battle is thought to be in the Devauden area. Almost a thousand years later, on 15th October 1739, John Wesley preached his first sermon in Wales here. In his diary he recorded "About four in the afternoon I preached on a little green at the foot of the Devauden (a high hill, two or three miles beyond Chepstow) to three or four hundred plain people on 'Christ our wisdom, righteousness, sanctification, and redemption'". A bust of Wesley on the village green was unveiled on the 15th October 2013.

In 1815 James Davies established a school in the village on the site of what became the church of St James. Davies was born in 1765 at Blaen Trothy in Grosmont parish, the son of a farmer. After a short career in a lawyer's office he spent 15 years as a weaver. His marriage was unhappy and he became a pedlar and kept a small shop. In 1812 he became a schoolmaster at Usk before moving to Devauden in 1815. He built his own house and tended his garden and livestock. He was a stern disciplinarian and the education received by his pupils was very much a religious one. The Revd. Francis Busteed Ashley wrote his biography and commented "He was the means of rescuing Devauden from darkness, and before he died he had built a church and parsonage there. Dissenters sometimes tried to induce him to join them, but he used to say – "While I can work eighteen hours a day in the Church of England, I do not see any need to change"". A new school, the James Davies School was built in 1830 to be replaced by a Board School in 1879. It closed in 1986. In 1848, at the age of 83 Davies moved from Devauden to become the schoolmaster at Llangattock-Lingoed. He died the following year.

St James Church was consecrated as a chapel of ease in 1839, funded largely through the efforts of James Davies as recorded by 'The District Visitor's Book' 1840. "Now in his seventy-fourth year, James Davies has through life been an humble and assiduous schoolmaster at Devauden, where his example aptly enforced his emphatic instructions of the children in the doctrines of religion. It had long been his great sorrow that the neighbourhood surrounding this chapel was without a church: he determined to attempt the heroic labour of endeavouring to supply one. By years of privation, out of a very scanty income; by the sale of a most interesting memoir of his life, written by an excellent clergyman; and by the unceasing labour of years in collecting subscriptions, this humble and pious man has lived to see, like a second ' Man of Ross,' his pious wish fulfilled, and a chapel raised where 'the Gospel will be preached to the poor' to the end of time". Nicholson described it: "The Chapel of Devauden is an unpretending oblong building, having an entrance porch surmounted by a tower with one bell. To those who knew it as a school-room it was a matter of astonishment to see what the taste and judgment of the architect Mr. Wyatt could effect". The church remains in use.

The Wesleyan Methodist Chapel on Coal Lane was built in 1843. It has now been converted to living accommodation.

The village has expanded over the years with new housing around the green and the small estates of Wesley Way and Churchfields. The village hall facing the green was built in part on the site of the old village pound. There is an early 19th century pub, The Masons' Arms and the village has since 2010 staged an annual music festival in May.

To the south of the village lies the 3,300 acre Chepstow Park Wood, originally reserved as a hunting forest by the Earl of Norfolk in 1280. It was walled in 1630 and the mixed woodland is now managed by the Forestry Commission. It is popular with walkers and contains the remains of an enclosure, possibly a medieval motte and a prehistoric, largely intact cairn. Over the centuries the wood has been the haunt of outlaws and highwaymen.

Dingestow (Welsh: Llanddingad)

Dingestow lies just north of the A40, three and a half miles south-west of Monmouth on the Afon Troddi.

An ancient village, it was sparsely populated until the latter half of the 20th century. A monastic settlement was established by the local ruler, Dingat a son of King Brychan, in the 6th century and the church is built on a traditional Celtic llan. A stone church was built in the 9th century by Tudnab who gave it to Llandaff.

There are the remains of two castles in the village. In Mill Wood to the east, is a motte some 16 feet high overlooking the confluence of the Troddi and another stream. Dingestow Castle near the church was in the course of being built in 1182 by Ranulf Poer, Sheriff of Herefordshire when it was burnt by the Welsh in an attack which resulted in the death of Ranulf. There is evidence of its continued use when it would have been stone built but there is no sign of masonry.

The church was until the late 19th century dedicated to St Mary, but is now dedicated to St Dingat and St Mary. The 14th century church was almost entirely rebuilt in stages in the 19th century. In 1846 the tower was built by Thomas Henry Wyatt while in 1887-88 there was a major rebuilding to plans by Ewan Christian, a prolific church architect, though he is possibly best remembered for the National Portrait Gallery in London. The church has a nave, chancel, north transept, vestry and south porch. The church has a peal of six bells. There are some fine examples of stained glass and monuments to the Bosanquet family. In the graveyard is the three stepped base of a medieval churchyard cross, though the head is modern.

Dingestow Corn Mill was in use until the end of the 19th century. It was fed by a 1,000 yard leat from the Afon Troddi and situated to the south of Mill Farm.

Dingestow Court was built by the Jones family in the 16th century. The family were related to the Morgans of Machen and the Herberts and the Court was built around 1600. The Jones family continued in residence until the 18th century when Richard Jones, known as 'Happy Dick', described as "a fine athletic figure, stood 6ft. 3in. high and well-proportioned, fond of the amusements of the country, and an excellent shot", was the last member of the family to live there. The *Gentleman's Magazine* reported that "Having lived a gay life he chose at the latter part of it to marry a Miss Milbourne of Wonastow, a single lady aged sixty with a fortune of ten thousand pounds. Having taken possession of her property he is said not to have lived a second day under her roof". He sold the estate to George Catchmayd and converted the proceeds together with the £10,000 into an annuity and went to live in Usk. A Mr Gwynne, second master at the Free Grammar School at Monmouth wrote a ballad about Happy Dick which was published in the *Gentleman's Magazine* of 1796, the first verse runs:

> *HOW comes it, neighbour Dick,*
> *That you, with taste uncommon*
> *Have serv'd the girls this trick,*
> *And wedded an old woman?*

It was reported that Happy Dick sang the ballad with gusto.

Catchmayd sold Dingestow Court to James Duberly who rebuilt the house before his trustees sold it in 1801 to Samuel Bosanquet, the descendant of a Huguenot family who had fled to Britain in 1685 from Lunel near Montpellier in France, following the revocation of the Edict of Nantes by Louis XIV. The Bosanquets continue to live at Dingestow Court, which is considered to be one of the finest houses in the county. The house has been extended and modified over the years and is not open to the public, though the gardens can occasionally be visited. John Bernard Bosanquet acquired a fine library of ancient Welsh manuscripts which was acquired by the National Library of Wales in 1916 and edited by Professor Henry Lewis in 1942 and published as *Brut Dingestow*. The present owner of Dingestow Court is Samuel Anthony John Pierre Bosanquet, a past president of the Country Landowners Association.

The village retains its rural charm with plenty of greenery. There is a modern village hall and a caravan and camping site at Castle Farm. Seddon House is home to the Gwent Wildlife Trust.

Treowen to the north-east is another early 17th century house built by the Jones family. Sir Charles Jones of Treowen was a Roman Catholic who died in 1637 and left a bequest to the Church for the building of a chapel. The house contains a priest hole. Used as a farmhouse until 1993, it is now run as a country house hotel and available for holidays, weddings and conferences. It was the setting for a *Doctor Who* episode in 2012.

Dinham (Welsh: Dinam) Little Fort
Dinham is a deserted village north of the Royal Navy Propellant Factory Caerwent. The Dinham Valley runs south from Dick the Miller Wood, half a mile south of Shirenewton. It is mentioned in the Domesday Book and there was a castle here in 1128. The manor of Dinham was held by the Le Walley family, though Valentine Morris (see St Arvans) claimed that a moiety had been held by his family since 1140. It was purchased during the time of Queen Elizabeth I by William Blethyn, Bishop of Llandaff. His descendants lived at Great Dinham House. The bard, Caruth, lived at Dinham in the Dark Ages and claimed that Caradog (Caractacus) was buried there. Dinham was a parish in its own right with a church and in 1900 *Kelly's Directory* reported that the font was used as a pump trough at Great Dinham Farm while a stone coffin lid was built into a wall.

Some stone remains identified as the castle site are in Church Wood while a stable block and barn remain of the Great Dinham complex, the barn is thought to be on the site of the church and incorporates remnants of the church windows.

Dixton (Welsh: Llandydiwg)
Dixton is a small village three quarters of a mile north-east of Monmouth. The name according to Sabine Baring-Gould is derived from Dukestown, possibly from an early dedication of the church to St Tydiwg, with the name being shortened to 'Diwg'. Tydiwg was a son of Corun ab Ceredig (after whom Ceredigion is named) ab Cunedda and brother of SS. Carannog, Tyssul, Ceneu, and others. The Saint's name was Latinized to Tadeocus, and appears as such in a grant to Monmouth Priory.

The parish of Dixton included Dixton Newton together with Dixton Hadnock and Wyesham across the river.

The present church of St Peter's stands on the bank of the River Wye. Unusually, it remains part of the Church of England, falling under the Diocese of Hereford. This followed a vote by the congregation in 1920 not to join the Church in Wales when it became disestablished. Built on the site of St Tydiwg's Celtic monastery, the church dates from the 12th century with the tower, chancel and extension of the nave added in the 13th-14th century. The church was restored in the 1860s by John Prichard and John Pollard Seddon and today consists of a west tower topped by a spire, nave chancel, vestry and north and south porches. There are some fine stained glass windows and a Royal Coat of Arms dating from 1711. The nave and tower are rendered and whitewashed, giving an attractive appearance. St Peter's is however susceptible to flooding and a raised storage area has been constructed to protect perishable items. Brass plates mark the levels of earlier floods. In the graveyard are the remnants of a churchyard cross with a modern shaft and crosshead.

Next to the church is the Agincourt School Annexe, originally the rectory dating from the mid 19th century.

Across the A40 is Dixton Mound, thought to be a motte dating from the 11th century.

To the north-west lie Newton Hall and Newton Court. The Hall dates from the early 17th century. The land was bought by Admiral Thomas Griffin, Commander-in-Chief of the East Indies Station, who also owned Goodrich Castle and his son George built Newton Court at the end of the 18th century. The family still occupy the Court.

Earlswood (Welsh: Coed yr Iarll)

Earlswood is a scattered community lying some three miles north of Caerwent in the parish of Shirenewton. The area was in the ownership of the Sheriff of Gloucester, Walter Fitzroger, giving the name Shirenewton (Sheriff's New Town). Walter's son, Milo Fitzwalter became Earl of Hereford in 1141 giving us the name Earl's Wood.

Originally part of the large Wentloog Forest, the Normans set about clearing the forest for cultivation. Earlswood remains a farming community. In 1791 the Earlswood Valley Methodist Chapel was built using local labour and materials. It stands, whitewashed, near Chapel Farm overlooking the Castrogi Brook. It remains in use and for many years relied on oil lamps for lighting though electricity has now been connected. The little Hope Christian Bible Chapel near the Old School was built in 1754 and extended in 1908. The Old School was a National School built in 1860 with schoolmaster's house attached. It is now a private dwelling. The Earlswood and Newchurch West War Memorial Hall stands nearby.

Elliots Town

Named after Sir George Elliot the founder of Powell Duffryn, Elliots Colliery in turn gave the village its name. The village is situated to the south-east of New Tredegar.

Sir George Elliot was born in 1815 near Gateshead and at the age of nine was working 14 hours a day underground. He progressed in the mining industry and at the age of 24 was manager of the deepest pit in England at Monkswearmouth. He began purchasing collieries in 1840 at the age of just 25. In 1860 he bought Kuper & Co, a wire manufacturing company and in partnership with Richard Glass formed the Telegraph Construction & Maintenance Co. which manufactured the submarine cables between Europe and America. In 1864 he moved to Wales and in a joint venture with other English and Scottish businessmen he purchased the mining interests of Thomas Powell of Newport to form Powell Duffryn which was to become the largest mine owner in Wales and eventually the largest mining company in Europe. Elliot was Member of Parliament for Durham North and later for Monmouthshire. He promoted Newport as a port to avoid the Bute interests in Cardiff and was also a promoter of the Pontypridd, Caerphilly & Newport Railway. He is credited with reducing the working hours of miners, restricting it to nine hours a day

The colliery was sunk in 1883-86 on the site of the Brithdir Colliery with a second shaft in 1888-91. Up to 2,800 men were employed at Elliots which eventually closed in 1967. The engine winding house and its Thornewill and Warham steam engine have been preserved and now form The Winding House Museum. The 1878 map also shows the Hope Colliery situated in the area of Jubilee Road but this colliery is not shown after 1885.

The village is much as it was in 1919 with the addition of some modern bungalows, but no places of worship. There is a post office but no other amenity in the village. The school stands between Elliots Town and New Tredegar.

Fleur-de-lis (Welsh: Trelyn)

The name of the village is said to be taken from a riverside pub, though there is no trace of any inn. The village lies immediately south of Pengam and is a mile and three quarters south of Bargoed. On the east bank of the River Rhymney, Fleur-de-lis was part of Monmouthshire until 1994.

It was a mining village with seven small collieries. There were two Gelli Haf Collieries, one opened by H.F. Jones and the other by D. Williams & Co, closed by 1896 and 1918 respectively. The other five were Gelli Haf Isa, Pwll yr Allt and Rhos, operators unknown, Trelyn operated by the Trelyn Coal & Coke Company which had closed by 1896 and Buttery Hatch which was opened by Thomas Powell in 1825 and in 1853 transferred to the sons of Thomas Prothero, and closed by 1880.

A mission church was built in 1872 with St David's parish church built in 1895-7. The church is in Pengam, though Fleur-de-lis became the parish in 1897. In the village, the English Congregationalist Chapel on High Street was built in 1903 and is still open. Mount Zion Methodist Church was built 1870 as a Primitive Methodist Chapel on Gelli-Haf Road. And is also still in use. Salem Independent Chapel on High Street was built in 1860 but closed in 1996 and has now been demolished and replaced by houses next to the community centre.

The Pengam & Fleur-de-lis Workmen's Hall was opened in 1911. Originally a two storey building, a third floor was added containing a gymnasium and boxing ring. Situated on High Street, it remains in use.

High Street contains a number of shops and takeaways as well as the community centre, James Club and Fleur de Lys Rugby Football Club (the Rugby Club using the French spelling). The Castle Inn is situated in Castle Street. The village has football and rugby pitches and two primary schools. South of the village is an industrial estate with a number of large factories including one used by British Airways Engineering.

The older part of the village is relatively small with a mix of housing including modern infill. There are some traditional terraces to the east while to the south are a number of new developments.

Forge Side (Welsh: Ger yr Efail)

Forge Side was established in the mid 19th century next to the site of the then new Blaenavon Iron and Steel Works, half a mile west of the town of Blaenavon. It is also the site of Big Pit Mining Museum.

The settlement was built on a grid system with the terraces called A Row, B Row and so on. Zion Baptist Church on Forge Road was built in 1875 and a schoolroom added in 1885.

Coal mining started in the vicinity with the Coity Pits in 1840 though some sections date back to 1810. These shafts were later used for ventilation of the Big Pit which was sunk in 1860 by Blaenavon Iron & Steel Co., the colliery taking its name from the size of the shaft. Big Pit employed up to 1,399 men at its peak in 1923. At the time of Nationalization in 1947 789 men were employed and this was further reduced by the closure in 1980. Three men died in an explosion in 1908 and another three died trying to rescue the horses as a result of a fire in the stables in 1913. No horses died in that incident. Big Pit opened as a museum in 2004 and immediately won Museum of the Year. It offers underground tours and is part of the UNESCO Blaenavon World Heritage Site.

Forge Side still maintains an industrial base with factories along Forge Road.

Gaerlwyd Grey Fort (also known as Gaerllwyd)
Gaerlwyd is a farming hamlet on a crossroads five miles south-east of Usk and five and a half miles north-west of Chepstow.

To the north-east of the B4235 is a ruined Neolithic burial chamber consisting of five upright stones supporting a broken, collapsed capstone. (The Ordnance Survey maps appear to place the chamber on the wrong side of the road, but the top is visible over the hedge.) Nearby is the mid 19th century Gaerllwyd Baptist Chapel, recently painted and still in use. Prior to 1920 maps described the chapel as Calvinistic Methodist.

Garn-yr-erw Cairn Acre
Garn-yr-erw is the highest village in Wales at over 390 metres or 1,279 feet above sea level. It lies on the slopes of Coity Mountain a mile and a quarter north-west of Blaenavon.

A former mining village it now consists of two terraces and some scattered houses overlooking the Garn Lakes but there was once a church, chapel, school and cooperative store together with more houses. The railway line connecting Blaenavon with the Monmouthshire and Brecon Canal at Gilwern ran along the valley beneath the village, while tramroads connected with the ironworks at Blaenavon and other pits scattered on the mountainside.

The Blaenavon Iron and Coal Company sank the Garn Pit in 1839, at first for ironstone but later for coal. Garn No. 2 opened in 1881 and connected underground with other collieries in the area. It continued in production until 1963, having merged with Big Pit in 1961. Up to 1,500 men were employed underground at the colliery's peak. The main complex was just to the east of the Whistle Inn. There was also the Waun Avon Slope Ironstone Mine to the west of the village but this was shown as disused by 1920.

In 1880 Mountpleasant Terrace and Garn-yr-erw Terrace (now known as

Upper and Lower Garn-yr-erw Terraces respectively) stood alone in the village apart from Blaen-y-Cwm Baptist Chapel which was built in 1847 and rebuilt in 1870. The chapel which stood at the north-western end of Lower Garn-yr-erw Terrace has been demolished. In the 1890s new housing was built in the form of Fairmount Terrace and Fairview Terrace to the north-west of the village along the B4248. These have since been demolished. Other individual houses date from this time as does St John's church which was built in the Neo-Gothic style similar to St Peter's Church, Blaenavon. The church has since been converted into private housing. A board school opened in 1894 on Garn Road to the south-east of the village together with a school house. It closed in 1971. The Welfare Hall and Institute was built in the early 20th century and was visited in November 1936 by King Edward VIII, less than a month before his abdication on December 11th. The hall is still in use.

The Whistle Inn to the west of the village today stands at the end of the Pontypool and Blaenavon Railway, a tourist steam line which has the distinction of being the highest standard gauge railway in preservation in England and Wales with the steepest continuous gradient. The Whistle Inn is of medieval origin, though has been rebuilt and was formerly known as the Garn Erw Bush Inn.

The village overlooks the Garn Lakes, two lakes reclaimed from former colliery waste heaps set in an area of 98 acres of nature reserve. Opened in 1997, there is now a wetland area in addition.

The surrounding mountainside is still littered with the remnants of the coal and iron industry.

Garndiffaith Wild Barren Cairn

Garndiffaith is today a northern suburb of Abersychan but was well established as a mining village in the 19th century. The area to the west of the village was extensively mined and many mines, bell pits, drifts were never recorded. The Golynos colliery was owned in 1850 by William Williams. It closed in 1913. There was a foundry at Golynos but this had closed by 1880. Other collieries operated at nearby Varteg and Abersychan.

St John's church on Stanley Road was built in 1932-6 by the Blackwood architect A.F. Webb on land donated by the Marquess of Abergavenny in 1915. It was closed and declared redundant in 2011. Pisgah Welsh Baptist

Chapel on Pisgah Road was built in 1827, rebuilt in 1831, 1850, and 1891, with a renovation in 1930. Still in use, a Sunday School was built next door in 1909. Bethel Primitive Methodist Chapel on Herbert's Road was built in 1849 and remains in use. New Tabernacle Calvinistic Methodist Chapel opposite The Avenue was built of corrugated iron in the 20th century, replacing a 19th century chapel which stood on Chapel Close. It is now used by The Veg Box. The Wesleyan Methodist Chapel was built prior to 1850 on Earl Street but has been demolished.

Garndiffaith Workmen's Hall was built in the 1900s and later converted to a cinema. Situated opposite the Hanbury Arms on Herbert's Road it has now been demolished.

Garndiffaith had two distinct building phases. The first in the mid 19th century, typified by the terraces of workers' housing and the second in the mid 20th century, largely to the north, but with infill to the south. There is a modern village hall, primary school and shops including an old style Cooperative store on Stanley Road.

Gelligroes The Grove at the Crossroads

Gelligroes is a small village a mile south of Pontllanfraith, taking its name from the farm.

The Gelligroes Colliery was started in 1874 but was abandoned by 1875. The Lloyd's Navigation Steam Coal Company resumed work in 1914 but abandoned it in 1915, a story that was repeated in 1917 when the Tredegar Iron & Coal Company began work but stopped in 1918.

Shiloh Presbyterian Church on Heolddu Road was built in 1813 and was renovated in 2011.The old school further up the hill has been replaced by modern housing. The Halfway House pub and restaurant is now on a quiet road but the old Sirhowy Tram Road and later the London and North Western Railway passed opposite its front door.

The Gelligroes corn mill operated from 1625. New machinery was installed in 1900 which has recently been restored to working order and the mill is now open to the public together with a candle factory. In the early years of the 20th century it was the home to radio enthusiast Arthur 'Artie' Moore who had lost part of his leg in an accident at the mill. He intercepted Italy's Declaration of War on Libya in 1911 which placed him on the front page of the *Daily Sketch*. In 1912 he heard the distress call from the *Titanic* but when he relayed the information to the police he was not believed. Subsequent publicity however brought Marconi to visit him at the mill and Moore joined the Marconi Company, finally retiring in 1947. Among his other achievements was the Echometer, invented in 1922, an early form of sonar.

Gilwern

Gilwern lies at the end of the Clydach Gorge as the Heads of the Valleys road levels out towards Abergavenny, three miles to the east. The Welsh name is Y Gilwern, derived from Cil meaning a place of retreat or corner while Wern is a swamp or mire. Another suggestion is that it was derived from Cil-Gwern meaning a corner of alders, the alder being a native of swampy areas.

Gilwern grew with the opening of the Brecon and Abergavenny Canal from Brecon to Gilwern on 24th December 1800. The remainder of the canal was opened in 1812 and connected with the Monmouthshire Canal giving access to Newport. A wharf was built at Gilwern with connecting tramroads to the Clydach Ironworks, Llanelly Forge and through the Clydach Gorge to Brynmawr.

The canal continues to have an important role in the village through its leisure use. Narrowboat and small motorboats are available for hire in Gilwern to explore the 33 miles of canal between Brecon and Cwmbran through some beautiful scenery. The canal crosses the River Clydach by means of a single arch aqueduct near the wharf.

As well as the canal, the River Clydach runs through the village and provided water power for the Dan y Bryn woollen mill and Rackham's Corn Mill, both now converted for living accommodation.

Hope English Baptist Church on Abergavenny Road was built in 1876 and is still in use as is the Congregational Church, now the Gilwern United Reformed Chapel on Main Road which was built in 1886. The Wesleyan Methodist Chapel on Main Road was built in 1848 but has been demolished and a shop now occupies the site.

The attractive village centre has three licensed premises, the Beaufort Arms, a 17th century coaching inn, the Bridgend Inn and the Corn Exchange Inn. There is a primary school and a range of shops. There have been a number of modern housing developments taking advantage of the pleasant surroundings and good road links.

Glascoed Green Wood

The scattered hamlet of Glascoed lies a little under three miles west of Usk. The church of St Michael was built as a chapel of ease by Thomas Henry Wyatt, David Brandon and R. Hancock Evins, the latter of Abergavenny, in 1848-50. It is a single cell structure with west door beneath a bellcote. Mount Zion Baptist Chapel was built in 1821 and is still in use. The nearby Fellowship Hall is built on the site of the High Cross Inn.

This was farming country and there has been some small scale individual development. Glascoed shared a school with Llanbadoc and Monkswood. Situated south of The Cross, it opened in 1892 and closed in 1985 when hopes of converting it to a village hall were dashed when the council approved plans by the owner, the Duke of Beaufort, to demolish the school and build two houses on the site.

Over several months in 1860 local residents invoked the spirit of the Rebecca Rioters by tearing down gates and fences that had been erected across Glascoed Common, known as Greenmeadow, in an attempt to enclose it. 28 residents were brought before Usk magistrates and while charges against four were dropped the remainder were brought before Monmouth Assizes in April 1861 were the jury found in favour of those charged with riot and dismissed the charge. The decision was greeted with great celebration in the village and with the ringing of the church bells at Usk. The *Pontypool Free Press* commented "The failure of the prosecution appears to afford general satisfaction in the locality, inasmuch as it was an attempt, under the most trumpery pretence, to fasten a criminal charge upon men who performed what they believed to be a public duty".

East of the village is the BAE Systems Glascoed complex. Originally developed for Royal Ordnance in the 1930s as a munitions filling factory, it has continued in this role and has developed an expertise in insensitive munitions, i.e. armaments that will not deteriorate and cannot be set off accidentally.

Goetre Farm Near a Wood

Goetre, also known as Goytre and Goytrey is a scattered parish six miles south of Abergavenny. It includes the hamlets of Penperlleni, Nant-y-derry and Newtown, the latter being the main centre of population and a development of the 1960s.

The small village of Goetre is centred around St Peter's church. St Peter's was first recorded in 1348 but was completely rebuilt by Thomas Henry Wyatt and David Brandon in 1846 at the instigation of Thomas Evans, the Rector from 1844-1886. The rebuilding incorporated some material from the original church including the Norman font reset on a Victorian base and the chancel roof. A west gallery was built which now accommodates the organ, gifted by the wife and children of the Revd. Evans in 1886. The organ blocks the west window. The 1903 east window is by Heaton, Butler and Bayne (whose works in Covent Garden is now a restaurant) in memory of the Revd. Thomas Evans. The vestry was included in the plans of 1846 but enlarged in 1981. Outside to the north, the churchyard cross was restored in 1932 on its original base in memory of the Revd. Henry Charles Penoyre Belcher M.A. rector 1919-1932. There is a second churchyard cross to the south of the nave, restored in 1905.

Along the road to the north-east of the church is Church Farm, the old school, built by Revd. Evans in 1854, and the Rectory.

Saron Baptist Chapel was built in 1826-7 and rebuilt in 1875 with the addition of a vestry cum schoolroom and a second gallery above the pulpit. Services prior to 1827 had been held in Wern Farm and Ty-mawr.

Capel Ed Calvinistic Methodist Chapel on Capel Ed Lane was built around 1807 on the site of Coedcae Farm. The unusual name is derived from Joshua chapter 22 verse 34 "And the children of Reuben and the children of Gad called the altar Ed".

Goytre Hall, is said to have been erected in 1446 for Thomas Herbert, son of the Earl of Pembroke. The present Goetre Hall Residential Home dates from the early 17th century with major additions carried out in the 19th century when it was the home of Revd. Thomas Evans. It stands half a mile to the north-west of the church off the A4042.

Nant-y-derry House is opposite the church with the gardens now operated as a nursery and garden centre. The house was built for Robert Farquar of the Blaendare Ironworks in Pontypool around 1830 and was the home of the daughters of Revd. Evans in 1901. The house was enlarged in the 1840s by Wyatt.

The hamlet of Nant-y-derry lies to the east of the railway. It had a station, built by the Newport, Abergavenny and Hereford Railway in 1854. It closed in 1958. There has been a public house shown on maps here since 1882. The Foxhunter was named after the horse ridden by Nant-y-derry local, Sir Harry Llewellyn in the 1952 Helsinki Olympic Games. Foxhunter won the only British gold medal of the games and the pub was duly re-named in his honour. It has now become a restaurant.

A little further to the east is Melin-y-coed, a three storey corn mill in use into the second half of the 20th century.

There was a school at Penperlleni designed by Wyatt, with the new school on School Lane opposite.

Goetre Wharf lies just under a mile to the west of the village on the canal which runs above the level of the surrounding land. The wharf together with an aqueduct and lime kilns was built between 1809 and 1812. Today it is a centre for pleasure craft on the canal with a tea room, restaurant and heritage centre.

Goldcliff (Welsh: Allteuryn)

Goldcliff is an attractive rural village with its church and pub set on the Gwent Levels four and a half miles south-east of the centre of Newport.

The village is thought to take its name from the mica in the cliffs bordering the Severn estuary which glitters in the sunlight, described by Giraldus Cambrensis in 1188 as "glittering with a wonderful brightness". The Welsh version Allteuryn has a modern attribution, translating as Cliff of Gold Coins. Evidence of Prehistoric man has been found in the mud of the Severn in the form of 8,000 year old footprints preserved in the silt and featured in an episode of *Time Team*. Erosion has taken its toll on Goldcliff Island and there is a submerged forest south of Hill Farm with a number of oak trees dating from around 5700 BC.

In 1113 Robert de Chandos founded a Benedictine Priory on what was then the headland near Hill Farm. Initially under the Abbey of Bec in Normandy, by the 15th century it was deemed an alien priory and in 1442 was granted to Tewkesbury Abbey and in 1450 to Eton College which retained ownership of the land into the 20th century. In the early 1330s the monastery was plagued by a series of disputes following a rebellion against the King and suffered a number of robberies by rebels. There was also a dispute over the succession of the Prior and in 1332 a monk from Tintern Abbey forged a number of Papal Bulls which led to rebels expelling the Prior and stealing what remained of the priory's treasures. Erosion was a problem and by 1424 the walls of the priory were under threat and half the church had already been lost. The monks have left their mark however in the form of three fish traps off the coast. The method used was to set wicker traps to catch salmon on the incoming tide, a practice which continued into the 1970s.

The area of the Severn estuary was hit by a major tidal surge in 1606 and a plaque in the church marks the highpoint of the flooding which is said to have drowned over 2,000 souls. (The date 1606 is by the Julian Calendar. The Gregorian Calendar replaced the Julian in Britain in 1752 and by this the date of the flood is 1607.)

The inlet of Goldcliff Pill is tidal as far as the village. The church of St Mary Magdalene was consecrated after the priory church was lost. The tower is 14th century but part of the single cell nave and chancel date to the 12th century, suggesting that the building may have been converted from other use. There was a major restoration in the late 19th century in the Victorian Gothic style. The interior was refitted in 2006-7. The three storey tower has a single bell while the large porch is thought to be medieval in origin. In the churchyard is the stump of a cross.

750 yards along Chapel Road is a medieval earthwork, possibly the site of a chapel connected with the Priory. It is shown on the 1883 Ordnance Survey map as Chapel (Site of) with a central mound surrounded by what was once a moat.

The majority of the houses along Goldcliff Road are modern, but Goldcliff House, Level House and the Farmers' Arms are shown on the 1883 map. The Farmers' Arms was said to have been haunted by Eve Roberts, the daughter of the landlord. The clashing of furniture, the rattle of moving dishes on the dresser and the clank of fire-irons on the hearth were heard at night and a woman in white was seen walking from the pub to the church. The vicar, armed with bell, book and candle called the ghost who appeared. Chased by the assembled villagers the ghost fled north, past Nash church throwing itself into a spring and disappeared. The spring is still known as Ffynnon Eve.

Opposite the Farmers' Arms is Fisher's Gout, one of the many ponds in the wetland area. 'Gout' is used in its archaic sense of a drop or splash. In 1878 an inscribed stone was discovered near Goldcliff Point, recording work carried out by Roman legionaries, recording that 31½ paces of sea wall were built by the 1st Cohort of the Century of Statorius Maximus.

Govilon (Welsh: Gofilon) The Place of the Smith

Govilon lies on the Brecon and Monmouthshire Canal two miles west of Abergavenny on the southern side of the A40. It owed its growth to the canal which opened in 1812.

There was a wharf and dry dock in the village while to the south in Cwm Llanwenarth was the Wilden Wireworks, a complex containing an iron foundry and nail factory. Established in the early years of the 19th century the wireworks had closed by 1886. Govilon Warehouse was built in 1812 and restored in the 1980s as part of a Work Experience Scheme. It served the connections to the canal of the Llanfihangel tramway, connecting to Abergavenny and beyond, and later another tramway from Crawshay Bailey's Blaenavon Ironworks.

The little stream of Cwm Llanwenarth known locally as Cwm Shenkyn provided the power for two corn mills in the village, the Upper Mill near Upper Mill Farm and the Old Mill in Mill Lane. Ty'r Factori Woollen Mill stood behind the Bridgend Inn. The Merthyr, Tredegar and Abergavenny branch of the London and North Western Railway opened in 1869 with a station at Govilon. It continued until 1958.

Govilon formed part of Llanwenarth parish and it was not until 1847-50 that a chapel of ease was built in the village. Designed by Thomas Henry Wyatt and David Brandon it was dedicated to St Catherine. In 1860 Govilon became a parish in its own right, known as Llanwenarth Ultra and the church, now known as Christ Church, was enlarged in 1870-72, with a new north aisle, tower, chancel, vestry, and organ chamber. The architect was John Dando Sedding. There are suggestions that the tower, which contains a single bell and is no higher than the nave, was never completed.

Llanwenarth Baptist Chapel was founded in 1652 and the chapel built, on what is now Station Road, in 1695. The land for the chapel was granted by Christopher Price, one of the leaders of the Baptist movement in the Abergavenny area. It is the oldest Baptist Chapel in Wales. It was refurbished in 1870 and continues in use.

On School Lane a National School was built in 1861. It closed in 1969 and was converted to the Robert Jeffrey Field Studies Centre.

Govilon once had 13 public houses; there are now two, the Lion Inn and the Bridgend Inn, renamed Tafarn y Bont. There is a school and playing fields and modern housing, but the main attraction in the village is the canal with its walks and canal boat hire.

Grosmont (Welsh: Y Grysmwnt)

Grosmont, nine miles north-east of Abergavenny, lies on the banks of the Monnow, which here forms the boundary with England. This now pretty, small village was once the third largest town in South Wales and was governed by a mayor and burgesses into the 19th century.

There is evidence of an Iron Age camp but in the years after the Norman Conquest the Great Hall of Grosmont Castle was built as an administrative centre. It was in the 13th century that the major fortification of the castle took place under Earl Hubert de Burgh after an attack by the Welsh under Llywelyn the Great. Following de Burgh's death in 1239, Grosmont became a Royal fortress, granted by Henry III in 1267 to his second son Edmund Crouchback, 1st Earl of Lancaster. The name 'Crouchback' refers to the cross he wore on his back as a participant in the 9th Crusade, crouch being derived from 'crux', the Latin for cross. Edmund made Grosmont one of his homes and his grandson, Henry of Grosmont was born in the castle and became the 1st Duke of Lancaster in 1351. Today the ruined castle is maintained by Cadw and open to the public daily. Surrounded by a dry moat, large circular towers cover the angles of the ramparts, within which are traces of the hall and other rooms. Of particular note is the surviving chimney.

Grosmont was granted a borough charter early in the 13th century, but in 1405, a year after he had been defeated in battle by the Earl of Warwick's forces at nearby Campstone Hill, Owain Glyndŵr's forces under Rhys Gethin burnt some 100 houses and although the Welsh troops were subsequently defeated by the forces of Prince Henry sent from Hereford, Grosmont never really recovered. Coxe comments: "The natives boast of its former extent, point out spots at some distance which formed streets of the town, and allude to a tradition, that the market was once held on the side of the Graig. But a more decisive proof of its former importance is derived from the numerous causeways, which diverge from it in several directions. Two of these causeways may be traced to the distance of a mile, one leading towards the Graig and the Abergavenny road, and the other, towards the extremity of the village, in the direction of Scenfreth and Monmouth, which is supposed by the natives to have been a street of the town. These roads are raised to the height of several feet, and though much dilapidated, are still in many places from nine to twelve feet broad; the stones are laid one on the other; several which I measured were not less than nine feet in length, and of proportionate breadth and thickness. Within the memory of the inhabitants, roads of a similar construction led in other directions, but have been demolished for the sake of the materials".

The main street climbs up the hill, lined with cottages and houses and the town hall. This hall replaced the earlier and larger timber framed structure in 1831, the gift of the Duke of Beaufort. It has a first floor assembly room with an open arcaded ground floor market hall. The external stone staircase was a later addition and the arcading on the southern side has been filled in. Nearby, the Angel Inn dates from the 17th century with the original stable block incorporated into the inn in the 19th century. There are other 17th century cottages and houses in the centre of the village.

The church of St Nicholas dates from the 12th century with the tower and other additions built by Edmund Crouchback for his mother, Queen Eleanor. Described by Cliffe as a miniature cathedral, it consists of an aisled nave, north and south transepts, a crossing-tower, chancel, and a chapel on the southern side with a north porch. The tower which is octagonal and topped by a spire was rebuilt in the 15th century. There were restorations in the 19th century for the chancel by Walter Parry James, John Pollard Seddon, Edwin Seward and George Thomas, with Seddon drawing up the initial plans. The nave remained largely untouched with the roof oak beams dated to 1214-44, the oldest accurately dated roof beams in Wales. The crown post rafter roof is a magnificent piece of early medieval construction. The timbers are thought to be part of a grant of 50 oaks made by the King to Hubert de Burgh for the rebuilding of the castle in 1227. A 19th century glazed screen now separates the nave from the transepts and chancel. The font is thought to be early 12th century and consists of an octagonal bowl on a drum pedestal. There are a number of ancient tombstones including a carved effigy of a recumbent knight. In the graveyard is the base and substantial part of the shaft of a medieval cross.

Outside the chancel was the grave of John of Kent, about whom stories and legends abound locally. According to some he made a pact with the devil and was able to perform miracles. He built the bridge over the Monnow to Kentchurch in a single day and as a boy working on a farm, was able to restrict crows in a roofless barn while he went off to the fair.

Grosmot Church Nave

He is said to have stabled his horses in a cellar at Kentchurch Court and was able to traverse the air on these horses with the speed of Lapland witches. He cheated the devil by being buried beneath the church wall. Another version suggests he was a monk, who transcribed a Latin text of the Bible for the Scudamore family of Kentchurch Court on vellum. His exploits can be explained by the impressions of an uneducated population of a man with superior knowledge of natural philosophy. Others believe that he was a bard of Owain Glyndŵr whose poems appear in Welsh manuscripts. Yet another theory is that he was Owain Glyndŵr, who had sought refuge with his daughter who married the head of the Scudamore family and lived at Kentchurch Court across the Monnow. After the rebellion, Glyndŵr disappeared and his tomb has never been found.

The main part of the village is now a conservation area. York House, behind the Angel was the Duke of York Inn. The Old School was a Board School, designed by Hereford architect E.H. Lingen Barker and built in 1877 for the Skenfrith School Board. On the road leading from the school is a Mission Chapel with house attached, described on the 1889 map as belonging to the Plymouth Brethren. There is a tea room and shop near the church in a building next to the 17th century Greyhound Inn, converted to a private house in the 1920s. There has been some new development in the village away from the centre.

The site of the 1233 Battle of Grosmont, when the combined armies of Llywelyn the Great and Earl Richard of Pembroke attacked the camp of Henry III, is situated to the south-west of the village, some 600 yards from the church.

On the road to Kentchurch is the former early 18th century inn at Cupid's Hill, overlooking the valley of the Monnow. Below the old inn, the road crosses the old tail race of Grosmont Corn Mill, which was powered by a leat from the Monnow. The mill had two undershot wheels which have been removed. John of Kent's Bridge is just beyond.

Gwehelog Shot (as in shot silk)

Gwehelog is a rural community two miles north of Usk and within the parish of Usk. Much of the area was common land but part was granted to the Earl of Pembroke for enclosure in 1581. The main population lies on Wainfield Lane, leading north from the Hall Inn on the old Usk to Raglan road. Gwehelog Wesleyan Methodist Chapel was built in 1822 with a side room added in 1902. The village hall is a corrugated iron structure built in 1926 to the south of the Hall Inn. It has recently been refurbished.

Gwernesney (Welsh: Gwernesni)
Gwernesney is a scattered rural village two miles east of Usk. The Welsh name of Gwernesni alludes to the alder trees in the area.

The church of St Michael and All Angels lies off the B4235 along with the 16th century Church Farm House. The church dates from the 13th century with work carried out in the 15th century, which included the windows, and in 1853-5 by John Prichard and John Pollard Seddon. The latter work was for repairs and reseating and left the interior of the church in its original medieval form for which it has been Listed Grade I. Of particular interest are the chancel screen and the 13th century bells in the double western bellcote. In the graveyard is the base of a cross.

The parish covers a large area and includes the Usk Showground and the South Wales Gliding Club field. There is a pub, the Rat Trap Inn and a filling station. There is some modern housing but the area is farming country with scattered farms and cottages.

Hafodyrynys Island Farm or Island Summer Dwelling
Hafodyrynys is a small village a mile north-east of Crumlin on the A472 road to Pontypool. Until boundary changes in 1994 it was part of Monmouthshire but is now in Caerphilly.

The Taff Vale Extension of the Newport, Abergavenny and Newport Railway, opened in 1857, passed through the village with a tunnel avoiding the highest ground. The railway closed in 1964. In 1880 the only buildings shown are the Hafod-yr-ynys Inn, the cottage up the lane from the inn, Tunnelbank Cottages and the Rectory. By 1901 Herbert Street and Terrace had been built along with the chapel and houses around the inn. Hafodyrynys English Congregational Chapel was built in 1894 and is still in use. The Mill Court estate is a modern development of detached properties together with small terraces of three and four houses with a variety of two and three storeys. The recreation ground was created by the Hafodyrynys Miners' Welfare Association and is now the Hafodyrynys Rugby Club, but the tennis court which once stood between the hall and the playground has disappeared. The Village Hall was opened in 2008. In addition to the Hafodyrynys Inn there is the Happy Garden Fish Bar, a florist and service station. Three quarters of a mile south of the village is Blaengawney Farm, which produces a range of ciders under the Blaengawney and Hallets name.

Hafodyrynys Colliery was started by E. Jones in 1878, but it was not until 1914 when it was taken over by Crumlin Valley Collieries that it became fully operational. It employed up to 924 men and despite a multi million pound expansion in the 1950s when it was linked with Tirpentwys

Hafodyrynys Washery Tower

and Glyntillery Collieries to the east, geological problems led to the closure of the colliery in 1966. Four men died in a roof fall in 1962. A modern washery had been built as part of the expansion and this continued to operate into the 1970s, leaving an unusual monument, a concrete cylindrical structure on stilts with a concrete domed cap. This was the Slime Thickener, designed to remove water from the crushed coal. It was retained with the intention of converting it into a restaurant. Other remnants of the colliery and washery have disappeared.

Hollybush (also known as Holly Bush)
Hollybush lies some four miles south of Tredegar in the Sirhowy valley. A former mining village Old Hollybush Colliery was sunk in 1860 and taken over in 1868 by E.D. Williams. New Hollybush was developed in the 1890s. After Williams' death in 1895 the collieries employing up to 171 men were operated by his trustees until closure in 1921. New Hollybush was reopened in 1929 for pumping. An accident in 1881 caused the deaths of four men. There were coke ovens north of Railway Terrace dating from the early 19th century and further north at Pontgwaithyrhaearn, a 17th century charcoal iron furnace together with lime kilns and a foundry which ceased production circa 1760.

Holly Bush was a station on the Sirhowy branch line of the London and North Western Railway with a pub known as the Holly Bush. There was a Baptist Chapel at the entrance to Banalog Terrace, built around 1890, but now converted to a private house while the Congregational Chapel on Newport Road has been demolished. There was a Mission Room on Railway Terrace, now a bungalow. A mixed Board School was built in 1884.

The area south of the village is known as Ancient Druid and in 1832 at the Ancient Druid Inn James James, composer of the Welsh National Anthem, was born to Evan James the innkeeper. The Inn is reputed to be nearly 1,000 years old. A plaque commemorating James James was unveiled in 2005.

Signs of its industrial past have all but disappeared and there has been new housing with some prestigious properties taking advantage of the views and the many walks around this beautiful wooded valley.

Ifton (See Rogiet)

Itton (Welsh: Llanddinol)

Itton is a small scattered village three miles north-west of Chepstow. The church of St Deiniol is near Itton Court, while the main population is at Itton Common a little over half a mile further north. The Welsh name is Llanddinol derived from the dedication of the church, but the English name was known in 1668 as Hodytton, derived from the Anglo Saxon.

Itton Court was originally a fortalice or small outlying hilltop fortification built for Chepstow Castle and was held by Ralph de Bendeville under Earl Gilbert of Pembroke in the 12th century. By the mid 15th century the owner was John Gwilym Herbert, half brother of William Herbert, Earl of Pembroke. In the early 18th century the house was built incorporating the 14th-15th century gatehouse. In 1749 Itton Court was purchased by John Curre, who had married into the Turberville family of Glamorgan. The Curre family retained possession of Itton Hall, extending it in the 19th and early 20th centuries, until the death of Sir William Curre in 1930 and his widow, the former Augusta Selina Crawshay Bailey, in 1956. During this time, the Curre Hunt was established and was celebrated for its all white fox hounds. It has since been merged to form the Llangibby and Curre Hunt with the hounds still kennelled at Itton. After the death of Lady Curre the estate was left to the Order of St John of Jerusalem. The farms were sold off and Itton Court has now been divided into apartments.

The church of St Deiniol lies to the south of Itton Court. St Deiniol was the first Bishop of Bangor and a contemporary of St David. Sir David Trevor, in his poem, speaks of Deiniol as "one of the seven blessed cousins, who had spent part of his early life as a hermit on the arm of Pembrokeshire, but God called him to be a bishop, deficient though his education was". He performed many miracles. When thieves stole a ploughman's oxen, Deiniol yoked stags in their stead, and made the thieves "lie upon the ground like stones". A woman who had taken poison drank of the water of his well, and immediately threw up "numberless worms". (Baring-Gould). Deiniol died according to the Annales Cambriae in 584, and was buried on Bardsey Island.

The church dates from the around 1300. There was a major restoration in 1869 by Henry Woodyer, financed by the Curre family and the windows and roofing date from this time. The tower was hit by lightning in the 18th century causing the upper part to be rebuilt. There is the socket stone and part shaft of a churchyard cross to the east of the church.

The main centre of population, amounting to no more than 30 houses, is at Itton Common, half a mile north-west of the church. Itton Village Hall was built in 1901 in the Arts and Crafts style and is a listed building

Kemeys Commander (Welsh: Cemais Comawndwr)

Kemeys Commander lies three miles north-west of Usk on a bend in the river. Kemeys may be derived from the Welsh Cemais meaning bend, while Commander refers to the Commandery of the Knights Templar which once held the church. Burke however asserts that the Norman de Camays family was rewarded with Kemeys Inferior and Kemeys Commander after their efforts in the conquest of Monmouthshire.

The church is first mentioned in 1254 as St John's, but the current dedication is All Saints. It is a small single cell structure with the nave and chancel divided by a 15th century oak screen. There are no windows on the northern wall and two relatively small windows in the southern wall. The former chancel door has been blocked. The east window is 15th century as is the western timber framed porch. The western double bellcote is thought to date from the 19th century refurbishment by Richard Creed, though one of the bells is 13th century.

West of the church are the 17th century Church Farm and cottages, while to the south is the 16th century whitewashed Church House. This was the former parsonage for All Saints consisting of two rooms with naturally curved timbers forming the ridge of the roof (known as a cruck truss). The rooms are divided by a post and panel partition on which there are 17th century paintings. The building continues into the barn.

On the B4958, opposite the Church Lane turning to Kemeys Commander is the 36 hole Alice Springs Golf Club. Further north-west along the B4958 the road crosses the River Usk by the 1905 chain bridge. This is a rare example of a bowstring girder road bridge. The Chainbridge Inn lies on the eastern side of the bridge while the small building on the western side is the toll house for a previous bridge. The Pont Kemys Camping and Caravan Park lies on the western side of the river.

Kemeys Inferior (Welsh: Cemais)

This former parish lie three miles north-east of Caerleon on the eastern side of the River Usk and the A449 dual carriageway. Edward Kemeys, the lord of the manor settled at Kemeys Manor in the 13th century. The house which stands on the slopes of Kemeys Graig was largely rebuilt in the Tudor period before George Kemeys sold it in 1700. The family was well connected through marriage, with links to the Lewis family of St Pierre, Lewis the Van and the Herbert family. According to Burke, among the direct descendants was Oliver Cromwell. The Manor is now a country house restaurant. On top of the ridge, George Kemeys built the three storey tower known as Kemeys Folly. It was restored in 1910 and today is occupied as a private house. The Norman church of All Saints was demolished in 1960-62. Its outline can still be seen between the river and the A449. It consisted of a nave, with western bell-turret and south porch, a north aisle and chancel. In 1850 the wooden carving of the rood figure of Christ crucified was discovered in the blocked up rood staircase.

Kilgwrrwg (Welsh: Cilgwrrwg)

Kilgwrrwg is a scattered village a mile south-west of Devauden. It is first mentioned in the *Liber Landavensis* written around 1125, "King Ithael son of Morgan, and his sons Ffernwael and Meurig, sacrificed to God, and to St. Dubricius, St. Teilo, and St. Oudoccus, and to Bishop Berthgwyn, and all his successors at Llandaff, three uncias of land altogether, in the middle of Cwm Cerruc, that is, the village which was Guroc, with all its liberty, and all commonage in field and in woods, in waters and in pastures". The Norwich Taxation survey of 1254 also lists it as founded by Guroc. Knight in *South Wales: From the Romans to the Normans* suggests that the derivation is 'Villa Guroc'. Three uncias of land is approximately 1500 acres.

It is an ancient, now deserted, village with the church one of the most isolated in Wales, set in a Celtic llan reached along a footpath across a stream and two fields from Kigwrrwg House. James Davies the schoolmaster of Devauden found that at Kilgwrrwg, nearer to the Devauden, "the little church was in decay, rain and snow penetrated through the roof into the body of the building, and a neighbouring farmer folded his sheep within the walls of God's house. On twelve Sundays in the year, and on those only, was public worship performed in that church; and on those occasions the accumulated filth of sheep and cattle was shovelled out the day before". Davies together with William Jones the assistant curate set about persuading the parishioners to repair the church but found that it was still too distant for the people of Devauden who continued to spend the Sabbath "in idleness and sport".

Set on a knoll, the church of The Holy Cross had no dedication until 1979. The walls are thought to date from the 13th century but there were renovations in 1718, 1820, 1870 and 1979-80 when new roof timbers were installed and the original roof tiles refitted, coinciding with the new dedication. The 1820 work was carried out under James Davies while the major alteration in 1870 was the responsibility of John Prichard. This work included a new porch, new nave north window, reseating and general repairs to roof and walls. The church is constructed of the local red sandstone with a stone slate roof and is lit by candles as there is no electricity. The double bellcote now contains a single bell dated 1698. It was donated by William Nicholas, whose well preserved tomb is on the south east side of the church. The east window is a War Memorial containing the names of those in the parish who died in the Great War. Richard Morgan, serving aboard *HMS Garland* died a day before the Armistice came into effect in 1918. In the churchyard is the only intact cross in the county, set on a small socket, the cross, over six foot high, is carved from a single block of stone and considered to be pre-Norman. Services continue to be held in the church.

Kilgwrrwg House which dates from the 16th century was originally a two unit house with barn attached. There is a scattering of farms but no village, at the time of the re-hallowing of the church in 1979 there were just 11 inhabited houses.

Langstone (Welsh: Llangston)

Langstone today is a large village four and a half miles east of the centre of Newport, straddling the A48. The village lies to the north of the M4, though the church and the Lang Stone, from which it takes its name, lie to the south of the motorway. The Lang Stone is a broken Bronze Age monolith though much of the original stone has been removed.

Langstone formed part of the Villa Segan estate of Marchiud whose son Asser, according to the *Liber Landavensis*, "by treachery slew Gulagguin, and to make amends to the family and his peace with God, he and his father Marchiud, in alms for the soul's health of the slain man, granted the Villa to God and St. Peter, and the triad of Llandaff Saints, into the hand of Bishop Gulfridus" in 940.

The church lies along Langstone Court Road. The 13th-14th century church has no patron saint and all attempts to trace the original dedication have failed. The lintel above the west door has the date 1622, together with the names of the bishop and churchwardens, suggesting that there was a rebuilding or extension at that time, though the trefoil lancet window high above the door is of 14th century origin. The bell in the bellcote is also dated 1622. A south porch was added, possibly in the 16th century and in 1897 the north chancel chapel and south vestry were added in a restoration which included a new east window.

Langstone Court is now known as Langstone Court Farmhouse with parts dating from the 15th century. In the grounds are the remains of a motte and excavations have revealed that the mound was topped by a masonry wall, suggesting that there would also have been a bailey. The castle was in use between the 13th and 15th centuries.

At Cat's Ash to the north of the village was St Curig's chapel, possibly a former chapel of ease but now incorporated into Cat's Ash Farm. There was also a United Methodist Chapel on Coed-y-Caerau Lane. Chapel Cottage is now in ruins. Langstone Methodist chapel is now situated on Cat's Ash Road 200 yards north of the A48.

The village in 1891 had a population of just 184, in an area of 1,345 acres. Expansion began in the 1930s with the building of houses along the A48 and Cat's Ash Road. Since 1990 expansion has been dramatic with new business parks and housing estates with commuters attracted by the now semi-rural environment and the ease of access to the M4 and A449. There is a local primary school, but relatively few other amenities.

The New Inn now has a motel attached and to the west of the village there are a number of hotels at Junction 24 of the motorway. These include the Celtic Manor Resort with its Golf courses and other facilities. Originally based on Coldra House, until 1700 the home of the Vanne family, but rebuilt in the early 1860s as a home for Thomas Powell Jnr, whose father was a prominent colliery owner. The Powell collieries formed the basis of Powell Duffryn. Thomas Powell Jnr and his family were murdered in 1869 while on safari in Abyssinia. Between 1869 and 1915 the house had a number of tenants but in 1915 it was purchased by Sir John Beynon, the son of Thomas Beynon of Castleton. Sir John gifted Coldra House to the local Health Board in the 1930s and it opened as the Lydia Beynon Maternity Hospital on 1st January 1940. It continued as a maternity hospital until 1975 and in 1982 opened as a hotel. The hotel and leisure complex has expanded since that time. It is perhaps appropriate that the owner of the Celtic Manor, Sir Terry Matthews was born at the Lydia Beynon Maternity Hospital.

Little Mill

Little Mill lies between Usk and Pontypool on the A472, roughly midway between the two towns as the inn named the Halfway House suggests. The village stands on the Berthin Brook which supplied the water power for the corn mill which gives the village its name. The three storey building had an internal wheel and much of the machinery remains. A second external wheel was installed in 1929 to provide electricity. A leat from the brook also provided power to the tannery, 120 yards to the west, which had closed by 1886. East of the Halfway House was a smithy, which after 1920 became a saw mill. There is an evangelical church and a village hall. Until 1955 the village had its own station, Little Mill Junction, on the Newport to Hereford line which opened in 1854 and still runs to the west of the village. The junction was with the Coleford, Monmouth, Usk & Pontypool Railway opened in 1857, which ran to the south of the Berthin Brook. The village has seen rapid expansion in recent years with developments to the north of the main road.

Llanarth

Llanarth is a small estate village three miles north west of Raglan. The name is thought to derive from Llan Garth meaning church on the ridge. According to the *Liber Landavensis*, Iddon ab Ynyr King of Gwent granted his house in the village of Llan Garth to Teilo in the first half of the 6th century.

The church is dedicated to Teilo and dates from the Norman period consisting of a narrow nave, south porch, chancel and embattled tower on the western end topped with crocketed pinnacles. The tower has a ring of eight bells. The building underwent extensive restoration in 1851, while roof repairs were carried out by Griggs & Vaughan 1926-7. There are burials of the Jones and Herbert family and the medieval base of a churchyard cross to which a modern shaft and cross head have been added. The church held its last service in July 2013.

The Llanarth Estate was owned by the Jones family. Burke traces the family back to Herbert Count of Vermandois, who is mentioned in the Battle Abbey Roll as accompanying William the Conqueror in 1066.

Following generations were prominent in English history. His son, Herbert Fitz-Herbert served as Chamberlain and Treasurer to Henry I, and his son in turn served as treasurer to King Stephen and was Archbishop of York. It was the practice of the Normans for the surname to reflect the father's Christian name with the suffix Fitz, similar to the Welsh ap. One member of the family, Herbert Fitz-Matthew was killed in an action against Llewellyn Prince of Wales in 1205. A large stone was thrown down on him by the Welsh and he is buried at Margam Abbey. His son, Peter Fitz-Herbert married Isobel, daughter of William de Braose and widow of Dafydd ap Llewellyn Prince of Wales. William de Braose was lord of Brycheiniog (Brecknockshire) but was hanged by Llewellyn after being found in bed with Llewellyn's wife Joan, the natural daughter of King John. Adam Fitz-Herbert, a junior member of the Herbert family, acquired land at Llanlowell near Usk through his grandmother and his heirs adopted the Welsh practice and were known John ap Adam and so on until William ap Thomas alias Herbert acquired Raglan Castle by marriage. He was knighted By Henry V at Agincourt in 1415. His second cousin David ap Jenkin married the daughter and co-heir of Thomas Huntley Esq. of Treowen and Llanarth. David was killed in 1469 fighting for the Lancastrian cause under William Earl of Pembroke. His grandson was John ap Thomas whose son adopted the name of William Jones. Still adherents of the Roman Catholic Church they supported Charles I and Sir Philip Jones of Treowen was a Colonel in the King's army leading troops raised in Monmouthshire. The Jones family made Llanarth Court their home after the death of Sir Phillip Jones in 1659. (Treowen is situated in Dingestow.)

Llanarth Court was rebuilt around 1770. On 12 November 1846 John Jones, who had been born at Llanarth in 1818, married the Honourable Augusta Charlotte Elizabeth Hall, daughter of Benjamin Hall, 1st Baron Llanover. Two years later he adopted the name John Arthur Edward Herbert by Royal Sign Manual on the grounds that he was the senior member of the Herbert family. In 1848-9 the architects W. & E. Habershon remodelled the house in the Italianate style. John's son was Major-General Ivor John Caradoc Herbert, 1st Baron Treowen of Treowen and Llanarth C.B., C.M.G., K.StJ., M.P. for South Monmouthshire between 1906 and 1917 when he was raised to the peerage.

Llanarth Court was given to the Roman Catholic Church in 1948 by Fflorens Mary Ursula Roch, daughter of Baron Treowen and used as a school until 1990 when it was sold to the A.M.I. Healthcare Group and is today a private hospital under Partnerships in Care. The grounds were laid out in the style of Capability Brown by Samuel Lapidge at the end of the 18th century and many features remain, though the lake was created in the mid 19th century. The impressive gatehouse dates from 1863.

In the grounds is the Roman Catholic Church of St Mary and St Michael, the oldest Roman Catholic parish church in the Cardiff Archdiocese. It was built around 1750 for the Jones family as a chapel, but built in secret and disguised as a tool shed. The 1791 Roman Catholic Relief Act permitted the building of chapels but prohibited steeples and bells. Initially a single cell structure, the apse was added in 1930. The white washed walls are set with some fine stained glass, German in origin dating from the early 16th century and installed in the 1880s and surrounded by contemporary glass. The depiction of St Therese of Lisieux is 20th century as are the apse windows designed by Margaret Agnes Rope. There is a gallery at the south-eastern end of the church which together with the extension and bellcote, was installed after The Catholic Relief Act of 1829. Outside is a cross topped by a medieval cross head with depictions of the Virgin and Child and the Crucifixion. The church is in the hospital grounds but belongs to the Cardiff Archdiocese.

The Llanarth Estate remains in private ownership.

Llanbadoc (also known as Llanbadog and Llanbadock)

Llanbadoc is a village situated across the river from the town of Usk. It takes its name from the church, dedicated to St Madoc. There is some dispute as to the identity of this saint. Browne Willis identifies him with Madog ab Gildas. Baring-Gould however suggests that early spellings, Lampadok, in the *Taxatio Ecclesiastica* of 1291, Lanpadoc in 1306-7 and Lampaddoc, in the 14th century appendix to the *Book of Llan Dav*, point to a Saint Padog, though he fails to identify this saint further. Welsh mutation would also suggest that the correct identity of the saint is Padog, as 'P' mutates to 'B'. In the 19th century maps and other sources give the dedication as St Madocus.

St Madoc's church (also known as St Madog's) lies on sloping ground between the road to Llangybi and the River, its tall thin 15th century west tower prominent from the road. The earliest part of the existing church dates back to the 13th century, though Richard de Clare endowed a church here in the 12th century. John Prichard was responsible for a major refurbishment and enlargement in 1872. This included an additional north aisle and vestry and most of the fittings. The chancel screen and rood-beam is a 1920 War Memorial, while the reredos dates from 1905, by the Cardiff firm of Veall and Sant with the statues carved by W. Henry Wormleighton of Cardiff. The pulpit was designed by Prichard, based on that of Beaulieu Abbey and carved by Crisp of Leamington. The font is medieval.

Alfred Russel Wallace, naturalist and co-founder with Darwin of the theory of natural evolution, was born in Kensington Cottage, between the bridge at Usk and the village of Llanbadoc, in 1823 and baptized in the local church. On Saturday 20th May 2006 a memorial to him of 350-million-year-old Carboniferous limestone with fossils on its surface, sponsored by the Wallace Fund, was unveiled by Wallace's grandson Richard, in the company of Lord Raglan.

West of the church is the Twyn Bell Iron Age promontory fort, now incorporated as a garden feature in Twyn Bell House. The Bell public house once stood to the north of the church but disappeared as the line of the road was altered. Church Cottages south of the church occupy the site of the village smithy. Alongside the river is Llanbadoc Island Common, providing a car park, children's play ground and picnic area.

North of the village is the bridge across the Usk with the little octagonal Toll House of 1837.

Llanbeder

Llanbeder is a hamlet now forming the eastern end of Langstone on the A48 east of Newport. It takes its name from the church of St Peter which was already in ruins in 1882. Most of the housing is modern. Tregarn Mill is situated to the south of the old church and was a working corn mill into the 20th century.

Llancayo (Welsh: Llancaeo)

Llancayo is a farming hamlet a little over a mile north of Usk on the eastern side of the river. There is no church and it has been surmised that the name is a reference to the Llancayo Roman Temple, as Llan Caeau. Llancayo Farm is the site of a large Roman Marching Camp enclosing 20.2 hectares including the Roman Temple and bisecting a Bronze Age barrow cemetery. The temple or mausoleum has been identified from aerial photography and appears to have been built on the site of an Iron Age shrine. A Roman road has been identified, again by aerial photography, to the south of Llancayo Farm.

The most prominent structure in Llancayo is the 1819 windmill, possibly the largest in Wales and capable of grinding 100 sacks of flour weekly. It suffered a fire in 1830 when the miller left the mill running while he went to market and returned to find that a change of wind had caused the gears to overheat. It has recently been restored as living accommodation with a new cap and sails. The building next to the mill was the drying kiln and this too has been converted to living accommodation.

The Llancayo estate belonged to Edward ap Jenkyn in the 16th century. In 1697 it became the property of Sir Hopton Williams, MP for Monmouthshire 1705-1708 and a most unsavoury character. Sir Hopton, who later inherited Llangibby Castle, was a faithless and violent husband, abandoning his wife and children and living as man and wife with an Anne Warner, who also suffered from his violence, in Westminster. In 1705 his wife began divorce proceedings only for Williams to sell off her possessions leaving her destitute. Williams also claimed Parliamentary Privilege, causing the divorce action to lapse. In the early 19th century the estate was acquired by Edward Berry, a Yorkshireman and a wealthy London velvet merchant. He had married a Huguenot and on a visit to France at the time of the French Revolution, she was arrested and guillotined. Berry and his daughter escaped back to London. He retired to Court St Lawrence at Llangovan before moving to Llancayo and building the three storey Regency style Llancayo House. During Word War II it was used as a convalescent home and has recently been restored and is available for bed and breakfast and as a wedding venue.

Apart from farms and Llancayo House there are a small number of terraced farm workers' cottages.

Llanddewi Fach Little St David's Church
Llanddewi Fach is a small scattered farming community situated some two and a half miles east of Cwmbrân. The church of St David occupies a Celtic llan. This late medieval building was restored by John Pollard Seddon in 1856-7 but was declared redundant in the 1990s and converted

to a private house. It consists of nave, chancel, south porch and a double western bellcote though the bells have been removed. According to the Revd. Rice Rees M.A. Professor of Welsh at St David's College Lampeter, writing in the *Church of England Magazine* in 1838, the parish of Llanddewi Fach along with Caerleon formed part of the Diocese of St David's, an arrangement dating from the time of St David when he was Bishop of Caerleon. In 1864 John Edward Jones became vicar of Llanddewi and his son, Arthur Llewelyn Jones, better known as Arthur Machen, was brought up in the rectory. Machen was an author specializing in horror, fantasy and supernatural fiction. Machen, while working as a journalist published *The Bowmen* in the *Evening News*, an imaginary account of phantom archers from the Battle of Agincourt rising up and firing their arrows at the Germans. The account was taken by many as factual and began the legend of the Angels of Mons.

Llanddewi Rhydderch

Llanddewi Rhydderch is an attractive, growing, rural village three miles south-east of Abergavenny. Built on a north facing slope the village is centred on the church of St David. Rhydderch was a common male name in medieval Wales and is used to differentiate between the different Llanddewis. The church is Norman in origin, with the first recorded priest being Edulf, in 1071. The tower is 12th century, heightened in the 15th century while the chancel dates from the 14th century. The church was refurbished in 1862 by John Pollard Seddon. The tower is topped with a bell-stage in the form of a half timbered wall beneath a tile roof with a further stage of oak lattice beneath a pyramidal roof of stone slate and a weather vane. The east window has a modern stained glass window by John Petts, of the Tree of Life, installed in 1988.

The Particular Baptist Chapel was built in 1827 and extended in 1859. There is a record of Protestants meeting at the home of John Williams a local farmer in 1819 and a member of the congregation, Thomas Richard Edwards, went as a missionary to India. He learnt the native language and preached at the bazaar in Barisal. His book *Bazaar Preaching* was published posthumously in 1939.

There has been a considerable amount of new building in the village which remains small and rural and retains a village green. The National School built in 1867 has now been converted to a private dwelling.

Llanddewi Skirrid (Welsh: Llanddewi Ysgyryd)
The church of St David by the great divided hill

Three miles north-east of Abergavenny, Llanddewi Skirrid lies beneath the Skirrid or Ysgyryd Fawr, part of the Black Mountains and within the Brecon Beacons National Park. The mountain, also known as Holy Mountain, is 1,594 feet in height with an elongated ridge along which passes the Beacons Way footpath. At the north-eastern end is an elongated defensive enclosure marked by a bank. At the summit within a smaller enclosure are the ruins of the medieval St Michael's Chapel, a Roman Catholic Church, used during the 17th century persecution of Roman Catholics. A Papal Brief of Clement X, dated 20th July 1676, granted a plenary indulgence to "all the faithful of either sex who being truly penitent and having confessed and communicated shall on the feast of the Dedication of St Michael the Archangel, between first vespers and sunset of the feast in any year, devoutly visit the church or chapel of St Michael on the Mount of the Diocese of Llandaff...and shall there piously pray to God for the concord of Christian princes, the extirpation of heresies, and the exaltation of Holy Mother Church". John Arnold of Llanvihangel-Crucorney testified before the House of Commons that "He hath seen a hundred Papists meet at the top of a high hill called St Michael's Mount where there is frequent meetings eight or ten times a year...Mass is said and sometimes sermons preached there". Major J.A. Herbert donated the upper part of the mountain to the National Trust in 1939.

There are a number of legends attached to the Skirrid. The first is that the mountain was split in two during the hours of darkness during the Crucifixion. The second is that Jack O'Kent bet the Devil that the Skirrid was higher than the Malvern Hills. When the Devil discovered he was wrong he gathered earth from the top of the Skirrid in his apron to raise the Malverns but when the cock crowed his apron strings broke and the contents formed the second peak known as Little Billy. Yet another story attributes the stones at Trellech to a competition between Jack O'Kent and the Devil throwing stones from the Skirrid. (See Grosmont for Jack O'Kent.)

In 1843 Crawshay Bailey purchased the manor of Llanddewi Skirrid, and the farms of Llanddewi Court, Dan-y-Skirrid and Skirrid Pentre. The Bailey Estate was sold in 1920. At the foot of the mountain is Llanddewi Court, now converted into a modern courtyard housing complex.

St David's Church apart from the tower was rebuilt in 1879 by John Prichard the whole cost being borne by Crawshay Bailey II of Maindiff Court. The tower dates from the 14th century though the castellated parapet is a Victorian addition. The east window is a memorial to Crawshay Bailey II (1841-1887). The nave was rebuilt on the original floor plan, but the chancel and porch are larger than those they replaced. Outside are the remains of a late medieval churchyard cross, with socket stone and shaft. A broken off wheel-head cross head lies nearby.

The timber and corrugated iron village hall stands on the cross roads south-east of the church, another gift of Crawshay Bailey II. The main populated area of the village lies to the west in Brynygwenin. Here there was a small Primitive Methodist Chapel built in the last 20 years of the 19th century, now a private house.

The Walnut Tree Restaurant opened by Franco Taruschio in the 1960s was celebrated as one of the finest restaurants in Britain. Following Franco's death it fell on hard times, featuring on Gordon Ramsay's *Kitchen Nightmares* TV series. It was taken over by chef Shaun Hill and in 2009 was named Best Restaurant in Britain by Gourmet Britain and is one of four Michelin starred restaurants in Wales.

Llandegveth (Welsh: Llandegfedd)

Llandegveth is a small village a little under three miles east of Cwmbrân. It takes its name from the church of St Tegfedd. Baring-Gould records that "Tegfedd, or Tegwedd, daughter of Tegid Foel, lord of Penllyn, in Merionethshire, was the wife of Cedig ab Ceredig ab Cunedda Wledig, by whom she became the mother of St. Afan Buallt. Tegfedd is patroness of Llandegfedd or Llandegveth, near Caerleon, where she was slain by the Saxons".

The church which stands in a Celtic llan dates from the 12th century and was sympathetically restored in 1875-7 by E.A. Lansdowne of Bristol with the ancient door and windows replaced in the new walls. The church has two bells set in an alcove above the west porch. Inside there is a set of early 19th century box pews on the northern side of the nave. The chancel arch and the rebuilding were financed by John James of Lansor in memory of his parents, John and Sara James who are buried beneath the arch.

Lansor is a 16th century house which takes its name from the nearby Sor Brook. The original name was Glan Sor. It was previously the seat of the Meyrick family. It is situated just past the Pont Sor on Treherbert

Road. Cwrt Perrot near the church is now a working farm. The house was built in 1683 for Revd. Gregory Perrot, Rector of Llandegveth who died in 1741 aged 86. The Perrot family held extensive estates in Monmouthshire and Glamorganshire at that time.

The Sor Brook runs alongside the road through part of the village, making an attractive setting.

There are a number of old cottages as well as some modern houses and bungalows but the village remains very small. There is a pub cum restaurant, The Farmers' Arms.

Llandenny (Welsh: Llandenni)
Llandenny lies some two miles south of Raglan on the western side of the A449. The name would indicate the Church of St Tenni but the present church is dedicated to St John the Apostle. The *Liber Landavensis* gives the name of 'Ecclesia Mathenni Mustuir Mur,' i.e. 'The Church of Tenni's Field belonging to the Great Monastery' (the Archmonastery of Llandaff). The manor is still known as Mathenny alias Llandenny (Baring-Gould). In the Taxationes it is Mahenni (1254) and Mykenni (1291). There is however no other record of a St Tenni.

The church of St. John is a Grade I Listed building. Set on a small hill, the oval graveyard suggests a Celtic llan. It is essentially a late medieval building, though there are traces of a 9th century Saxon structure. The main part dates from the 14th and 15th century. It was restored by John Prichard and John Pollard Seddon 1860-65 with the tower refurbished in 1901 by G.E. Halliday as a memorial to the 2nd Lord Raglan. The roof was renewed in 2009. There is a chancel, nave, vestry and south porch while the western tower, with its embattled parapet and north-east stair turret, contains six bells. In the graveyard is a restored cross.

This attractive village had three pubs in 1901, The Crown, now Rumpus House, The Raglan Arms which is still open and the Victoria Inn where the Old Victoria Orchard now stands. At that time it had a smithy, post office, shop and butcher, all of which have closed. The village had a station on the Coleford, Monmouth, Usk and Pontypool line which closed in 1955. The track forms the route of the A449 dual carriageway. The village school opened in 1864 for boys and girls. It closed in 1951 and was given to the village by Lord Raglan for a village hall. There is only a small amount of new building in the village.

Three quarters of a mile south of the village lies Cefn Tilla Court, a large mansion built in 1616, with the Herbert Arms above the fireplace in the Great Hall. During the English Civil War it was the headquarters of General Sir Thomas Fairfax during the siege of Raglan Castle. The house had a number of owners including Crawshay Bailey. In 1858 it was purchased by a group of 1,623 of the late Lord Raglan's 'friends and admirers and comrades', as a memorial to him and presented it to Richard, the 2nd Lord Raglan and his heirs in perpetuity.

FitzRoy James Henry Somerset was the fifth son of the Duke of Beaufort, born in 1788. He served under Wellington in the Peninsular Campaign and at Waterloo, rising in rank from Lieutenant in 1805 to Lieutenant Colonel in 1812. At Waterloo he was wounded and had his arm amputated, demanding its return so that he could remove a ring given by his wife. He served as MP for Truro and continued to rise in the ranks of the army, a Major General in 1825 and Lieutenant General in 1829. He was was raised to the peerage as Baron Raglan of Raglan in the County of Monmouthshire on 11th October 1852, apparently only accepting the honour when Queen Victoria discreetly paid the expenses. In 1854 Lord Raglan was appointed to lead the British troops sent to the Crimea. In September of that year, a joint Anglo French army under Lord Raglan and General Jacques St. Arnaud defeated General Alexander Menshikov's Russian army at the Battle of Alma. At the Battle of Balaclava later that year he gave an order to the Earl of Lucan which led to the Charge of the Light Brigade. Although successful, Lord Raglan was blamed by the British press for the sufferings of the army in the Crimean winter. He died from dysentery in June 1855. He was succeeded to the title by his second son.

Cefn Tilla Court was completely remodelled for the 2nd Lord Raglan, by Sir Matthew Digby Wyatt and his brother Thomas Henry Wyatt, in Tudor style.

The 5th Lord Raglan, a historian and antiquarian died childless in 2012, but while the title passed to his nephew Geoffrey Somerset, the estate was left to another nephew, Henry Van Moyland of Los Angeles. He put the Court up for sale, together with a unique collection of military and family artefacts. The sale was halted by a challenge to the will by Geoffrey who sadly died in 2013 and the sale of the Court was withdrawn.

Llandevaud (no official Welsh spelling but possibly Llandyfawg)

Llandevaud is situated a mile east of Langstone, lying between the A48 and M4. The spelling has been given as Llandevad and Llandevan; however derivation of the name is obscure. The church of St Peter stands on the A48, some distance from the village. It was reopened in August 1843 having been completely rebuilt, yet a description of the village in 1868 states that there are some ruins of an old church. There is reference to a chapel of ease and Chapel Farm and Chapel Lane would suggest the location of a chapel other than St Peter's.

The church is located down a lane past the Forester's Oaks on the A48 half a mile from the village. It was rebuilt in the Early English style with nave, chancel, south porch and western bellcote. The font is from the original 13th century church. The East window of 1897 is a memorial to Canon Edwards, Vicar of Caerleon and Llandevaud while the oak reredos was carved by one of his daughters. In 1993 a Rowan tree was planted near the church gate by the Rt. Rev. Rowan Williams, then Bishop of Monmouth and subsequently Archbishop of Canterbury to mark the church's 150th anniversary. Church services are held regularly and St Peter's is now part of the Penhow Group of churches.

The village has grown substantially over the last 50 years with dormer bungalows and some substantial houses. There is a small common towards the southern end of the village.

Llandogo

Llandogo is a picturesque village set on a hillside on the western bank of the Wye, six miles south of Monmouth. The river is tidal as far as Llandogo and by 1840 much of the village was owned by the Gough family who operated a fleet of sloops and trows on the river.

The name is derived from the dedication of the church to St Oudoceus, Welsh Euddogwy. He was the nephew of St Teilo and succeeded him to become the 3rd Bishop of Llandaff in 580. Llaneuddogwy, now Llan-dogo is the only church that regards St Oudoceus as patron other than the Cathedral Church of Llandaff, where he shares the honour with SS. Dyfrig and Teilo and SS. Peter and Paul. The land was granted to Oudoceus by King Einion, after whom it was occasionally called Llaneinion. A charter in the *Liber Landavensis* records a Lech Oudocui or Stone of Oudoceus as a boundary marker in the gift.

The village was a port and boat building centre. Flat bottomed boats or trows were built here and traded between Monmouth and Bristol. The village and boat gave the famous Llandoger Trow pub in Bristol its name. The boat trade died with the building of the Turnpike road and more significantly the railway.

The church of St Oudoceus (called Odoceus by the Church in Wales) was built in 1859-61 by John Pollard Seddon on the site of the original Celtic church. Situated between the road and the river, it has an octagonal bellcote, with a thin tall spire topped by a weathervane. The bell is from the *William and Sarah*, the last of the Chepstow barges on the Wye. It has a three aisled nave, west and south porches, a chancel and vestry. An organ chamber was added in 1889-90. Originally there was an additional Sanctus bellcote above the chancel but this has been removed. A drawing of the church was exhibited at the Paris Exhibition of 1867. Styled in 13th century Gothic, the interior is richly decorated with the Devonshire marble reredos by William Clarke of Llandaff and mosaics by James Powell and Sons of the Whitefriars Foundry, London. The chancel walls were painted by a German artist to a design by John Coates Carter, Seddon's partner. The wall surrounding the churchyard is also a Grade II Listed monument.

In 1881 the village had a Particular Baptist Chapel on the hillside. This appears to have been replaced by 1901 with Hephzibah Baptist Chapel on the main road, now the Wye Valley Arts Centre. The old village school is now known as Gallery House and to the rear was the late 19th century Lion Saw Mill. The railway from Chepstow to Monmouth operated between 1876 and 1964. It passed between the church and the river and between the railway and the river is The Holm Farm. Nearby was a saw pit and windlass.

The village once had three inns, The Ship Inn near the river, The Lion Inn on the hillside and The Sloop Hotel on the main road, the only one still trading.

The Gough family who operated the boats built The Falls, also known as the Priory, in 1840. Designed by Wyatt and Brandon, Robert Baden-Powell holidayed there in the 1880s. It was later used as accommodation for walkers before being converted to a residential care home. Cleddon Hall, on the hillside was originally known as Ravenscroft, the home of Lord and Lady Amberley, the parents of the philosopher Lord Bertrand

Russell who was born there in 1872. Lord Amberley was the son of Lord John Russell, the British Prime Minister. The Amberleys were an unorthodox couple, Lady Amberly was said to have an affair with the children's tutor with her husband's approval. They were prominent in the Women's Suffrage movement and Lord Amberley was a proponent of birth control.

Cleddon Shoots is an area of woodland and there is the Cleddon waterfall, with walks from the village.

The village store is Brown's, operated by the family since 1921. There is a modern school and a village hall, opened by The Princess Royal in 2003.

Llanellen (Welsh: Llanelen)

Llanellen lies some two miles south of Abergavenny between the Monmouthshire and Brecon Canal and the River Usk. It takes its name from the church dedicated to St Helen. The village has increased in size since the 1960s with new housing developments. It has also been by-passed by the B4269.

The 13th century church was largely rebuilt in 1851 by John Prichard, when the tower was demolished and the nave extended to the west. A large bellcote was erected over the west window and has a crenellated parapet topped by an ornamented spire, itself topped by a cross. The chancel roof is Victorian but the nave retains its late 16th century wagon roof, while the font is medieval.

The three arched Llanellen Bridge was designed by John Upton of Gloucester and built in 1821.

The old school at Llanellen of 1862 was designed by Prichard and Seddon. It was presented to the parish by Sir Thomas Phillips, who was the son of Thomas Phillips of Llanellen House. In 1838 he was elected Mayor of Newport and in that capacity read the Riot Act on 4th November 1839 when 7,000 Chartists rioted in the town. He was shot in the arm and hip outside the Westgate Hotel. The crowd dissipated after being fired on, leaving 17 killed. Phillips was knighted on 9th December in recognition of his 'individual exertions in maintaining her majesty's authority'. He was voted the Freedom of the City of London in 1840. A leading Parliamentary lawyer, Phillips gained considerable wealth and became a coal owner and land owner in South Wales. He was a great philanthropist, and supporter of national education. He died in London in 1867 and is buried in the churchyard at Llanellen

The village used to have a pub, the Hanbury Arms, but due to the influence of Lady Llanover who was Lord of the Manor, this had closed by 1900 and replaced by a coffee tavern. Lady Llanover was greatly influenced by the Temperance Movement and forced the closure of all public houses on her estates. There is a village stores and farm shop while the old smithy is now a craft and gift shop serving Welsh teas.

Llanelly (Welsh: Llanelli)

Llanelly is a tiny village perched on the hillside a mile north-west of Gilwern, with views extending over the Usk valley. The village takes its name from St Elli, who according to Baring-Gould was a pupil of St Catwg at Llancarfan and one of the three disciples who persuaded Gwynllyw, King of Gwent to mend his wicked ways. He succeeded Catwg at Llancarfan. Some have suggested that the dedication is to a St Ellyw or Elyw, who is supposed to have been a granddaughter of Brychan Brycheiniog. But Baring-Gould maintained that there is no evidence whatever that anyone of that name belonged to the Brychan saintly clan.

The church is surrounded by minor roads and the graveyard extends to the south and west beyond these roads. The church itself is surrounded by a circle of Yew trees, suggesting pre-Christian origins of the site. The present church was built in the 13th century with the west tower and chancel added in the 14th century. The south porch and north aisle were added later. It was restored in 1867-68 by Joseph Nevill of Abergavenny while in 1897 Baldwin of Brecon added the slated broach spire and the gable to the turret stair. The nave and chancel roofs were replaced in 1910-11. The east window is by James Powell of Whitefriars and depicts the Good Shepherd, with local landmarks including the Sugar Loaf, and the Blorenge. Outside is the four step base of a churchyard cross.

There are just a few buildings surrounding the church, including the former Five Bells public house. The community of Llanelly covers a large area, including Clydach and Gilwern.

Llanfaenor Manor Church

Llanfaenor is a tiny village two miles north-west of Llangattock-vibon-avel. Rees identifies Llanfaenor as Llannuannar, a church mentioned in *Liber*

Landavensis, Llyfr Teilo, with Llanllwyd as its chapelry. The village has over the years has also been known as, Llanvannah, Llanmocha and Llanbocha. Whatever the name, the church had fallen into decay by 1859, as this description of the village in *The Church Builder* shows: "Turning down a narrow lane more resembling a watercourse than a road, I walked for some time, and then suddenly came upon a scene I shall never forget. In the fore-ground a village green, with a small barn in the centre, and around it a few scattered cottages, whitewashed and thatched; in the background a splendid view of distant mountains, the dark blue Graig conspicuous amongst them. Some old people were standing at their doors, sunning themselves in the early morning, and enjoying the quiet, which was only broken by a distant sheep-bell or the who-ho! of some carter, encouraging his sleek animals to drag their burden through the deep ruts of the neighbouring lane". The barn referred to was the church and the writer continues "it might by courtesy be termed a church, in as much as one end possessed a little wooden place of shelter wherein hung a bell". The church was renovated in 1861 and: "The little barn chapel had disappeared. In its stead, I saw a pretty church, with porch, nave, chancel, and bell-gable, built of warm coloured stone with white atone dressings. I entered. There was nothing more to be desired, altar, lectern, handsome font, low open seats, all had been provided by the pious care of one whose taste and zeal will long be remembered in that neighbourhood; and, better still, the church was crowded with a reverent congregation". The church, now converted to a private dwelling was one of eleven dedicated to St Beuno, a saint born in Powys, educated at Caerwent, according to Baring-Gould though others suggest Bangor on Dee, eventually settling at Clynnog Fawr on the Lleyn Peninsular before his death in 640. The church which was renovated 1955 by Reginald Lewis Edmunds of Blaenavon, had a nave, chancel south porch and western bellcote as shown in the 1862 sketch on the next page.

The village was the site of the Glendower Oak. This tree had a 27 foot girth, described as a stump in 1901, but as very much alive in *Country Life* in 1963! The village pump still stands on the green in front of the church.

At Little Mill Farm half a mile to the west of the village are the partial remains of a corn mill, with a leat from Llymon Brook powering an internal wheel.

Llanfaenor Church

Llanfair Kilgeddin (Welsh Llanfair: Cilgedin)
St Mary's Church at Cedin's Cell

This small village lies on the B4598 four miles north-west of Usk. The church is situated a mile to the north of what is now the village which has a Church in Wales primary school. Until recently this was shown on maps as St Mary's Yard though the village has expanded with new housing. In a field, opposite the entrance to the village, is an eight foot high motte, a cliff alongside the River Usk providing defence to the east and a ditch surrounding the remainder.

The church of St Mary the Virgin is signposted off the B4598 at Pantygoetre Farm. It lies amid fields and is well worth a visit. It is a Grade I Listed building but was declared redundant in 1982 and is now in the hands of The Friends of Friendless Churches. Medieval in origin, it was largely rebuilt in 1873-6 by the distinguished Arts and Crafts architect

John Dando Sedding. In 1888-90 the interior was decorated with large and colourful sgraffito panels by Heywood Sumner of the Art Workers' Guild. Sgraffito is the Roman system of applying layers of plaster tinted in contrasting colours to a moistened surface. The work was commissioned by the Revd. Williams J. C. Lindsay in memory of his wife Rosamond Emily Lindsay, who died in 1885 and depicts the Benedicte prayer with a further depiction of Christ above the chancel arch. These panels were restored in 1986-8 by Brian Morton.

The interior retains a late medieval pointed timber wagon roof and some medieval glass. There is a nave with south porch and western double bellcote above the west door and window, chancel with north vestry. Outside is a restored churchyard cross.

Llanfair Court north of the village dates from the 16th century with alterations in 1815 and again in 1855. Until 1925 it was a rectory but was acquired by Captain Geoffrey Crawshay, a descendant of the Crawshays of Cyfarthfa and founder of Captain Crawshay's Rugby Team. His son, Colonel Sir William Crawshay was a British agent during World War II and carried on the connection with the rugby team.

Llanfihangel Pont-y-Moel, St Michael and All Angels Church at the Bare Bridge

Not to be confused with Pontymoel, the suburb of Pontypool, Llanfihangel lies a mile and a half east of Pontypool some 300 yards west of the roundabout on the A4042 signposted to New Inn. There is the Jockey Garage, the 17th century Horse and Jockey thatched inn and the church.

The church is thought to be medieval in origin, but heavily restored in the 19th century. There are wagon roofs to both nave and chancel, thought to be 16th century. An unusual feature is that the entrance to the pulpit is through the vestry via the archway which originally led to the rood stair. This was apparently a design alteration implemented by the Revd. Christopher Cook, the longest serving rector in Wales. He retired in 1925 at the age of 98, having served as rector for 74 years. He died two years later at the age of 100. There is a memorial to him in the church. Externally the church has retained the tradition of lime-washed walls, but tradition has not been followed on the roof which has a combination of concrete tiles, imitating stone slates, and artificial Welsh slates.

Llanfihangel Tor-y-Mynydd
St. Michael's Church in the Mountain Hollow
This small scattered village lies two and a quarter miles north-west of Devauden in rich farming country. The name is slightly confusing as there are no mountains in the vicinity but the church lies below Star Hill.

The Grade II* Listed church of St Michael is signposted off the Devauden to Llansoy road. Although not identifiable in the *Norwich Taxatio* of 1254, it is likely to be one of four churches dedicated to St Michael but not given a location. The first recorded rector was in 1307. The church has a number of 15th century features and was restored in 1854 by John Prichard and John Pollard Seddon. The wagon-roof of the nave dates from the 16th century while the semi-circular chancel arch is late 15th century. Although the altar is Victorian, the stone pre-Reformation altar with its five dedication crosses stands to the side. The western double bellcote is Victorian, and the church has a nave, chancel and south porch. Further restoration was carried out in 2006-7 and while the church is kept locked, the key is available from the vicar or vicar's warden (details on the church website).

Church Farm adjacent to St Michael's dates from around 1600. Even older is the Star Inn which dates from the 15th century. It was where horses were changed on the coach road from Chepstow to Raglan. John Wesley stayed here and described it as "a good small inn". More recently it was the CAMRA Country Pub of the Year 2012/2013 and 2013/2014.

Llanfoist
Llanfoist lies a mile south of Abergavenny, between the Monmouthshire & Brecon Canal and the Heads of the Valleys dual carriageway. To the south is the Blorenge Mountain rising to 1,834 feet.

According to Iolo Morganwg the village takes its name from Ffwyst, a saint of Gwent, without pedigree, although he has been identified as a priest from the college of St Seiriol on Anglesey. The *Norwich Taxatio* of 1254 however uses the name Llanfoist and the church is dedicated to St Faith, presumably the nearest English sounding name to the Welsh.

Until the beginning of the 19th century Llanfoist was a small village with a number of larger properties and scattered farms. The site of the church is almost certainly Celtic. A yew tree blown down by a storm in early 2012 is thought to have been more than 1,000 years old and Gwenllian, daughter of Iestyn ap Gwrgan who married Ynyr, King of Gwent lived at Llanfoist at the time of Edward the Confessor.

The village developed with the opening of the canal in 1812. Tram lines connected the canal at Llanfoist with the coal and iron works at Blaenavon, using a series of inclines and tunnels across the Blorenge. There were also quarries above the canal and lime kilns.

Charles Edwards established a brewery in 1874. It was taken over by Buchans, the Rhymney brewer in 1945. Beer production ceased and Llanfoist Table Waters were produced until 1958 when production moved to Rhymney although the name was retained and Llanfoist Bitter Lemon won a gold medal at the British Bottlers' Institute in 1962.

By 1881 Llanfoist had a school and three pubs, the Waterloo Inn, formerly Waterloo House, itself the former Maerdy or reeve's house, the Bridge End Inn on the banks of the Usk and the Llanfoist Inn. The latter two remain, with the Llanfoist Inn now known as the Spice Lounge.

Between 1943 and 1945 radiators for Spitfires were produced at the Coopers Filters factory north of the Heads of the Valleys Road, an area now scheduled for housing.

From the 1960s the village has seen a major expansion with new housing developments, the Waitrose supermarket and council depot. There is also McDonalds Nursery Garden Centre and a village hall.

The church of St Faith dates from the 13th century and is set on the slope of the circular churchyard. It was largely rebuilt in 1872 at the expense of Crawshay Bailey II, in memory of his father who had retired to Llanfoist, buying Llanfoist House in 1851. The church has a nave, chancel, south porch and north vestry. The western double bellcote is Victorian, as is the chimney stack and the unusual central octagonal ventilator above the nave. In the churchyard is a medieval cross missing its head and a memorial to Crawshay Bailey and his wife Ann in the form of a pink granite obelisk. Buried in the churchyard is the novelist Alexander Cordell who died in 1997. Among his works were *Rape of the Fair Country*, *The Hosts of Rebecca* and *Song of the Earth*, which cover the history of industrialization of the South Wales valleys.

Llanfoist House lies to the west of the village. 17th century in origin it has now been split in two to form Llanfoist House and Hall.

Llanfoist Wharf is now frequented by pleasure craft but was once the link between the tram road and the canal.

Witchcraft ceased to be a punishable offence in England and Wales in 1735 but even before this trials for witchcraft in Wales had been rare. In certain areas however the superstitions and fear of witches continued. In 1827 John Prosser, shoemaker and parish constable, William Watkins, farmer, Thomas Jenkins, his servant, and Henry Evans, blacksmith, appeared before the Monmouth assizes charged with riot, and committing an assault upon Mary Nicholas. Nicholas a woman of 90 was believed to be a witch and was dragged by the four accused, pursued by a group of up to a 100, to Watkins' Llanfoist farm and forced to kneel down at the heels of a sickly colt on which they accused her of having cast a spell. She was forced to bless the colt. She was then scratched with a briar rose to see if she bled and stripped to the waist in search of a witch's teat. A benign tumour on her head was taken as a sign of witchcraft and hair was taken to see if it would burn. The four accused were found guilty of assault.

Llanfrechfa Church at a Hilly Place

Llanfrechfa is a small village two miles south-east of Cwmbrân. All Saints Church dates from the late medieval period but was enlarged when it was rebuilt, apart from the tower, in 1873-4 by Charles Buckeridge. There are three carved figures from Oberammergau removed from the chapel at Llanfrechfa Grange. The large carved stone reredos has a carved relief of The Last Supper by James Redfern, 1874. There is a large total immersion font in addition to the octagonal font and some fine stained glass windows by the London firm of Clayton and Bell. The crenellated tower is of three storeys and there is a nave with a north aisle, chancel, north-east vestry and south porch.

In 1921 the churchwarden, 73 year old William Richards was battered to death and robbed in his cottage. His murderer was never apprehended.

Llanfrechfa Grange lies three quarters of a mile to the north-west of the church. It was built in 1848 for the Newport businessman Charles Prothero by the architect John Harris Langdon of Newport. It was purchased in 1860 by Frank Johnstone Mitchell who had married Elizabeth Harcourt Rolls of The Hendre, Llangattock-Vibon-Avel. They enlarged the house and built a chapel using stained glass by William Wailes, a disciple of Pugin, from All Saints Church, Margaret Street, London. Mitchell died in 1915 and the Grange was over time transformed into a hospital and extended. Mitchell rebuilt, at a cost of several thousand pounds, the parish church of Llanfrechfa.

The 1862 school has been demolished while the Gate Inn dates from the 1890s.

Llangattock Lingoed

Llangattock Lingoed is a small rural village five miles north-east of Abergavenny on the Offa's Dyke footpath. The first part of the name is derived from the dedication of the church to St Catwg. Lingoed is more difficult and various suggestions have been put forward over the years. The earliest reference in the *Liber Landavensis* is to Ecclesia de Lancaddoc Kellenny, but by 1348 it is to Lancadok Lyncoyd. The most likely explanation is that it refers to the nearby Grange of Llyncoed, belonging to the Abbey of Dore, 'llyn' meaning lake or pool and 'coed' meaning wood.

The church of St Catwg/Cadoc is a Grade I Listed building. It stands in the sloping churchyard with the exterior white-washed. It is thought to be Celtic in origin, though it is difficult to give a precise date for the current building other than the work carried out by John Prichard in 1876. Internally there is a finely carved rood beam surviving from the 15th century rood screen. Both nave and chancel have wagon roofs. In the chancel are two 17th century oak box pews. Above the chancel arch is a depiction of the Royal Coat of Arms of Queen Anne, with a squint to the left of the arch and a piscina to the right. There is a nave, chancel, west tower and south porch. The three storey tower is tapered with a castellated parapet and stair turret. Outside is the five-step base and socket stone of a medieval churchyard cross. Between March and October horseshoe bats may be seen around the church.

There was a school here in the 18th century where James Davies the schoolmaster of Devauden was educated. In 1848 at the age of 83, he returned to teach at Llangattock Lingoed at the new National School built for and named after him. Davies endowed the school with £400. He died in the village the following year and is buried in the graveyard. The old school is north-west of the Old Rectory.

The Hunter's Moon Inn was formerly known as the Carpenter's Arms and dates back to the 14th century. The village smithy was on the T-junction north-east of the church.

A quarter of a mile south of the church is Cwm Farm where there is a purpose built cider house of 1754, complete with a cider mill and press.

A son of Lewis Morgan of Old Court, Llangattock Lingoed, was Sir Thomas Morgan. Sir Thomas had fought in the 30 Years War in the Protestant cause, along with Fairfax and Monck and in 1645 became Governor of Gloucester for the Parliamentarians. He captured Chepstow and Hereford and directed the siege of Raglan Castle until the arrival of Sir Thomas Fairfax. After the Restoration he was appointed Governor of Jersey by Charles II and frustrated French designs on the island. According to George Wöosung Wade, in his book *Monmouthshire* written in 1930, his younger brother was Sir Henry Morgan, the buccaneer and Deputy Governor of Jamaica. Others suggest that Henry was Thomas's nephew and dates of birth would tend to confirm this.

Llangattock Nigh Usk (also known as Llangattock-juxta-Usk and The Bryn) (Welsh: Llangatwg Dyffryn Wysg)

Llangattock Nigh Usk is a small village four miles south-east of Abergavenny, between the A40 and the River Usk. Described in 1868 as "a small rustic place", there has been some building but it lies on a No Through Road.

The Grade II* Listed church of St Catwg, after which the village was named, lies at the southern end of the village next to the Old Rectory and Rectory Farm. The main features of the church date from the 15th century, but this was due to a rebuilding as there is evidence of an earlier structure. In 1827 the church was re-roofed by the Gloucester engineer, John Upton and there was a further refurbishment in 1865-6 by John Prichard. The rood stair survives and the font is of the late Norman period, but the main fittings are Victorian. There are some good medieval tiles. The nave and chancel are under the single open roof structure of 1827. The four storey tower is topped by a pyramid roof with a ball finial. Outside is the hexagonal four step base of a churchyard cross with a restored crosshead. The railway passes between the church and the River Usk.

Penpergwm House at the entrance to the village was built in 1845 as a rectory and is now a residential care home. The village school was built in 1876 but closed in 2010 and has been converted to offices. There is a modern village hall and a post office.

Llangattock-Vibon-Avel (Welsh: Llangatwg Feibion Afel)
St Catwg's Church of the Sons of Abel

Llangattock-Vibon-Avel is a scattered village three and a half miles northwest of Monmouth. The parish covers a large rural area and is probably best known for The Hendre, the home of Baron Llangattock, John Allan Rolls, father of the Hon Charles Stewart Rolls, joint founder of Rolls Royce.

The church of St Catwg/Cadoc is found by taking the Newcastle road off the B4233. It is signposted off this road and stands near Llangattock Manor. Plans for the restoration of the church were drawn up by Thomas Henry Wyatt in 1852-3 and the same architect was used in 1875 to add the north aisle, extend the chancel and add a south porch and organ chamber. In 1866 the church furnishers Cox & Sons redecorated the church at the expense of John Etherington Rolls. The extent of these works makes dating the nave and chancel difficult, but the tower is 14th century. In the graveyard are tombs of the Rolls family including that of Charles Stewart Rolls who apart from his collaboration with Royce became the first Briton to die in an aviation accident when the tail of his Short-Wright No.5 biplane broke off in mid air during a display at Bournemouth in 1910.

The Rolls family originated in Bermondsey where, in 1746, Aaron Rolls was a victualler at St Thomas à Watering on the Kent Road. In 1767 his son John married Sarah Coysh who inherited property in London and Monmouthshire. The Hendre Estate was bequeathed to her by her uncle Henry Allen who died in 1767 and is commemorated in the chancel of St Mary's Church in Monmouth. John and Sarah Rolls maintained their home at The Grange in Bermondsey but in 1794 John was appointed High Sheriff of Monmouthshire. He died in 1801 and was succeeded by his only surviving son, also John. In 1803 he was appointed Lieutenant Colonel of the Loyal Southwark Volunteer Infantry, having earlier that year married Martha Barnet, only daughter and heiress of Jacob Barnet. They added 3, Bryanston Square to their residences and in 1830 began the enlargement of The Hendre as a shooting lodge. In 1837 John was succeeded by his eldest son, John Etherington Welch Rolls, born in 1807. He was a Justice of the Peace and Deputy Lieutenant of Monmouthshire, serving as High Sheriff in 1842. He employed Thomas Henry Wyatt to enlarge The Hendre, building on the work of George Vaughan Maddox. The Hendre estate extended to 1,000 acres complete with a deer park said to contain 1,000 deer, surrounded by a tall iron fence. There was a pineapple house, an ice house and lakes stocked with rare breeds of duck. John Etherington's younger brother Alexander lived at Croft-y-Bwla in Monmouth where he was mayor.

Expansion of The Hendre continued under John Allan Rolls who inherited the estate from his father in 1870. Work was carried out by Wyatt and later by Aston Webb. In 1877 he also rebuilt the 17th century Llangattock Manor next to the church, intending it as a dower house, though it became the vicarage. In the same year Rolls commissioned Wyatt to build the school, now the Montessori Infants School. In 1868 John Allan Rolls married Georgiana Marcia Maclean in London. She was the daughter of Sir Charles Fitzroy Maclean, 25th Clan Chief of Clan Maclean. Rolls was appointed High Sheriff of Monmouthshire in 1875, and served as MP for Monmouthshire from 1880-1885. In 1892 he was raised to the peerage as Baron Llangattock of The Hendre in the County of Monmouth. A noted philanthropist, he donated to the town of Monmouth a public hall, gymnasium, and isolation hospital. He served as Mayor of the town in 1896-7 and was granted the Freedom of the Borough in 1901. He was also a breeder of shire horses, Hereford cattle and Shropshire sheep. An antiquary, he financed the restoration of a number of the county's churches. Lady Llangattock also had an interest in history and acquired a large collection of Nelson memorabilia which she bequeathed to the town of Monmouth to be housed initially in the gymnasium funded by her husband. This building is now known as the Nelson Rooms while the collection is now housed in The Nelson Museum and Local History Centre, occupying the old Market Hall.

Lord and Lady Llangattock had four children, The Hon. John Maclean Rolls (1870-1916) 2nd Baron Llangattock; who died from wounds received in action at the Battle of the Somme, Henry Alan Rolls (1871-1916) who was a sickly child and returned home from university after a nervous breakdown, Eleanor Georgiana Rolls and Charles Stewart Rolls. The latter studied mechanical and applied science at Trinity College, Cambridge. He travelled to Paris in 1896 to buy his first car, a Peugeot Phaeton. He was one of the first three car owners in Wales and in 1900 brought the Duke and Duchess of York, later King George V and Queen Mary, to The Hendre for their stay, by car. After a short career with the London and North Western Railway in Crewe, he set up a motor dealership C.S. Rolls & Co. in Fulham in 1902. A year later he was introduced to Henry Royce and within months they formed a partnership. The first Rolls-Royce car was unveiled at the Paris Salon in December the same year. In 1906 he broke the record for the Monte Carlo to London journey in a Rolls Royce and also won a race at Yonkers in New York, again gaining publicity for the marque. As well as his interest in cars, Charles while still at Eton wired the servants quarters at The Hendre for electricity. He also designed the pumping station supplying the house with water and the gasworks for lighting as well as garden machinery including a steam roller. Rolls' interest later switched to aviation. In 1903 he was a founding member of the Royal Aero Club and became the second person in Britain to be licensed to fly balloons by it. That same year he won the Gordon Bennett Gold Medal for the longest single flight time. He qualified to fly powered aircraft in January 1909 with the French Aero Club, being awarded license No.23, internationally recognised under the Fédération Aéronautique Internationale. He was later awarded the 2nd license to be granted by the Royal Aero Club. On 2nd June 1910, he became the first man to make a non-stop double flight across the English Channel and he was awarded the Gold Medal of the Royal Aero Club. The following month he was killed in an air crash at Hengistbury Head near Bournemouth while taking part in an air show. His statue by Sir William Goscombe John stands in Agincourt Square, Monmouth.

With the death of the 2nd Lord Llangattock at the Somme, the title became extinct. The family connection with The Hendre ended in 1980 and the house is now the centre for the 18 Hole Rolls of Monmouth Golf Club with function rooms available for weddings and conferences.

Llangovan

Llangovan is a tiny rural village three miles south-east of Raglan. At the heart of the parish is the church of St Govan, Church Farm and nearby Springfield Farm.

St Govan is associated with Bosherston in Pembrokeshire and Baring-Gould denied a link with this church. It stands on a traditional raised Celtic llan and dates from the Norman period. Grade II* Listed, the church is closed and leased by a wildlife trust as it is now home to a colony of horseshoe bats. Access is possible only in the winter months. It has a nave with a western bell-turret enlarged in the 17th century, a south porch, provided by John Jenkin of Llangovan in his will of 1625, a chancel and north vestry. There was a refurbishment in 1890-91 by Henry Prothero of

Cheltenham. There are barrel vaulted roofs to nave and chancel, with shutters to the nave windows for the protection of the bats. The churchyard has a medieval cross-base of five steps and socket stone, topped by a cross head mounted in 1903.

Church Farm dates from the end of the Tudor period.

Llangua (Welsh: Llangiwa)

Llangua is a small scattered village on the River Monnow, a mile and a half north-west of Grosmont. It takes its name from St Ciwa. Baring-Gould asserts that: "The Welsh genealogies know nothing of her, which shows that most probably she was not of Welsh origin. The church of Llangiwa or Llangua, in Monmouthshire, now dedicated to S. James, is generally supposed to have been dedicated to her. It occurs as Lann Culan in the Book of Llan Dav, in the grant by Cynfyn, son of Gwrgant, in the time of Bishop Cerenhir, about the ninth century, and as Languwan and Langywan in the fourteenth century additions to it. In the *Norwich Taxatio*, 1254, it is spelt Lagywan. Kigwa or Ciwa is almost certainly Cuach, the nurse of S. Ciaran, and a notable abbess in Ireland".

Following the conquest of the area, William Fitz Osbern (Lord of Breteuil in Calvados), gifted the manor and church at Llangua together with all the tithes of the Forest of Grosmont, tithes of the toll at Striguil and half of all the tithes of all the cows, pigs, coin, fisheries, standing corn and honey in all the lands between the Rivers Usk and Wye to the Benedictine Monastery he had founded at Lyre in Normandy. A monastic cell was established at Llangua, called variously a monastery or priory. It was granted to the Carthusian house of Sheen at Richmond on the Thames in 1414 after the Parliament of Leicester transferred ownership of 'alien' religious houses to English based monasteries. It was dissolved in 1539 but all physical evidence has been lost though it is thought to have been situated near the site of Great House Farm.

The church of St James remains in the Church of England as part of the Hereford diocese. Standing between the A465 and the River Monnow the small late 15th century church has a half timbered belfry turret. Inside the nave and chancel have wagon roofs. There are two aumbries and a carved figure of St James on the south wall of the nave. A major refurbishment was carried out in 1954-5, by the architect Ernest Alfred Roiser and financed by for Ivor Bulmer-Thomas, former chairman of the

Redundant Churches Fund in memory of his wife. This included the installation of the post and panel partition with painted figures from a redundant chapel at Whitford in Devon. The church remains in use though services are only held regularly once a month. Outside is the three stepped base off a medieval churchyard cross with a modern head.

The Abergavenny tramroad was built in 1827 for the transport of coal. It crossed the Monnow at Langua Bridge, north of the church. The bridge was built by R.G. Thomas and consisted of four arches. The tramline eventually opened in 1829 and 10.5 tons of the first load of coal was distributed free in Hereford. The bridge is now incorporated into the road bridge.

Llangwm Church in the Valley

Llangwm is divided between Llangwm Uchaf and Llangwm Isaf (Upper and Lower), situated three miles east of Usk on the B4235.

There are two churches in the village, St Jerome's which served Llangwm Uchaf and St John's, Llangwm Isaf, though they are only a quarter of a mile apart.

St John's church is first recorded in the 12th century, but by 1840 it was in ruins. It was rebuilt in 1849-51 by John Prichard. The nave and chancel are contained in a single shell, with a chancel arch inserted between them with a small bell above the chancel and a west door and porch. The church was said to have been in ruins for 100 years before its rebuilding and the two parishes had been combined.

St Jerome's is the larger of the two churches but it has been declared redundant and is now in the care of The Friends of Friendless Churches. First recorded in 1128, it is to be found at the end of the lane east of St John's. It is Grade I Listed and has an exceptionally fine, rare, carved rood screen and loft, said to have survived the Puritans because of the church's remoteness, though Walter Cradock, a leader of the Puritans and supporter of Cromwell was born in Llangwm and in 1655 was appointed vicar. He preached the celebratory sermon in Parliament on the fall of Charles I's headquarters in Oxford in 1646 and is buried in the chancel. There is no memorial to Cradock, but there is one to Richard Creed, his son-in-law who died in 1690. Creed was secretary to Admirals Blake and Montagu and later the schoolmaster at Llangwm.

The church was restored in 1863-9 by John Pollard Seddon, largely rebuilding the porch and nave. Further work was carried out on the chancel by Ewan Christian in 1871 and more recently preservation work has been carried out by the Friends (2013-14). The tower is positioned to the north of the chancel. Seddon's contribution at St Jerome's included the pulpit and font which represent some of his finest work. He also restored and coloured the rood screen, his drawing of which was exhibited at the Royal Academy and Architectural Association in 1878.

Llangwm Baptist Chapel on Chapel Lane was built in 1840 on land given by Cradock Gwynne Watkins. An earlier Baptist chapel was at Golden Hill where in the latter part of the 17th century Thomas Quarrel became the minister, serving Llangwm and Llantrisant. Quarrel had been a Baptist minister in Shrewsbury in 1662, but moved to Llangwm when he was ejected from Shrewsbury. He lived at Ty-gwyn to the south of the village, now in ruins. Peniel or Pen-y-well Chapel stood for many years in ruins amid the tombstones on Golden Hill.

The National School was built in 1870 on the Llansoy road, designed by Seddon. It is now a private house. The Parish Hall stands on a crossroads nearby.

At Camp Farm, south of the village on the B4235 are the remains of a ditched motte now forming a garden feature. A mile and a half south-east of the village is the Iron Age Gaer Fawr Hillfort. Extending to some ten acres it is one of the largest hillforts in the county. The Bridge Inn at Llangwm closed in 2010 and efforts of the local community to have it re-opened have so far proved to be in vain.

The village remains small although there has been some expansion with mainly bungalows built well back from the road.

Llangybi

Llangybi is located some two and a half miles south of Usk on the Caerleon to Usk road. The older part of the village was to the east of the road while new developments have taken place to the west.

Llangybi takes its name from the dedication of the church to the Cornish Saint Cybi. In Cornwall he founded foundations at Duloe and Tregony. Cybi was the son of Selyf, King of Cornwall, and St Gwen, the sister of St Non the mother of St David. Following his father's death there was a failed attempt to place him on the throne and Cybi fled to Morgannwg where at first he was not well received, but was eventually granted two sites for churches by King Edelig, Llangybi and Landauer Guir.

He did not remain long in the area, travelling first to St David's and then to Ireland where he fell out with St Fintan and was forced to return to Wales where he set up a church at Llangybi in Caernarvonshire and later settled at Caer Gybi, Holyhead. The church dates from the 13th-14th century with new windows in the 15th century. It was refurbished in the 17th century and again in 1909-10 when the architect was W.H. Dashwood Caple of Cardiff. Medieval wall paintings dated to 1450 have survived including 'Christ of the Trades' or 'Sunday Christ', a depiction of Christ wounded by the tools of people who worked on Sundays. Entry is through the door in the west tower, with nave and chancel of equal width. The interior is lime-washed and light and airy. The priest in charge in 1423 was the chronicler, Adam of Usk. Adam was a native of Usk and under the patronage of Edmund Mortimer, 3rd Earl of March and Lord of Usk, attended Oxford University and became a Doctor of Law. After lecturing at Oxford he was one of those commissioned to justify the deposition of King Richard II on legal grounds. He left for Rome in 1402, returning to Wales in 1408. He died in 1430 and is buried in the Priory Church at Usk. He is remembered for his *Chronicle of English History from 1377 to 1421*, a period when he met Kings and Popes as well as dealing with the law. Across the road south of the church is St Cybi's Well, which still feeds the stream that runs alongside the road to the Usk. South-east of the church is a standing stone of unknown date.

The White Hart Inn is effectively two houses dating from around 1600, but evidence suggests that the two have always been linked. The inn existed prior to 1600 and formed part of Jane Seymour's wedding dowry for Henry VIII. Cromwell is reputed to have stayed here during the English Civil War and T.S. Elliot visited in 1935 and mentioned the Inn in his poem *Usk*: "Do not suddenly break the branch, or hope to find The White Hart over the white well". The white painted, now ruined village well was near the Inn.

Bethel Particular Baptist Chapel on Ton Road was built in 1837 and refurbished in 1902. It has now been converted for residential use. Also on Ton Road is Craigwen, built in 1831 as the village school. Funds were provided by the Williams family for its building and maintenance. It became the teacher's house in 1894 when the parish school was built next door. The parish school has now been converted to living accommodation. The other house of note in the village is New House, on the northern outskirts. This large house dates from 1710.

In Llangybi on the night of 17th June 1878, William Watkins, Elizabeth, his wife, and their children. Charlotte, Alice, and Frederick were murdered. Their inquest was held at The White Hart Inn. Joseph Garcia, a 21 year old Spanish seaman, was arrested in Newport on the 19th of June in possession of William Watkins' shoes and other items. He was convicted of the murders at the Autumn Assizes and hanged at Usk on 18th November 1878.

North of the village, to the side of a private road, stand the remnants of Tregrug Castle. An earthwork castle it was superseded by Llangibby Castle and a bowling green was established on the top. Tregrug derived its name from the commote of Tref-grug. Llangibby Castle was built in the early 14th century, to the west of Tregrug Castle and the scant remains are now surrounded by woodland. A new mansion, known as Llangibby Castle was built by the Williams family, together with the 17th century Llangibby House, between the two castles, with extensive gardens. Both House and Castle were demolished in 1951. Roger Williams, High Sheriff of Monmouthshire, acquired Llangibby Castle in 1545. During the English Civil War, his grandson Sir Trevor Williams, a protestant, was captured by the Roundheads in 1643, while acting for the King. He then appears to have changed sides, as in 1645 he was arrested by the King for hindering recruitment to the Royalist cause in South Wales. He was released on bail, only to assist the Roundheads in the capture of Monmouth. He changed sides again, helping to capture Chepstow Castle for the King and was forced to renounce his baronetcy after Cromwell was victorious. He had a long running dispute with the Marquess of Worcester, which continued after the Restoration, when in 1680 as a Member of Parliament, he accused Worcester of manning Chepstow Castle with papists. Worcester, by now the Duke of Beaufort sued him for libel in 1684 and Williams was fined £20,000 and imprisoned. He was elected as Member for Monmouthshire again in 1689 even though he was still in the King's Bench Prison. He died in 1692. He had married Elizabeth Morgan, daughter of Thomas Morgan of Machen and they had two sons. Sir John Williams died in 1704 and was succeeded by his notorious brother Sir Hopton Williams (see Llancayo). Sir Hopton served as MP between 1705 and 1708 but then retired to Llangibby, his time spent improving the gardens and planting the avenue of trees between the Castle and the River Usk which can still be seen today. The estate eventually passed by marriage to the Addams-Williams family who still own the estate. The name of Llangibby is known in Australia where Chris Addams-Williams has established the Llangibby Estate Vineyard in the Adelaide Hills. The *Llangibby Castle* was a ship in the Union Castle Line, built in 1929. During World War II she served as a troop ship and was damaged by German bombing at Liverpool in 1940. In 1942 she was torpedoed by a German U-boat, but made it to the Azores and eventually to Britain via Gibraltar with a damaged stern, steering by her engines. Repaired, the *Llangibby Castle* took part in the allied landings in French North Africa, Sicily and Normandy. After the war she resumed passenger services until 1954.

Llanhennock (Welsh: Llanhenwg)

Llanhennock is a small village a little over a mile and a half north-east of Caerleon. According to Iolo Morganwg the church was built by Taliesin in the 6th century in honour of his father, St Henwg. This is the only mention of St Henwg and other accounts suggest that Taliesin's adopted father was Elffin.

The church today is dedicated to St John the Baptist and dates from the 15th century. It stands on a Celtic llan in a prominent position overlooking the lower Usk valley. It was largely rebuilt in 1863 by John Prichard and John Pollard Seddon when the north aisle and vestry were added as was the parapet of the west tower. There are the remains of a medieval churchyard cross.

The Old Rectory is now a Cheshire Home and the school, provided by Sir Digby Mackworth is now a private house but retains its bell turret.

The village retains its inn, the Wheatsheaf, but the old smithy is now a private house.

Glen Usk is a neo-classical mansion half a mile to the east of the church, built in 1820 for Sir Digby Mackworth of the Gnoll, Neath. The house enjoys views over the River Usk and has extensive gardens, remodelled in the 1920s.

Llanhilleth (Welsh: Llanhiledd) Also known as Llanhiddel

There are two centres for Llanhilleth. The older part of the village is centred on the 9th century church of St Illtyd, a mile and a half south of Abertillery. The main settlement lies a further half mile to the south.

The name is derived from Llan Heledd, the 'e' changing to 'i' to account for the local Gwenhwyseg dialect. Listed by Baring-Gould as a Virgin, there is no record of this saint in the Welsh saintly genealogies. And it is not a common Welsh name. Heledd is Welsh for a brine or salt pit as in the Welsh name for Nantwich in Cheshire, Yr Heledd Wen.

The oldest part of the village is around the church of St Illtyd and the complex of Castell Taliorum. The local tradition was that Christianity was brought to Llanhilleth by St Paul, but there is no evidence of a Celtic church being established here before the 9th century. The church which is built on a traditional circular Celtic llan dates from the early 13th century when it was under the control of the Cistercian Abbey of Llantarnam. St Illtyd's has a western tower with saddleback roof, nave and chancel, but no vestry. Entry is through the tower.

St Illtyd's ceased to be the parish church in 1911 and in 1984 the church was deconsecrated and offered for sale. It was purchased for £1 by Mrs Gladys Hale, then owner of the Carpenters' Arms. She was however unable to raise the funds for renovation and it was purchased by Blaenau Gwent Borough Council in 1990 and restored with advice from Cadw. The graveyard remains consecrated ground belonging to the Church in Wales.

There are the remains of two castles near the church. The more obvious is the motte of a motte and bailey castle, known as St Illtyd's Castle Mound or Twyn Motte. It may be the site of Castell Hithell which was destroyed in 1233. Behind what was the Carpenters' Arms are the scant remains of Castell Taliorum, a 14th century masonry castle which was occupied for a short period. Excavations in the 1920s revealed two towers, one round tower with a diameter of 18 metres and the other to the west a cruciform structure 23 metres across. The site was levelled in the late 19th century revealing Roman pottery and coins suggesting that there may have been an earlier fortification on the site.

Until recently this small village had a pub and consists of just a few houses and farms.

The main settlement of Llanhilleth grew dramatically in the last two decades of the 19th century. In 1880 there were a number of cottages, small terraces, Llanhilleth House, the Union Foundry public house and Zion Independent Chapel. The Western Valleys Section of the Monmouthshire Railway was built along the line of the old canal and completed in the early 1850s. The station was reopened in 2008.

Llanhilleth Colliery began in the 1850s with the sinking of the first shaft to the south of the village and west of the railway. A second shaft was sunk in 1865 and by 1896 the colliery under the control of Partridge Jones

& Co employed over 800 men. After a temporary halt to production, there were 1,800 men employed in 1908. Numbers gradually declined and in 1947 there were 736 miners. The colliery closed in 1969.

Zion Independent chapel on the High Street was built in 1877 and rebuilt in 1890. It is still in use as Zion Congregationalist Church also known as Zion Miners' Chapel. The Wesleyan church on High Street was built in 1905 but has been converted to residential and commercial use. A chapel on Hafod-Arthen Road was built between 1901 and 1920 but has since been demolished.

St Mark's Church on Brooklyn Terrace was built 1897-99 by the Cardiff architect C. Telford Evans. A large church on two floors in the Gothic style it has a nave and chancel and a double bellcote. It now serves Llanhilleth and Aberbeeg in the Tillery ministry.

The mountain above the village was said to be the haunt of an ellyll or mischievous fairy known as the Old Woman of the Mountain. Wirt Sykes relates that: "Those who saw this apparition, whether by night or on a misty day, would be sure to lose their way. The popular tradition in that district was that the Old Woman of the Mountain was the spirit of one Juan White, who lived time out of mind in those parts, and was thought to be a witch; because the mountains were not haunted in this manner until after Juan White's death. When people first lost their way, and saw her before them, they used to hurry forward and try to catch her, supposing her to be a flesh-and-blood woman, who could set them right; but they never could overtake her, and she on her part never looked back; so that no man ever saw her face".

Llanishen (Welsh: Llanisien)

Llanishen enjoys an elevated position, overlooking the Usk valley, four and a half miles south-east of Raglan, on the Devauden to Trellech road which formed the boundary of the Trellech Grange of Tintern Abbey. The village takes its name from the original dedication of the church to St Isan, described as such in the plans for the rebuild in 1851-54 by Prichard and Seddon. The *Liber Landavensis* gives it as Lann Nissien and Baring-Gould believed that the "Norman ecclesiastics read into the name that of Dionysius or Denis". In a Tintern charter the Monmouthshire church occurs as "the Church of Dionysius of Lanissan". The current dedication is to St Dennis, though there is no saint with this spelling of the name.

Little is known of St Isan, who was a monk at Llantwit Major and is identified with Abbot Isanus, but his festival is not entered in the Welsh calendars. The church which stands on sloping ground has a nave, chancel, vestry, south porch and a western bellcote, topped with a small spire. The rebuilding in the 1850s replaced the earlier thatched church.

Bethel Bible Christian Chapel was built in 1841 nearly a mile north of the church. It is now a private house. Llanishen Wesleyan Methodist Chapel was built in 1820 on Church Road. It has been converted and extended for residential use and shows little sign of its original purpose.

The Carpenters' Arms dates from 1700. The village smithy was opposite, now a garage and village shop. The village Board School opened in 1877 but closed in 1987. The building on Church Road is now a private house. There is a modern village hall. There has been some new building in the village, which remains small and surrounded by farmland.

Llanllowell (Welsh: Llanllywel)

Llanllowell is a tiny village a mile and a half south-east of Usk. Apart from the church there is the rectory and Great House Farm. It was a lordship held initially by the Fitz-Herberts.

The church is dedicated to St Llywel, a disciple of Dubricius, and later of Teilo. It occurs as Lanlouel in the Taxatio of 1254. It is a single cell structure dating from the 13th century, refurbished in 1871-4 by John Prichard and William White and in 1964 by Reginald Lewis Edmunds of Blaenavon. Prichard and White's plans included a north vestry which was never built, but they did rebuild the east and north walls. The font is medieval and there is a projection on the front wall to accommodate a rood stair. As well as the south porch there is a priest's door in the chancel. St Llywel's is now part of the Usk group of churches and services are still held in this pretty little medieval church.

Llanmartin (Welsh: Llanfarthin)

The village lies under a mile south-east of Langstone, and north of the M4. A mainly agricultural area there has been some small development off the Magor Road.

The church of St Martin was rebuilt in the Perpendicular style in 1858. It is mentioned in the Doomsday Book but the earliest surviving part dates from the 13th century when it served as the chapel for Pencoed Castle as well as the parish church. There was a Morgan Chapel built in 1541 which contained the tombs of the Morgan family and their successors at Pencoed Castle. By 1801 the chapel was in ruins, the lead from the roof having been sold off. William Coxe reported that an elaborate alabaster tomb of Sir Walter Montagu was scarcely discernible. The chapel was replaced by the vestry on rebuilding and only the elaborate tomb of Sir Thomas Morgan remains. This shows 14 children in prayer with a central figure bearing a coat of arms. The tower and chancel arch date from the 15th century with the upper part of the tower rebuilt. The church has a chancel, nave, south porch and vestry in addition to the battlemented tower. The old rectory is now known as Hollyberry Hall.

Bethel Calvinistic Methodist Chapel near Court Farm was built in 1838 and rebuilt in 1891 but has since been demolished. In 1661 Richard Blinman, an Independent and native of Chepstow who had emigrated to New England in 1640 with a group of Welsh men and women, was indicted at Monmouth Assizes, for unlawful assembly at the church in Llanmartin, and bound over for £40, after his return to Wales in 1659.

Court Farm Barn was built in 1675 and is now The Old Barn Inn, having been converted in 1988. Court Farm dates from around 1700 while in the field to the west is an enclosure defined by the three arms of a moat.

The village had a smithy on Waltwood Road, now a private house.

Pencoed Castle stands to the east of Llanmartin. The earliest mention of it in the records is in the reign of Henry III, when a Sir Richard de la More was the owner. The castle and estate continued in the possession of the family of De la More for about a century, before it passed to that of Kemys. Sir Walter de Kemys was recorded as its lord in 1306 and 1337. During the reign of Henry VII it belonged to Sir Thomas Morgan (1453-1510), eldest son of Morgan ap Jenkin ap Philip of Langston, a branch of the family of Morgan of Tredegar. It was Sir Thomas and later his grandson, also Sir Thomas Morgan, who were mainly responsible for converting the castle into a Tudor manor house. Sir William Morgan who inherited in 1565 was a soldier and adventurer. He was also a Member of Parliament for Monmouthshire Boroughs in 1572. He had sold the St Brides estate at Langstone in 1577 and when he died in 1583 the Exchequer ruled that he had died in debt to the government to the extent of 2,000 marks. His estate was seized but Sir Walter Montagu of Boughton, who had married Anne, Sir William's niece and heiress, was allowed to farm the estate until the

Pencoed Mansion 1801 by Sir Richard Colt Hoare

debt had been cleared. Pencoed passed through numerous hands over the years, becoming increasingly dilapidated. In 1914 it was purchased by David Thomas, Lord Rhondda who began renovations, but following his death in 1918 his widow built a smaller house nearby. The tower dates from the early building which was a moated castle but the gatehouse and main building are Tudor. The roof and windows were restored but not the interior. Plans were put forward in 2007 for conversion but have not been pursued. In addition to the three storey main block there are stone barns. The castle is not open to the public.

Llanover (Welsh: Llanofer)
The main part of the village of Llanover lies on the A4042, four miles south of Abergavenny, though the church of St Bartholomew lies to the east in what is known as Old Llanover. The original parish of Llanover covered a large area of some 4,700 acres including Blaenavon, four miles to the west. According to Iolo Morganwg the village takes its name from the founding of a cell by St Gofor, a hermit. Baring-Gould however suggests that the spelling Lanmouor in *Liber Landavensis* points to a

name of Myfor. Another suggestion is that Llanover is a corruption of Llanddwfr meaning the Church of the Waters,

The village is dominated by the Llanover Estate. Benjamin Waddington moved to Ty Uchaf at Llanover in 1792. His younger daughter Augusta married Benjamin Hall, grandson of Richard Crawshay in 1823. Hall's father, also Benjamin, had married Crawshay's daughter and had been made a partner in the business and given the Abercarn Estate by his father-in-law. The marriage of Augusta and Benjamin united the neighbouring estates and they built Llanover House in 1837. Designed by Benjamin Hopper, it was a three storey mansion, intended by the Halls as a centre for Welsh culture. It was demolished in 1936. Benjamin became MP for Monmouthshire 1831-37 but then transferred to Marylebone where he served until raised to the peerage in 1859, taking the title Baron Llanover of Llanover and Abercarn. He had been created a baronet in 1838. As Sir Benjamin Hall he was the first President of the Board of Health between 1854 and 1855 and First Commissioner of Works from 1855-1858, in which role he supervised the installation of the bell known as Big Ben, which according to many is named after him. From 1861 until his death in a shooting accident in 1867, he served as Lord Lieutenant of Monmouthshire.

Lady Llanover survived her husband by 29 years and was an enthusiastic supporter of the Welsh language and culture. She encouraged the use of the traditional triple harp which was frowned upon by the non-conformists because of its association with dance. She promoted the Welsh costume and through it the Welsh flannel industry. Staff at Llanover were required to wear Welsh costumes and the image of the Welsh woman in shawl and high hat is largely attributable to her. She learnt Welsh and collected manuscripts, including those of Iolo Morganwg and supported eisteddfodau, winning a prize at Cardiff in 1834 for her essay *The Advantages resulting from the Preservation of the Welsh language and National Costume of Wales,* for which she used the nom-de-plume Gwenynen Gwent (the Bee of Gwent). Lady Llanover was a staunch protestant, funding Calvinistic Methodist churches. She was also a supporter of the Temperance Movement, closing all public houses on her estates.

Lord and Lady Llanover's daughter, Augusta married the Roman Catholic Arthur Jones of Llanarth in 1846 and their son was Ivor Herbert, 1st Baron Treowen.

Lord and Lady Llanover are buried at St Bartholomew's church. The Llanover Estate remains in the family.

St Bartholomew's is built on an ancient, possibly pre-Christian site near the River Usk, on the eastern side of the Llanover Estate. The nave appears to be the oldest part of the surviving church and Norman in origin. The chancel dates from the early 14th century and the tower early 16th century. The tower was home to the village school until 1835 when a new school was built to the south-east. The font is Norman and there is an unusual Royal Arms of William IV over the chancel arch. There are rood loft stairs and a piscina while many of the pews are inscribed with the names of local farms. According to the guide to the church the pulpit was salvaged from St Bodolph's church, London in 1988. Outside there are the remains of a churchyard cross. Opposite the church there is a suspension footbridge crossing the Usk where, in 1881, there was a boat house.

Hanover Congregational Chapel was built in 1744 and rebuilt in 1839. A schoolroom was added in 1868 and the chapel was refurnished in 1893. It remains in use. Lady Llanover's Calvinistic Methodist Chapel was built in 1898 on Old Abergavenny Road. It is now used as a retreat for church and community groups and is available for weddings and meetings. Llanover House had its own chapel in the grounds, known as Coldbrook Chapel.

Ty Uchaf is a late 18th century three storey house built for Benjamin Waddington and replaced Court Farm as the main house of the Llanover Estate.

Tre Elidyr is a group of cottages was built in 1922 around an open green containing the village war memorial. It is named after Sir Benjamin Hall's great grandson, Captain Elidyr J.B. Herbert, who was killed on active service in Palestine during the First World War. Designed by Alfred Powell the development included a new school, opened in 1925. A more modern development runs off it.

The Llanover Estate is still run as a commercial enterprise, with business units, property lettings and a garden school running courses and one-off lectures.

Llansoy (Welsh: Llan-soe)

Llansoy is a small, rural village three and a half miles south-east of Raglan. It takes its name from St Tysoi, a pupil of St Dubricius, mentioned in the *Liber Landavensis*. Little else is known of Tysoi; but he is in all probability the Soy who was one of the clerical witnesses to a grant to the monastery of Llancarfan in the time of Abbot Paul. Baring-Gould notes that although the village is named after Tysoi, the church had no dedication and records of the 1857-58 refurbishment give the dedication to St Michael. Ordnance Survey maps give the dedication as St Siso up to the 1920s.

The church today is known as St Tysoi's and is built on a circular Celtic llan. The building dates from the 15th century with the squat, crenellated tower built in 1688-9. There is a nave, chancel, west tower, south porch and north vestry. In the nave wall there is a projection for the rood stair and both nave and chancel have 15th century barrel roofs. In the porch is a polygonal stoup. Most of the fittings are from the 1857-8 restoration by John Pollard Seddon and John Prichard.

Llan-Soe Wesleyan Methodist Chapel was built in 1867 but has now been converted to a private house. The National School was erected and opened in 1867, for 40 children. It is now the village hall.

The village had a pub, the Cross Keys, which with the well, shop/post office and smithy formed the centre of the village, all have now closed. There has been modern development on a small scale, north of the church and St Tysoi Close.

Arthur Evanson, born in the village, was selected to play rugby for Wales in 1881, but chose to play for England, as his brother Wyndham had already done. He played for England against Wales in 1882 at St Helens Swansea, in the second match between the two countries, converting two tries in England's victory.

Llantarnum

Llantarnum today is a suburb of Cwmbran on the south-eastern outskirts of the town. It is included as the abbey played an important part in the history of the county. The full title is Llanfihangel Llantarnam. 'Llantarnam' it is suggested is a corruption of Nant Teyrnon, being the ancient name for the river known today as Afon Lwyd. A Cistercian Abbey was founded here in 1179 by Hywel ap Iorwerth of Caerleon and initially known as Caerleon Abbey. It was a daughter house of Strata Florida Abbey. At the time of the Dissolution there were just six monks. In 1561 the abbey was purchased by William Morgan of Pentrebach whose son, Edward Morgan, an MP and High Sheriff, built a mansion on the site. The Morgan family were staunch Roman Catholics and the second baronet, Sir

Edward Morgan gave shelter to Saint David Lewis, the Jesuit priest who was hanged and disembowelled at Usk following his arrest on 17th November 1678 at St Michael's Church, Llantarnam.

The Abbey was eventually inherited in the early 19th century by Reginald John Blewitt, a barrister, the founder of the Monmouthshire Merlin in 1829 and the Monmouth and Glamorgan Bank in 1837. He was Mayor of Newport 1837-8 and MP between 1837 and 1851. Using the architect T.H. Wyatt, he rebuilt the abbey in 1834-6 at a cost of £60,000. In 1851 the Monmouth and Glamorgan Bank collapsed and Blewitt fled the country. Legal proceedings dragged on until 1895 when the abbey was purchased by Sir Clifford Cory, chairman of the Cardiff coal owners and exporters, Cory Bros. & Co. Cory died in 1941 and the abbey was used as an American Army depot. In 1946 it was purchased by the Sisters of St Joseph of Annecy, as their British headquarters and it remains a nunnery. Of the original abbey, only the cells, converted to stables remained. A new chapel was built in 1857 and the house was renovated. In the grounds are the remains of the medieval tithe barn.

Across Turnpike Road from the Abbey, St Michael's Church has its origins in the 12th century, but dates mainly from the 15th century. There is a Tudor west tower, south porch, nave, chancel, and a large arcaded chapel to the north of the chancel, dating from the 16th century for the Morgan family. The church was restored in 1869-70 by E.A. Lansdowne and in 1921 by Sir Harold Brakspear who removed plaster to reveal medieval murals. The church was originally dedicated to the Blessed Virgin Mary & Mary Magdalene, but by 1535 it was known as the 'chapel of St Michael near the monastry'. The 16th century Welsh poet Sawnder Sion, known as the 'Lion of Llantarnam', is buried beneath the choir while in the churchyard is the grave of John Fielding who, as Private John Williams, won the Victoria Cross at the Battle of Rorke's Drift in 1879. The John Fielding pub in Cwmbrân is named after him as is the nursing home where he died in 1932, aged 75. The churchyard cross has a modern crosshead and shaft.

Near the church is the Greenhouse pub, dating from 1719. Above the door is a carving of an inn scene showing two tiny figures smoking pipes, at a table with glass, candle and tankard and the inscription:

'Y Ty Gwyrdd 1719 Cwrw da a seidir i chwi Dewch y mewn chwi gewch y brofi'
'The Green House 1719 Good Beer and Cider Come you in and try'

Llanthony (Welsh: Llanddewi Nant Hodni)

Llanthony is a small village some eight miles north of Abergavenny in the valley of the Afon Honddu (formerly Nant Hodni) or Vale of Ewyas, in the heart of the Black Mountains. The name is a corruption of the Welsh Llanddewi Nant Honddu

According to legend, St David had established a chapel here and many years later a monk recorded that, while out hunting, William, a knight retainer of the Earl of Hereford in the reign of William Rufus, took shelter in the ruins. This knight "laid aside his belt, and girded himself with a rope; instead of fine linen he covered himself with hair cloth; and instead of his soldier's robe, he loaded himself with weighty irons. The suit of armour, which before defended him from the darts of his enemies, he still wore as a garment to harden himself against the soft temptations of his old enemy, Satan; that as the outward man was afflicted with austerity, the inner man might be secured for the service of God. That his zeal might not cool, he thus crucified himself, and continued his hard armour on his body until it was worn out with rust and age." The knight's fame spread and many wealthy and powerful nobles visited, including Hugh de Lacy who established a church dedicated to St John the Baptist. By 1118 a priory of the Augustinian Canons was granted the site. In 1135, the community of 40 canons were driven off by what Giraldus Cambrensis called "a barbarous people". They escaped to Hereford and Gloucester but returned after peace was imposed and, under the patronage of the de Lacys and the Crown, began what was to be one of the most impressive medieval buildings in Wales. After the Dissolution of the Monasteries in 1538 the priory fell into ruin, but at the end of the 18th century it became an attraction for those seekers of the 'picturesque'. Sir Richard Colt Hoare witnessed the collapse of the west window on his visit of 1803. In the early 19th century the estate was owned for a time by Colonel Sir Mark Wood who also owned the Piercefield estate (St Arvans). Wood converted the south west tower into a shooting box and the western range into a house for his steward. In 1807 it was acquired by the English writer and poet Walter Savage Landor. The latter attempted to create a 'Picturesque' landscape and mansion but failed and left the country, with his assets going to his creditors, principally his mother and the Llanthony estate remained in the family for over a century. There are extensive ruins of the church and chapter house, with the old cloisters being incorporated

Llanthony Abbey by Sir Richard Colt Hoare

into the Llanthony Priory Hotel. It is thought that the first pointed arch in the country was used here. The parish church of St David had been created in the 18th century from the former infirmary and contains a 12th century font. Alongside the road is a 17th century barn which was originally the great gatehouse. South of the priory is the old mill and smithy complex, and the Half Moon Inn.

This beautiful area is now a centre for pony trekking, hill walking and mountain biking.

Llantilio Crossenny (Welsh: Llandeilo Gresynni)

Llantilio Crossenny is a small village set in rich farmland six miles east of Abergavenny. According to legend St Teilo stood with a cross on a mound and prayed, helping King Iddon put the invading Saxons to flight. The *Liber Landavensis* records "And St. Teliaus came with him to a mountain in the middle of Crissinic, near Trodi, where he stood and prayed to Almighty God that he would succour the plundered people; and his prayer was heard, and a great victory was obtained". The Book records the parish name as Sancti Teliaui de Cressinic.

A Celtic church was built on the site which was almost certainly a pre-Christian place of worship and later the Normans built Llantilio Castle, now known as Whitecastle, two miles to the north-west.

In the 13th century Llantilio Cwrt was built at the junction of the B4233 with the Whitecastle road. The Cwrt was moated in the 14th century and was the principal residence of Dafydd Gam. There is a great deal of uncertainty about the history of Dafydd, who was the son of ap Llewelyn ap Hywel Fychan ap Hywel ap Einion Sais of Penywaun near Brecon. His name of Gam suggests that he had a squint or had lost an eye. The family served the de Bohun family who were both Earls of Hereford and Lords of Brecon and the loyalty continued when Henry Bolingbroke married Mary de Bohun and became Lord of Brecon. Dafydd is alleged to have killed Richard of Slwch, a relative, on Brecon High Street and fled from the area, seeking refuge with Henry's father, John of Gaunt. Henry was crowned in 1399 and in 1400 Dafydd was a king's esquire with an income of 40 marks a year. In 1401 he was rewarded with lands in Cardiganshire seized from supporters of Owain Glyndŵr. In 1404 he is said to have attended the Welsh Parliament at Machynlleth, when Owain Glyndŵr was proclaimed Prince of Wales, with the intention of killing Glyndŵr but was captured in the attempt and imprisoned at Glyndyfrdwy, only being released after payment of ransom in 1412. Other sources suggest that he was released shortly after the attempt and took the lead in the defeat of Glyndŵr's forces at the Battle of Pwll Melyn near Usk on 5th May 1405. This version suggests that he was captured in 1412 and released on payment of a ransom and a promise not to bear arms against Glyndŵr. In 1415 he was with Henry V at the Battle of Agincourt where he was said to have saved the King's life but was himself killed and supposedly knighted on the field of battle. There may be some confusion between Dafydd and his future son in law, Sir William ap Thomas, who also fought at Agincourt, as did his daughter Gwladys' first husband, Sir Roger Vaughan who died there. The son of Gwladys and Sir William ap Thomas adopted the name of William Herbert and became 1st Earl of Pembroke. A stained glass window in the church has a Latin inscription which, translated, reads 'David Gam, golden haired knight, Lord of the manor of Llantilio Crossenny, killed on the field of Agincourt 1415'. Davy Gam is listed by the Herald as one of the dead in Shakespeare's *Henry V*. The Cwrt continued to be occupied through the 15th century but later became a park lodge before being abandoned in the 17th century. All that remains today of Hen Gwrt (Old Court) is the moat.

A new Llantilio Court was built in 1775 by John Lewis, a lawyer of Llwyn Ffortun and High Sheriff of Monmouthshire in 1757. He inherited a small leasehold estate in Llantilio through his wife, Mary Powell. Mary's great-grandfather was Walter Powell, a local attorney and steward to the Earl of Worcester. Mary had been involved in a scandal over an affair with an organist named James Parry and John Lewis had represented her. Llantilio Court passed to the eldest grand daughter, Mary Anne Lewis who married John Barnard Bosanquet in 1804. Bosanquet who later became a Judge of the Court of Common Pleas was the third son of the Bosanquets of Dingestow. They died without issue and the Court eventually passed to Colonel Henry Morgan-Clifford, the MP for Hereford, 1846-1865, in 1847. He sold Llantilio Court to Sir Samuel Jackson, Baronet of Birkenhead, grandfather of Sir Henry Mather Jackson, in 1873. The house which lay to the north of the church had gardens extending to the west and south of the church. The Court was demolished in 1922 and its foundations are now grassed over.

The church of St Teilo dates from the 12th century, though there was almost certainly a wooden Celtic church on the site from the 6th century. Sancti Teliawi Crissinic was confirmed to Llandaff by papal privilege in 1119. A large, impressive church, the crossing tower dating from the late 12th century denotes its importance. In the 14th century the chancel was rebuilt and the north transept was enlarged to form the Lady Chapel. This became known as the Cil-lwch Chapel when owners of Great Cil-lwch, (Great Killough) including the Powells and Medlycotts were buried there. Within the chapel there is a depiction of The Green Man, a pagan fertility symbol. In the 15th century the upper set of windows or clerestory was added to the nave. The spire dates from 1708-9 when the four great timbers from a single 60 foot tree were used to support the ring of six bells as well as the new spire. In 1978-9 two further bells were added. There was a restoration by Prichard and Seddon in 1856 which included new windows in the nave's south wall and new seating. Interestingly, an 18th century map shows the church as St Michael's. The very tall nave contrasts with the small chancel arch with the doorway which would have given access to the rood loft above the arch.

Outside the church the ruined churchyard cross with its four step base and socket stone, now forms the base for the war memorial.

During the time of Cromwell, the diarist, William Powell of Llantilio Crossenny commented on the organized Puritan campaign. "The new preachers began at lantilio". Among those preaching were Henry Walter,

Jenkin Jones, the fiery Breconshire Baptist, Wroth Rogers, originally a tailor at Llanfaches but by this time governor of Hereford, George Robinson, an approver named in the Propagation Act, who preached 'damnac'om', John Morgan of Tintern, a county sequestrator of royalist property, Philip Williams of Monmouth later appointed minister of Llanvapley and even an unknown smith of Malpas was heard 'expounding'.

It was during this time that Llantilio Crossenny Free Grammar School was founded, though it gradually became an elementary school. Commissioners commented "As it stands in a country place about halfway between Monmouth and Abergavenny with a population consisting only of labourers and small farmers, there is little or no need for Latin or mathematics, or indeed any subject which cannot be learned before a child is ten or twelve years of age".

The village had a smithy, corn mill, post office and the Hostry public house. A corn mill operated on the same site from 1557 to 1914 and the building remains.

Llantilio Castle, now known as White Castle was one of three castles built by William Fitz Osbern, Lord of Breteuil, between 1067 and 1075. The others being Grosmont and Skenfrith. White Castle was never used as a lord's residence though apart from a short period the three castles were held by a single lord. The original fortification would have been an earth mound topped by timber defences. In the latter part of the 12th century Roger of Grosmont strengthened the fortifications, but it was Hubert de Burgh who was responsible for the impressive stone castle when he was granted it by King John in 1201. Described as a 'place of great renown and magnificence', White Castle resisted the attacks of Llewellyn ap Gruffydd in 1262 but was subsequently strengthened with the addition of the curtain wall and more round towers. It was during the 13th century that the castle walls were whitewashed, giving it the name White Castle. The castle's importance declined with the peace that followed Edward I's subjugation of the Welsh and by the 16th century the castle was in ruins. It was sold to the Duke of Beaufort by the Duchy of Lancaster in 1825 and gifted to the nation in 1922. Now in the care of Cadw it is one of the best preserved castles in South Wales. Entrance is through the outer ward with its five towers. There is a bridge over the moat to the inner ward, with two towers forming the gatehouse and a

Llantilio Crossenny White Castle

further four towers. To the south of the inner ward there is a further moated area or hornwork.

Great Killough is a late-medieval hall-house, Grade II Listed, a little over a mile south-west of the village. The manor of Killough was held in the 15th century by William, Earl of Pembroke and remained in the family for six generations. In the 17th century the house was owned by the Powell family and in the early 18th century, the Duke of Hamilton before being purchased by the Duke of Beaufort's agent Thomas Medlycott. More recently it was the home of John Frazer Ingledew, High Sheriff of Gwent in 1983.

Llantilio Crossenny stages an annual festival of music and drama in May, with concerts held in the church or a barn.

Llantilio Pertholey (Welsh: Llandeilo Bertholau)

Llantilio Pertholey is a small village a mile and a half north-east of the centre of Abergavenny, now by-passed by the A465 Hereford road. The village lies in the valley between the Sugar Loaf Mountain to the west and the Skirrid Fawr Mountain to the east. The name is derived from the dedication of the church to St Teilo, with Pertholey and the Welsh Bertholau being corruptions of the original name of Lann Teliau Porth Halauc recorded in the *Liber Landavensis* which records that 'King Idon granted in alms for the health of his soul, and the souls of his ancestors. Kings and Princes, to God, and St. Peter, and to Archbishop Teilo" Lann Maur, otherwise called Lann Teliau Porth Halauc. Port Halauc means defiled entrance and possibly refers to burials on the site.

St Teilo's consists of a nave with an integral chancel, north and south aisles, a north tower, south porch and three chantry chapels. The Grade I Listed church dates from the 13th century with the Triley, Neville and Wern-ddu chantry chapels built in the 16th century. Carved oak arcades separate the Triley and Wern-ddu chapels from the chancel. There was a major restoration in the 1890s by Frederick Robertson Kempson and Charles Busteed Fowler. William Douglas Caröe designed the chancel panelling in 1920 including the reredos which forms a war memorial. The medieval churchyard cross was also restored as a war memorial. A fire in 1974 destroyed the organ while in 1981 the Tredilion Room designed by R. Merton Jones was added, providing facilities for small meetings and refreshments. There are a number of stone monuments sculpted by members of the Brute family of Crickhowell.

Thomas Jones, incumbent of Llantilio Pertholey celebrated the translation of the Bible into Welsh with a poem in 1588 titled *Diolch am y Beibl yn Gymraeg*.

James Davies, the schoolmaster of Devauden was a frequent visitor to Llantilio Pertholey where his cousin was a farmer. In one of his visits, "he was pained by witnessing what was then usual in country churchyards – the playing of ball against the north wall of the church; a practice which he regarded as inconsistent with reverence for the house of God, a feeling that was deeply implanted in his character, and was manifested in an age when irreverence was extensively prevalent. He thereupon addressed a letter to the parish clergyman, entreating, with affectionate earnestness, that he would employ his authority to put a stop to a practice, which conduced to irreverence, and was often productive of serious disorder and gross profanity".

The village once had a pub, the Old Mitre Inn, opposite the church, and a smithy. There were two corn mills on the River Gavenny, Brooklands and Triley Mill with the latter still standing, half a mile north of the church. There is a new housing development on the Woodlands Garden Centre site. The Llantilio Pertholey Church in Wales Primary School is located at Maerdy.

At Great Bettws Farm, two and a half miles to the north-west is the little 12th century chapel of ease to St Teilo's church. The single cell building with its bellcote, topped by a cross, was rebuilt in 1829 by John Pratt. There were further renovations in 1901-2 by Charles Busteed Fowler when the side entrance was blocked and a new doorway constructed beneath the bellcote. Church services are still held there.

At the hamlet of Pantygelli a mile to the north-west on Old Hereford Road is the Crown Inn.

Llantrisant Church of Three Saints

Two and three quarter miles south-east of Usk, nestling between the A449 and the River Usk is the little village of Llantrisant. There is an alternative spelling of Llantrissent, which more closely resembles the local Welsh pronunciation and was in use in old maps.

The Grade I Listed church of Saints Peter Paul and John stands in the middle of the old village which was by-passed in the 1960s. Sir Joseph Bradney suggested that the original dedication was to Saints David, Teilo and Padarn. The building dates from the 14th century with the tower and south porch 16th century. It was restored in 1881 by A.E. Lansdowne of Newport and Bristol, though previous plans for reseating drawn up in 1867 by John Pollard Seddon were rejected by pew owners. The scissor truss nave roof is particularly impressive and there is an inscription on the west wall '1593 ER XXXV', said to mark a royal visit. The nave is wide with a narrow chancel arch. The octagonal font bears the 1673 inscription 'Iohn Iones'. The east window by Geoffrey Robertson is from 1981 and depicts Christ and a Lamb. There is a marble sarcophagus plaque to John Gardner Kemeys of Bertholey and Plantain Garden River, Jamaica, who died in 1830. A 19th century drawing shows the tower with a pyramid roof, but today it has a flat roof within the crenellation. The churchyard cross has a modern shaft on a four-step cross-base and socket stone.

Bertholey lies a mile and a half south-east of the village. The house was built originally for Edward Kemeys MP in 1616. The family were descended from Stephen de Kemeys, who held land in the county in the 13th century. Coxe in his history writes "Bertholly house, which deserves to be visited for the extreme beauty of its situation. It stands on a gently rising ground, above the lower road leading from Caerleon to Usk, and commands a most delicious view of the fertile vale and the distant mountains. The lawn and adjacent grounds are richly clothed with hanging groves of ancient oaks and below the Usk forms a curve, which is almost a complete circle. The irregular shape of the house well accords with the romantic scenery with which it is surrounded. I have seen few situations more pleasing and striking. This house was an ancient seat of a branch of the Kemeys family, and came, by a marriage with the heiress, to a Mr. Gardener, who assumed the name of Kemeys, and is since dead. The estate was mortgaged to Mr. Rigby to a very considerable amount, and has been appropriated by government for the liquidation of his debts."

In 1891 Bertholey was the residence of John Cory, but in 1905 it was destroyed by fire and only rebuilt in 1999. Bertholey was a chapelry. The chapel, dedicated to St Bartholomew is now in ruins above the road leading to Bertholey.

In the village are a number of buildings dating from the 17th century, including Ty Mawr. The Royal Oak has closed but the Greyhound, three quarters of a mile north of the village remains open.

Llanvaches (Welsh: Llanfaches)

The village lies to the north of the A48, eight miles east of Newport. It takes its name from the original dedication of the church to St Maches, a daughter of St Gwynlliw and sister of St Catwg. According to legend, she had her head 'smote off' by robbers intent on stealing her finest ram. The robbers confessed to St Tathan, Abbot of Caerwent who established a church at the place of her murder. The church today is dedicated to St Dubritius, an early Bishop of Llandaff.

The church which consists of a nave, chancel, west tower with saddleback roof and south porch, dates from the 14th century. It was restored in 1850 and further work, including the roofing was undertaken in 1908. The tower is 14th century as is the font.

The rector at Llanvaches between 1611and 1638 was William Wroth. In 1630 Wroth appears to have had a 'conversion' to Puritanism and in 1633 refused to read out the Book of Sports, a list of those activities permitted on a Sunday, as required by Royal Decree. Wroth was brought before the Court of High Commission in October 1635 and after procedural wrangling was ejected or resigned his living in 1638. He formed the first Independent Church in Wales, though there was no building at this time. His fame as a preacher spread and he attracted congregations from

Somerset, Gloucestershire, Herefordshire, and Glamorgan. Tabernacle Chapel was built at Carrow Hill, a little under a mile to the south of Llanvaches, some time after 1638. Wroth died in 1642 and Walter Cradock was later the pastor at Llanvaches, followed in 1648 by Thomas Ewins, a London tailor. In 1802 a new chapel was built when the location moved to its present site just north of the A48 on Tabernacle Lane. A Memorial Hall was incorporated in 1924 and Tabernacle is now the United Reformed Church. The building is said to have used material from the 17th century Carrow Hill building. Bethany General Baptist Chapel was built in 1809 and rebuilt in 1905.

North of the village, beyond the modern houses on Castle Rise are the remains of Llanvaches Castle, one of six castles surrounding Wentwood Chase. There are traces of a rectangular castle with banks and masonry. At the side of Millbrook Lane are the arched outlets of an early 19th century limekiln.

The village has grown substantially in recent years with new developments to the north and south of the church.

Llanvair Discoed (Welsh: Llanfair Iscoed)
St Mary's Church Beneath the Wood

The beautiful village of Llanvair Discoed is situated beneath two hills, Mynydd Llwyd, or the Grey Hill, and Allt yr Arfaid, or Wolves' Cliff, six miles west of Chepstow, to the north of the A48.

The village is mentioned in the Domesday Book as Lamecare. A castle was built above the village, by Pagan Fitzjohn, Sheriff of Hereford under Henry I and King Stephen. He died in 1137. A stone castle was built in the late 13th century by Ralph de Monthermer, 1st Baron Monthermer, Earl of Hertford, Earl of Gloucester. Monthermer married the widow of Gilbert de Clare and his titles of Hertford and Gloucester were taken from him on the death of his wife, the daughter of Edward I in 1307 and he was created Baron Monthermer in 1309. In the late 15th century ownership passed to Sir Richard Pole, a relative of Henry VII. His son was Henry Pole, 1st Baron Montague who was executed for treason in 1539. Richard Pole married Margaret Plantaganet, 6th Countess of Salisbury a title she held in her own right. She was executed in 1541 for her Roman Catholic sympathies and Llanvair Castle passed to the crown. It came into the possession of Edward Woodward in 1610 who sold it to Rhys Kemeys.

The later history is contained in the following extract from William Coxe's *Historical Tour of Monmouthshire* which also gives a description of the castle in 1800.

"The finest view of the ruins is to the south, where the round tower and the high broken walls exhibit a more magnificent appearance, than could he expected from a nearer approach. The view from the south-east, in a field called the warren, is more picturesque, presenting the round tower mantled with ivy, and some strait walls with several arched windows, 'Bosom'd high in tufted trees'.

In 1170 Lanvair, or as it was then called Lanveire, was possessed by Sir Robert Pagan, knight. It afterwards came to a branch of the ancient Kemeys family, by marriage with the heiress of the Pagans, and was the seat of George Kemeys, who lived in the reign of James the first. Dying without issue, he bequeathed it to Sir Nicholas Kemeys of Kevenmably, on the frontiers of Glamorganshire, who was created a baronet in 1643, and killed in defending Chepstow Castle."

Today the ruins are overgrown and stand in a private garden above the church.

Llanvair Discoed Church and Castle 1800 by Sir Robert Hoare

St Mary's church stands on rising ground beneath the castle ruins. It was rebuilt in 1865, replacing the small medieval church shown depicted by Sir Richard Colt Hoare. Further rebuilding of the west end of the nave and south porch was carried out in 1881-4 by Ewan Christian, but the east gable wall is medieval, as is the door. There is a nave with a western bellcote, south porch, chancel and north vestry. The vestry is not shown on Ewan Christian's plans and is a later addition. In addition to the porch, there is a priest's door in the south wall of the chancel and an additional door in the vestry. In the porch is a stone with the engraved message:

> 'Who Ever hear on Sonday,
> Will Practis Playing at Ball,
> it May Be before Monday,
> The Devil Will Have you All'

The three storey Court House was, according to the plaque above the porch, built in 1635, though a later date is thought likely. Above the doorway is the inscription "It is better to write the name of the Most High on stone than with ink". It formed part of the Court House Farm estate and on the other side of the road is the square dovecote and late 18th century threshing barn.

The Woodlands Tavern in the centre of the village was formerly the King's Arms. The village has seen some modern development, mainly in-fill and in keeping with the village.

On Grey Hill, a little under a mile to the north-west of the village are the remains of a Bronze Age stone circle with nine erect and a number of fallen stones. There is a seven foot monolith and, on the highest point, a Bronze Age round barrow. There are also signs of an enclosure and ancient field system.

Llanvapley (Welsh: Llanfable)

Llanvapley lies four miles east of Abergavenny on the B4233. The church is dedicated to St Mable who is mentioned as a virgin saint of Gwent by Iolo Morganwg. No other information is known and this is the only church dedicated to her.

The church is 15th century but was re-roofed in 1758 when the nave roof was lowered while there were further restorations by A.M. Wyatt of Monmouth in 1861, E.M. Bruce Vaughan in 1904 and R.L. Edmunds of

Blaenavon in 1950. There is a piscina with double bowl and the rood stairs, but most of the fittings are Victorian. St Mable's has a west tower, nave, south porch, chancel and a north vestry which was added after the 1861 renovations. Outside there is the four step base and socket stone of a medieval churchyard cross.

The village had a pub, the Red Hart, but sadly this closed despite the efforts of local residents. The village does have a thriving cricket club with the attractive pitch surrounded by trees and has the Llanymynach Brook flowing alongside. There has been some new building in the village, which remains small.

Llanvapley Court is a Georgian style house, remodelled with a Victorian gable built on the site of a 16th century house though some believe that a Roman villa was once positioned here.

A corn mill and smithy are shown as still operating in the village in 1920. The mill race was some 600 yards long, giving a head of 20 feet.

Llanvetherine (pronounced Llanverin) (Welsh: Llanwytherin)

Four and a half miles north-east of Abergavenny, this small village takes its name from the original dedication of the church to the little known Welsh Saint Gwytherin. A grant of the church, under the name Ecclesia Gueithirin, was made to the Church of Llandaff, in the time of Bishop Nud in the 9th century. Like the similarly dedicated church in Denbighshire Llanvetherine church it is now dedicated to St James. The village is named as Llanvetherine or Llanverin in an *Archaeologia Cambrensis* article of 1847.

The church is dedicated to St James the Elder otherwise known as St James the Great, one the twelve apostles and brother of St John. The present church dates from the 15th century, with the tower heightened in the 16th century. There was a restoration in 1870 by Charles Buckeridge, when the wagon roof of the nave was renewed and the chancel arch rebuilt. Much of the church furniture dates from this time. The east window of 1905 depicts the Adoration and incorporates fragments of medieval glass while the modern north nave window depicts St James and St Gwytherin. In the chancel is a tomb lid with the figure of St Vetteeinvs (St Gwytherin) carved on it in relief, raised about two inches from the rest of the stone, and in the dress of a clergyman in priest's orders, as worn at the time the person represented lived. *Archaeologia Cambrensis* in 1847 described it as being in the churchyard, though in *The Monthly Review* or *Literary*

Journal, Volume 24 of 1797 it was said to be in the chancel. Both accounts describe it has having been found many years before when digging a grave. The stone, measuring "six feet eight inches long, two feet eight inches wide at the eastern end, where are the feet of the figure, and two feet six and a half inches at the other end; and is in thickness about five inches", was moved in the 1970s from the porch to the chancel. There is a nave, chancel, west tower and stone tiled south porch. The belfry overhangs the rest of the tower. Outside is the four step base and socket stone of a medieval churchyard cross. To the south the graveyard is bounded by a tributary of the Afon Troddi.

Archaeologia Cambrensis in 1847 also makes mention of a holy well of great repute in the village, a chalybeate spring with remains of baths, but all trace has apparently been removed.

The Monthly Review or *Literary Journal* gave details of a custom in the village: "Thus in obscure parts of the kingdom a memorial of practices, bearing a very remote date, may be preserved; in support of which it is added that, among the common people in this parish, when persons appear as chief-mourners at a funeral, a dirty cloth is tied about their heads".

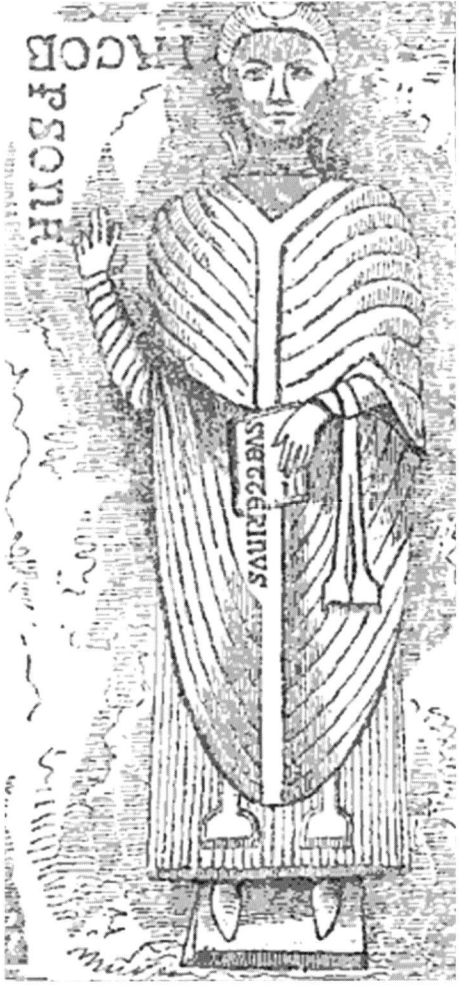

Llanvetherine Church St Veterinus Tomb

Cwmmerra Particular Baptist Chapel was built in 1856 in Caggle Street (road littered with sheep-dung from the Welsh 'cagl'), which is the main centre for the, albeit tiny, population. The King's Arms Inn has closed and is now a private house. Two new houses have been built to the north-west of the church and there is a small caravan site opposite.

Llanvihangel Crucorney (Welsh: Llanfihangel Crucornau)

Four miles north-east of Abergavenny, now by-passed by the A465, Llanvihangel Crucorney lies beneath the Skirrid Mountain which gives the village its name of St Michael at the Horned Hill. The village is mentioned in the *Norwich Taxatio* of 1254 as Sancti Michaelis de Crukorneo.

The Skirrid Inn claims to be the oldest public house in Wales and one of the most haunted. There is a record of an inn here in 1110, but the building appears to date from the 17th century with some good ship's timbers. The upper floor was used as a courtroom and local tradition has it that 182 men were hanged in the pub, the last for sheep stealing in the time of Cromwell. The rope marks on the oak beam over the stairwell on the first floor claimed to be from those who had been hanged add to the story. In addition to the Skirrid there is the Rising Sun to the north of the village.

Llanvihangel Court is a late 15th early 16th century house, enlarged in 1599 by Rhys Morgan a great-great-grandson of William Herbert of Raglan Castle, First Earl of Pembroke. In 1608 his son Anthony Morgan sold Llanvihangel Court to Edward Somerset, 4th Earl of Worcester. In 1627 it was purchased by Nicholas Arnold, son of John Arnold of Llanthony. He served as Member of Parliament for Monmouthshire between 1626 and 1629 when Charles I dispensed with Parliament. He was Lord Lieutenant of the county in 1633. Nicholas was a keen breeder of horses and built the stables at the Court. He was succeeded by John Arnold, who, fiercely Protestant, fell out with the Duke of Beaufort and was charged along with Sir Trevor Williams (see Llangibby) and fined £10,000, which he was unable to pay and spent time in prison. He Served as MP for Monmouthshire and Southwark at various times before his death in 1702. His son died without issue and in 1726 his daughters sold the Llanthony and Llanvihangel estates to Edward Harley whose son succeeded to the Earldom of Oxford in 1741. After a number of owners Llanfihangel Court was purchased in 1945 by Colonel and Mrs H.S.P. Hopkinson a descendant of Edward Somerset 4th Earl of Worcester who had owned it the 17th century. Today this Grade I Listed building is available for weddings and functions and the house and gardens are open at certain times of the year.

The church of St Michael and All Angels dates from the 12th century with the tower and chancel 13th-14th century. The tower was heightened in the 16th century when the porch was added. There was a refurbishment in 1833-5 by William Powell of Abergavenny and another in 1884-7 by Richard Creed of London. In 1974 the nave roof was renewed at a lower level by the Cheltenham architects Roiser & Whitestone. The wagon roof to the chancel dates from 1887 and the pews, chancel arch and east window also date from this time. In the nave is an Elizabethan relief tomb slab. The four storey tower is crenellated. During the 17th century the vicar, Owen Price was ejected by the puritans for "malignancy and drunkenness".

Zoar Particular Baptist Chapel was built in 1837 and has been converted to living accommodation, unlike the sadly neglected Hope Calvinistic Methodist Chapel which was built in 1866. Both chapels are in the hamlet of Pandy where there is the Old Pandy Inn and a railway station. The Lancaster Arms is now a guest house. Glan Honddu, a Georgian gentleman's residence is now the Park Hotel. The Pandy fulling mill supplied wool to the Llanover estate for the production of flannel. While two weirs and a mill race are shown on the 1889 map, there is today no sign of the mill.

West of Pandy is Trewyn, a manor house rebuilt by the Delahaye family in 1692. In the mid 18th century it was owned by the Shaw family and on the death of William Shaw in 1772, Jeremiah Rosher, who married Shaw's widow, purchased the estate. The Roshers had made money in the East End of London and Kent as lime and timber merchants. In 1895, Jeremiah Lilburn Rosher sold the manor and estate to Philip Bartholomew Barneby, 2nd son of William Barneby of Saltmarshe Castle, Herefordshire. After various alterations Trewyn has been restored to its 1692 appearance. A 'Chapel of St Martin at Trewyn' is listed in the records of Llanthony Priory, but no chapel is mentioned in the Trewyn Estate records. In the grounds is a large, octagonal 17th century dovecote with a turret.

The River Honddu flows to the north and west of the village. It is crossed at Penybont by a bridge built in 1827 by the county, replacing a two arched 17th century bridge similar to the pretty little Pont Rhys-Powell near the Queen's Head inn a mile and a quarter north–west of the village. There are a number of attractive buildings, including the old corn mill, though the wheel has been replaced by a turbine.

To the west of the village is the Abergavenny to Hereford railway line. This started as a tramline from the Brecon canal at Govilon, reaching Llanvihangel Crucorney in 1811. The next stage to Monmouth Gap opened a year later, but the final twelve miles to Hereford was not completed until 1829. The horse drawn trams gave way to the steam age after the tramline was purchased by the Abergavenny and Hereford Railway in 1845. The route changed in places and north of the village at Wern-Gifford part of the old 3'6" trackway survives in the form of an embankment with stone sleepers.

There is a modern development at Wern-Gifford while in the village itself are a number of modern 'character' properties nestling amongst the older farm buildings and cottages.

A mile south-west of the church is a small settlement around the old Llanvihangel station. Along Penyclawdd Lane is Penyclawdd Court and castle. The Court was built on the site of the castle bailey. The castle mound is partly surrounded by the wet moat. It is thought to have been one of a number of small castles built by Roger de Hastings in the time of William the Conqueror following a barons' revolt. The Grade I Listed Court was built in the early 16th century and extended in the early 17th century. It was sympathetically restored in the late 20th century and was for a time open as a country inn.

Llanvihangel Gobion, also known as Llanvihangel nigh Usk (Welsh: Llanfihangel Gofion)

This rural village lies some four and a half miles south-east of Abergavenny.

At the entrance to the village from the B4598 is the Steel Horse Café, a biker friendly, licensed café. This was formerly The Charthouse restaurant, the Herbert Arms and originally the Carpenters' Arms beer house and post office.

Gobion Manor dates from the 16th century with the Gunter Coat of Arms over the door. There is evidence of a larger building with moat and round tower on the site, but the Manor was built by the Gunter family, with William Gunter born around 1370 being the first of seven generations of the family to hold the property. Peter Gunter was a knight who had supported Bernard de Neufmarche in the conquest of Brycheiniog and the defeat of Rhys ap Tewdwr. Manor Farm lies between the Manor and the road.

The Grade II* Listed church of St Michael is located down a lane. Surrounded by trees it appears to have been refurbished at the same time as Gobion Manor, though the tower and lack of decoration point to an early date. The font is 16th century while the roof is similar to that at Llangattock Nigh Usk in being a single structure, suggesting renovation in the 1820s by John Upton of Gloucester. The outer south wall has a projection for the rood stair and a priest's door to the chancel. The substantial three storey tower has a roof similar to that at Llangattock Nigh Usk though the pyramid is topped by a weather vane. There is the stump of an octagonal cross shaft on a large socket stone and square base, all that remains of the churchyard cross.

South of the village the road crosses the River Usk by means of the handsome Pant-y-Goitre Bridge. A turnpike bridge of 1821, it was designed by John Upton of Gloucester and has three arches. The central piers have cutwaters and one large and two smaller circular holes designed to reduce weight and increase strength, a development of the technique first employed at the Old Bridge in Pontypridd. The abutments are pierced by a small hole and by circular tunnels, allowing for the passage of cattle. At the road junction just north of the bridge was the toll house, now demolished.

East of Gobion Manor is Mozerah Calvinistic Methodist Chapel, built in 1837 and still in use.

Llanvihangel near Rogiet (See Rogiet)

Llanvihangel-Ystern-Llewern (Welsh: Llanfihangel-Ystum-Llywern)

This small village is situated four and three quarter miles west of Monmouth. The derivation of the full name is obscure. 'Ystum' means a bend or meander, but 'Llywern' could refer to a fox, the forgotten name of the nearby stream or a local landowner. In 1291 it was referred to as 'Lanvihangel Estelweon' while an alternative local name in the 18th and 19th century was Llanvihangel-Taverne-Bach on account of the inn which once stood there. The name of the inn was Yr Onnen (the ash tree) which by 1901 was the village shop. There is a Tavern Cottage on the road to Onen.

The medieval church of St. Michael was restored in 1874-5, by T.H. Wyatt. It is in the Early English style, consisting of chancel, nave, south porch, vestry and a wooden turreted belfry, containing three bells. The belfry and the timber supporting frame were rebuilt by Wyatt and is a particular feature of the church. The wagon roof of the nave is late 15th century, while that of the chancel is by Wyatt. The font is 12th century. There are a number of monuments including a brass plaque to the memory of the historian Sir Joseph Bradney who died in 1933.

An infants' school was endowed by the Revd. Roger Thomas in 1730 with a house and land it was replaced in 1840 by the building 230 yards south-west of the church which is now a private house.

In 1667, the Quaker George Fox had "several blessed meetings" at Pant, the home of Walter Jenkins in the village where his father had been rector. Jenkins was a magistrate and had written the English version of *Y gyfraith a roddwyd allan o Zion* (*The Law Granted out of Zion*) in 1660. He was imprisoned in Cardiff and Monmouth jails for a while because of his beliefs. His grandson Elisha Beadles translated Jenkins' work into Welsh. In the 17th century a Quaker Chapel was built as an extension to the 16th century cruck framed hall-house at Pant to the west of the church. It was used as a Quaker Meeting House between 1668 and 1756. Later Pant was acquired by the historian of Monmouthshire, Sir Joseph Bradney who resided at Talycoed Court and noted that there had been a Quaker burial place in the orchard next to the house, on land given by among others Richard Hanbury.

There are just a few houses and farms in this scattered community.

Llanwenarth

Llanwenarth was until 1865 a large parish to the south west of Abergavenny. In that year a separate parish of Llanwenarth Ultra was formed, which included the village of Govilon and that area of the former parish on the right bank of the River Usk. Llanwenarth Citra as the smaller parish was known, with its church dedicated to St Peter, lies a mile and a half south-west of the centre of Abergavenny.

The name is difficult. 'Wen arth' would translate as 'White Bear', but there is a suggestion that it is a corruption of Gwengarth, a name mentioned in the *Vita Cadoci* as a member of the laity who witnessed various documents and granted land at Cradoc to St Catwg. The name was given as Llanvenarthe in 1563.

The church of St Peter is said to have been established here in the 6th century, but the present building dates from the 14th century, with the tower dated 1631. There was a major refurbishment in 1877-8 by John Prichard. The interior fittings are mainly 19th century, but the wagon roof in the nave is 16th century and there is a 14th century piscina in the chancel which is at a low level following the raising of the chancel floor by Prichard. The tower rises from within the nave roof with the west window blocked, suggesting that it was a later addition. There is a priest's door to the chancel. Outside there is a restored churchyard cross with the steps inscribed as a war memorial.

The former National School along the road from the church has been replaced by a house, with the only other houses being Church Cottage and Church House, behind St Peter's.

A ferry operated across the Usk until 1955. It consisted of a wooden boat pulled manually across the river by rope.

The Llanwenarth Hotel and Riverside Restaurant lies on the A40, a mile and a half north-west of the church.

Llanwern Church in the Marsh

The village of Llanwern which gave its name to the giant steelworks, lies three and a half miles north-east of Newport city centre, in a rural area. The old village consisted of a few cottages together with the Milton Hotel with the church a quarter of a mile to the south-east.

Llanwern House, to the east of the village, was a large three storey Georgian mansion built around 1700. The estate had been in the hands of the Walsh family but was purchased in 1630 by Lewis Van, a sheriff of Glamorgan. The Van or Vanne family lived at Coldra House until Llanwern House was built by Charles Van. His grandson, also Charles, married Catherine Morgan of the Tredegar House family. Charles Vann was MP for Brecon from 1872 to 1878. His daughter and heiress, Catherine, married Sir Robert Salusbury of Cotton Hall Clwyd in 1780. Sir Robert was MP for Monmouthshire 1792-1796 and for Brecon 1796-1812. In 1816 Salusbury went bankrupt and was detained in King's Bench prison, dying at Canterbury in 1817. He was succeded by Sir Thomas Robert Salusbury, 2nd Baronet who in turn was succeeded by his brother, Sir Charles John Salusbury (1792-1868) a man of letters and an antiquary who died without children.

From 1887 until his death in 1918 Llanwern House was the home of

David Alfred Thomas, born in 1856. David was the 15th of 17 children born to Samuel Thomas, a shopkeeper turned Rhondda colliery owner. David was educated at Clifton School and Cambridge. After graduating he went to the family owned Cambrian Colliery at Clydach Vale to study the economics of coal mining and attempted to form a combine of mines to control 80% of the trade and so regulate the price of coal. Unsuccessful in this, he entered politics as Liberal Party member for Merthyr Tydfil where he topped the poll in four elections. He failed to win a post in Campbell-Bannerman's cabinet of 1906 and returned to the Rhondda where he renewed his attempt to control coal production. He acquired controlling interests in the Glamorgan Coal Company, The Naval Company Limited and the Britannic Merthyr Coal Company Limited, forming the Cambrian Combine which brought him into conflict with the leaders of the South Wales Miners' Federation, leading to the strikes of 1910 and the 'Tonypandy Riots' of that year. During the First World War he undertook a mission for the government to the United States after which, in 1916, he was created the 1st Baron Rhondda, of Llanwern in the County of Monmouth. He became 1st Viscount Rhondda, of Llanwern in the County of Monmouth in 1918; the latter title carried a remainder to his daughter Margaret. In 1916 he was appointed President of the Local Government Board and in 1917 Food Controller where he introduced food rationing. He died in 1918 and in his will left £20,000 to Caius College Cambridge to provide 'Rhondda Scholarships'. The house was demolished in 1950. Thomas also acquired Pencoed Castle and its estate, making him one of the largest landowners in the county.

The church of St Mary sits on a Celtic llan though the building is 13th century. It is a single cell building with a substantial three storey tower with south porch. In the graveyard are the tombs of the owners of Llanwern House including a large monument to Viscount Rhondda.

Around the village are a series of medieval banks and ditches, thought to have been developed by the monks of Goldcliff in draining the surrounding land.

The village has seen some development in recent years but remains small.

The giant Llanwern steelworks was built by Richard Thomas & Baldwins Ltd and opened in 1962. It was the first oxygen-blown integrated steelworks in Britain with a hot strip mill, and was the first successful computer controlled steel mill. Steel making ceased in 2001 but, owned by Corus, a hot strip mill, two pickle lines, a cold strip mill and a hot dip galvanising line continue, producing 1.5 million tonnes of steel coil rolls a year. A redevelopment transforming the steel making plant into commercial and industrial units together with the development of 4,000 homes is scheduled to be completed by 2026.

Llechryd Stone Ford
Llechryd is a small village a mile north of Rhymney, just off the Heads of the Valleys road. It was named after a local farm though in the 19th century it was known as Rhymney Bridge. The Union Ironworks was established just south of the village in 1801. Housing was provided at Butetown 300 yards away across the county boundary on the western side of the River Rhymney. The founders of the ironworks were David Evans, Thomas Williams, John Ambrose and Richard Cunningham from Bristol. Richard Crawshay from Cyfarthfa, Benjamin Hall and Watkin George joined Williams and Cunningham and formed a new company in 1803. After Crawshay's death in 1810, Benjamin Hall became the sole owner. His son Benjamin, later Lord Llanover, became an MP and it is claimed that Big Ben is named after him. Iron production in the Rhymney area ceased in 1890, though by this time the works were sited further down the valley. Old Furnace Farm was the site of the stables. The Rhymney House Hotel was originally built as the manager's house.

Soar-y-Graig Welsh Independent Chapel was built in 1839 on the mountain north of the village but now stands roofless and derelict.

The London and North Western and Rhymney Joint Railway ran to the north of the village, the track now forming the route of the Heads of the Valleys road. The village has seen some expansion in recent years but remains small.

Lower Machen   (Welsh: Machen Isaf)
Lower Machen lies on the A468 five miles west of Newport. Originally this was the village of Machen, a title now taken by the larger, later development a mile to the north-west.

Lower Machen is a former estate village for Plas Machen, the residence of a branch of the Morgan family. The Morgan family traced its ancestry back to Cadivor, Lord of Blaencuch in the 11th century. By the time of

Henry VII, the Morgan surname had been adopted by Sir John Morgan, Knight of the Sepulchre and the family had acquired extensive estates through marriage, in particular by the wedding of Lewellin ap Ifor to Angharad, daughter and heiress of Sir Morgan Meredith, Lord of Tredegar. Sir John had married Jennet, the daughter and heiress of John Mathew of Llandaff. They had three sons, the youngest of which was Thomas Morgan, esquire to Henry VII. He was the first to be called of Machen. Thomas's son Rowland married Blanch, the daughter of William Jones of Treowen and on the death of Miles Morgan in 1578, inherited the Tredegar estate.

Plas Machen which stands to the east of the village was built in the 16th century and, after the acquisition of Tredegar House, became a subsidiary residence for the family until abandoned in 1800. Family members continued to be buried in the church into the 18th century. Machen was described as a "fair house" by Leland in 1575; it was partly demolished after 1800, to be restored in 1869 by Habershon and Pite.

The church of St Michael and All Angels is thought to have been built on the site of a Celtic pre-Christian religious site as a Gorgon's head from

Plas Machen 1800 by Sir Richard Colt Hoare

the central block of a pagan shrine was discovered during renovations in 1901. The building is medieval, mostly dating from the 15th century with a west tower, nave, chancel, south porch and the 18th century Morgan chapel. The church was restored in 1900-1 by C.B. Fowler of Cardiff. The Morgan chapel on the north side of the chancel contains memorials to eleven members of the family, including the following tribute to Sir William Morgan who died in 1731 at the age of 30.

> *'Though he came when young, to the Poffeffion of*
> *Power, Honour, art high Alliance, and a great Estate.*
> *Yet they neither made him forget himfelf,*
> *Nor his Father's Friends.*
> *He was a Stranger to Infolence, Oppreffion, or Ingratitude*
> *Humane, courteous, and benevolent.*
> *In his Converfation and at his Table,*
> *Sprightly, free, and engaging,*
> *A Lover of his Neighbours, compaffionate, and charitable;*
> *Amiable for thefe, and other good Qualities,*
> *And much lamented at his untimely Death.'*

The tower is topped by an embattled parapet and a pyramid roof with a weathercock. The acoustics of the church are said to be exceptional and the church hosts an annual music festival. Outside is the base and stump of the churchyard cross where John Wesley is said to have preached.

Machen House was built as the Rectory by the Tredegar Estate in 1831 for the Revd. C.A.S. Morgan, sometime Chancellor of the Diocese of Llandaff and chaplain to Queen Victoria as well as vicar of the parish. He was the younger brother of the 1st Lord Tredegar. The house in late Georgian style has an extensive Regency garden with a bee-bole, miniature lake with humped bridge and castellated corner features to the estate walls. The Revd. Morgan was responsible for establishing the church school built in 1834.

North of the village are the remains of the 12th century Castell Maredydd, a stone castle built by Maeredydd Gethin, prince of Gwynllwg. It was captured by the Normans in 1235.

At the western entrance to the village is the little early 19th century Toll House, a relic of the Caerphilly Turnpike road.

On the southern side of the village there have been finds of Roman material and evidence of building by the Romans over a prolonged period.

Lower Machen is today a conservation area and there has been very little development since the 19th century estate village was established. It is now by-passed by the busy A468 making it a very tranquil place.

Machen

Machen is a village formerly in Monmouthshire, situated three and a half miles east of Caerphilly on the River Rhymney. Morgan of Machen led the men of Gwent in the Battle of Bosworth in 1485 and the Morgans were to become an important family in the area establishing their home at Machen Place, Lower Machen before moving to Tredegar House on the outskirts of Newport. The name is difficult and there have been a number of suggestions over the years but Richard Morgan believes the most likely meaning is Plain of Cein.

There was a forge here in the 16th century with its blast furnace a mile south-west at Ty'n-y-coedcae and later a tin plate works which operated until 1886 on the south side of the river near Plas Newydd. An iron and brass foundry was still operating in the 1920s, north of the railway above the church. Barber on his tour of Monmouthshire in 1803 remarked "the country continues undulating and fertile to the vale of Machen, where the Rumney emerges from among wild hills and overhanging forests, and sweeps through the plain: a sprinkling of white cottages enliven the scene, which receives an additional effect from its picturesque church, and the steep acclivity of Machen hill, studded all over with lime-kilns".

To the east of the village is a large limestone quarry which was owned by Sir Charles Morgan of Tredegar House while Augustus Morgan, son of Sir Charles opened a coal mine across the river from the village in the 1840s to supply coal for the lime kilns belonging to the quarry. This colliery closed in 1860 after an explosion in 1858 killed three men and a boy. The colliery was later reopened as the Pentwyn Colliery in 1900 but closed in 1920. The Machen Colliery was situated a mile to the south-west of the village. It was opened in the latter part of the 19th century but was a small operation until it was taken over by the Pentwyn Glamorgan Colliery Syndicate but even then it employed no more than 101 men. It had closed by 1932. The Vedw Colliery, north of the village, operated between 1896 and 1908, employing a maximum of 73 men.

The Brecon and Merthyr Railway ran through the village with a station and a junction for the Caerphilly branch line. There was a railway works in the village which closed with the railway in 1956, though a line still services the quarry now operated by Hanson Aggregates. The viaduct which carried the railway across the Rhymney still stands.

The church of St John was built as a chapel of ease to St Michael's in Lower Machen (now in the Newport Council area). The church is in the Early English style, consisting of chancel, nave with a hammer beam roof, south porch and spire containing a clock and one bell. It was built in 1855 by W.G. and E. Habershon of London.

Siloam Baptist Chapel on Commercial Street was built in 1820 and enlarged in 1851. It has been demolished with a car park on the site. Adulam Independent Chapel on Lewis Street was built in 1846 and rebuilt in 1861. It has been demolished with houses built on the site. Ebenezer Baptist Chapel on Wyndham Street was built in 1820, rebuilt in 1851 and again in 1900. The chapel is still in use. The Emmanuel Assemblies of God Church in Forge Road is a modern building. Machen Wesleyan Methodist Chapel on the corner of Chatham and Llanarth Close was built in 1830 but has been demolished.

Machen today has expanded with new housing, but it retains a rural feel with plenty of greenery and still holds its annual agricultural show. There is a school, local shops and takeaways and the Forge and Hammer Inn and the White Hart. Sadly, the old Fwrrwm Ishta bar and restaurant was demolished in 2013 and the Tradesman's Arms was sold the same year.

Maesycwmmer Field Near the Footbridge

The spelling of the name Maesycwmmer predates the codification of the Welsh language which bans the double 'M'. The name is taken from Maes-y-cwmmer House, built in 1826 by the Revd. John Jenkins, a noted Baptist minister, theologian, editor, and publisher in the Welsh language. Born in 1779 at Llangynidr in Breconshire he moved to Hengoed in 1809 and was buried at Hengoed chapel in 1853.

Today Maesycwmmer is a largely residential village on the east bank of the River Rhymney opposite Hengoed. Historically a part of Monmouthshire, the village grew to house workers on the Maesycwmmer Viaduct, built to carry the extension of the Taff Vale Railway to the Newport Abergavenny and Hereford Railway. The viaduct which was originally called the Rhymney Viaduct and also the Hengoed Viaduct consists of 16 arches spanning 284 yards at a height of 120 feet above the river. Building which cost £20,000

'Wheel O Drams' sculpture

started in 1853 and was completed in 1858. The viaduct is now owned by Railway Paths Ltd and after restoration costing £870,000 in 2004 has opened as a cycleway and footpath. On the Maesycwmmer side is the *Wheel O Drams* sculpture by Andy Hazell, a 25 foot diameter ring of painted galvanised steel coal wagons, with railway and mining company logos.

In 1880 there was a chemical works to the east of the village between Main Road and the railway, while across the tracks was a foundry. On the banks of the river a corn mill was built in 1750, converted around 1850 to a woollen factory, the building for which still stands.

Zoar Calvinistic Methodist Chapel on Gellideg Heights was built in 1863. It is now used as a bathroom showroom. Mount Pleasant Baptist Chapel on Mount Pleasant was built in 1860. By 1920 it was a Wesleyan Methodist Chapel and today is Bethel Pentecostal Church. Mount Pleasant Evangelical Baptist Church was rebuilt on Main Road and remains in use. Zoar English Calvinistic Methodist Chapel on Main Road was built in 1906. In 2009 it was put up for sale. The large and impressive Tabor Congregational Chapel with its entrance on Tabor Road was built in 1829 and rebuilt in 1856 and 1876. It now stands disused.

St David's Mission Church stood between the railway lines to the north of the village on what is now Old Church Lane. It was replaced at some time after 1922 by All Saints Church on Victoria Road, but this has been demolished. Plans had been submitted for a new church of St Thomas in 1914 but were rejected.

There are two pubs in the village, The Maesycwmmer Inn and The Angel. The Albert Victor Hotel on Victoria Road was converted to a nursing home while The Butchers Arms next to the Angel on Thomas Street closed in 2009 and is now the Spice Tree Indian restaurant. There are a number of local shops and a primary school.

Magor (Welsh: Magwyr) Wall

Magor today is a large village seven and a half miles east of Newport, to the south of the M4. The picturesque old village remains its heart, around The Square and St Mary's church.

The Grade I Listed church is large, with nave, north and south transepts and aisles rebuilt in the 15th century with a refurbishment of 1868-9 by the architect John Norton of London. It is thought to have been founded in the 7th century, but the present structure dates from the 13th century. The church was granted by Gilbert Marshal, Earl of Pembroke to the Abbey of Anagni in Italy in 1238 but later transferred to Tintern Abbey. It was dedicated to St Leonard until 1868.

There are a number of interesting features in the church. The massive 13th century central crossing tower contains a ring of six bells. The north porch has a room above which was at one time used as a schoolroom. The north and south aisles are separated from the nave by three bay arcades with rectangular pillars. The chancel dates from the 13th century, but has a 19th century barrel roof. The stained glass of the 1880 east window is by Joseph Bell of Bristol. Outside are the remains of the two step base and socket of the churchyard cross and the 1857 National School and schoolhouse. The house is now a private residence while the school is used for community activities. There are also the ruins of a substantial house known as the Procurator's house, described in 1585 as a mansion house belonging to the vicar of Magor. Earlier records show that the vicar paid a rent to Tintern Abbey. The ruins date from the 15th century but there are references to an earlier house on the site.

Ebenezer Baptist Chapel on the square was founded in 1816 with a large extension built in 1993. There was a Wesleyan Methodist church on Main Road, which has now been converted into a private house.

On The Square is the four sided War Memorial with each side bearing a crest, the Red Dragon, the Welch, the Royal Arms, the Welsh Arms. On the west side is a medallion of David Thomas First Viscount Rhondda 1856-1918 by Allan G Wyon. Thomas's grandfather was born in Magor and Thomas resided at Llanwern House from 1887 until his death.

Around The Square are a number of 17th and 18th century properties, including the Golden Lion, while on Newport Road is the Wheatsheaf Inn.

In the 16th century Magor was regarded as a haven for outlaws. Rowland Lee, President of the Council of Wales and the Marches complained to Thomas Cromwell in 1535 that there were, living in the Lordship of Magor under the protection of Sir Walter Herbert five men who had committed wilful murder, eighteen who had committed murder, and twenty thieves and outlaws who had committed every variety of crime from the robbing of a man and his mother and putting them "on a hotte trevet for to make them schow", to a robbery of the cathedral of Llandaff, perpetrated by Myles Mathew a friend of Sir Walter.

The village has expanded considerably to become a commuting village and is now hardly distinguishable from nearby Undy. There have been demands for a railway station, replacing that lost in the 1960s. The centre however retains its old world village character.

Mamhilad (Welsh: Mamheilad)
Mamhilad lies two and a half miles north-east of Pontypool. The derivation and meaning of the name is unclear. It was first recorded in 1100 as Mam meliat.

The church of St Illtud was at one time chapel of ease to Llanover, but its history goes back to the time of St Catwg and earlier. The churchyard contained twelve yew trees when Coxe visited in 1800 when he noted one very old yew. This tree now has a circumference of over 30 feet making it the oldest tree in the county, estimated between 2,000-3,000 years old. According to the *Vita Cadoci* a monastery was established here and a portable shrine of St Catwg (feretrum et reliquiae) was moved to Mamhilad from Llancarfan to protect it from enemy attack. The shrine was however lost. The earliest written reference to the village was in 1100 when it was referred to as Mammeliat. The yews, coupled with the partly curved churchyard point to an early Celtic establishment. The present building dates from the 13th century and unusually retains its gallery, constructed from parts of the rood loft. There was a refurbishment by Prichard and Seddon in 1865. There is a weeping chancel and a south and west porch, the latter now used as the vestry. The western bellcote has two bells. Among the monuments are two incised effigies and a memorial to William Morgan in white marble. Morgan died in 1772 and in 1856 there was a court case involving his family when a Jacob Morgan, claiming descent from William's brother John, challenged in court the property of Pantygoitre, Mamhilad, passing to Revd. Iltyd Nicholl. Jacob's claim that John Morgan was William's brother was based on hearsay evidence while William's father's will had declared William to be his only son and heir. The case went before a jury at Monmouth Assizes and the claim was dismissed.

The 1680 gravestone of Aaron Morris has been used in the stile set in the 19th century churchyard wall. Within the boundary are the remains of the 15th century churchyard cross.

Mamhilad Farm House was originally known as Mamhilad House and dates from the 15th century with 17th and 18th century extensions and alterations, and a 19th century façade.

North of the church on the junction with Pentre Lane are the ruins of the 17th century Tithe Barn.

The village has the Star Inn, opposite the church, and the Horseshoe Inn three quarters of a mile to the north.

In 1814 a railway was constructed from the Brecknock and Abergavenny Canal (now known as the Monmouthshire and Brecon Canal) in the parish to the Usk Bridge at Abergavenny, a distance of six miles. It was known as the Mamhilad Railway. The canal runs to the west of the village.

Situated at Little Mill, Mamhilad was a Boys' Reformatory which consisted of a school and small farm opened in February 1859. Boys were sentenced by magistrates to a short term of imprisonment, usually with hard labour, followed by two to five years of compulsory detention in the reformatory.

Manmoel

The rural hamlet of Manmoel sits on Cefn Manmoel, the ridge between the Sirhowy and Ebbw valleys, two miles north-west of Aberbeeg. It takes its name from an Irish pupil of St Cadog named Macmoil, mentioned in the Life of St Cadog and there is reference to Ecclesia Mac moilo, indicating a church, in 1200.

Manmoel colliery, two miles south of the hamlet, was opened in the early 1800s by Sir Henry Protheroe who owned the local estate. It was purchased in 1810 by Benjamin Hall, father of Lord Llanover, who built a tram road connecting it to the Waterloo Colliery (Oakdale). It was a small colliery which continued in operation under different owners through the 19th century, employing 22 men in 1896 but was closed by 1901.

Manmoel has a pub, the Manmoel Inn, formerly the Full Moon and Paran Calvinistic Methodist church which was built in 1828 through the efforts of David Wynne who died in 1848 at the age of 92 and is buried in the graveyard. Paran still holds regular services. A school was built in 1880 to accommodate 53 children while to the north the village pound remains intact.

There is now no sign of the Ecclesia Mac moilo, said to have been built by St Cadog with an altar and enclosing rampart at the head of the Nant-y-felin brook. There is a near circular enclosure at Bragdy south of Macmoel, near Ty'r Capel (Chapel House) Farm.

Mardy (Welsh: Y Maerdy) Steward's House

Mardy today is a suburb of Abergavenny. In the 19th century it was a hamlet on the Hereford Road with a small number of villas, the Crown and Sceptre and New Inn and a post office. Mardy Park had been established by 1882.

To the east of the village is Maindiff Court Hospital, built in 1877 as a home for Crawshay Bailey Junior with Maindiff Farmhouse rebuilt at the same time. In 1924 the estate was gifted to Monmouthshire Asylum Committee for use as a hospital and the Court was rebuilt in the 1930s.

During Word War II it became the Maindiff Court Military Hospital and Prisoner of War Reception Centre with its most famous prisoner being Rudolf Hess. Hess was apparently given special treatment, being allowed to visit, with his guards, local sites of interest and was also entertained by Lord Tredegar at Tredegar House. It is now operated as a community hospital. Further east is Wernddu Farm, with its caravan park and Black Mountains Falconry Centre.

Markham

Markham lies a little under a mile north-east of Aberbargoed in the Sirhowy valley. The village takes its name from the Markham Colliery which in turn was named after Sir Arthur Markham, a director of Tredegar Iron Company. Markham Colliery in Chesterfield was part owned by his father Charles. The village enjoys an elevated position between the Rhymney and Sirhowy valleys with the scars of mining gradually being removed.

The first large pit at Markham was Abernant Colliery to the north of the village. It was opened by the Bargoed Coal Co. Ltd in 1888 and employed up to 500 men before closure in 1932.

Markham Colliery was sunk in 1910 by the Markham Steam Coal Company, a subsidiary of Tredegar Iron and Coal. Six men died in an explosion 12 months before the first coal was produced. By 1923 there were over 2,100 men employed at Markham. During World War II the colliery was linked underground with Oakdale Colliery to provide an escape route in the event of bombing. From 1979 coal produced at Markham reached the surface at Oakdale. The colliery closed in 1986.

The village dates from 1910 with the first terraces built to accommodate miners and their families. After World War II a large housing estate was built and there has been further development on a smaller scale in recent years including some bungalows at the south-eastern entrance to the village.

Only the Congregational Chapel in Pen-y-werlod Road has survived as a place of worship in the village, now under the banner of the United Reformed Church. St John's Church on Bryn Road has been replaced by houses; Markham Methodist Chapel on Abernant Road was housed in a terraced house but has now merged with the United Reformed Church. The Calvinistic Methodist Chapel on Abernant Road has been demolished while the Immaculate Heart of Mary, Roman Catholic Church, has been replaced by the three modern bungalows at the south-eastern entrance to the village.

The Markham Miners' Welfare Hall and Institute built in the late 1920s-30s are in separate buildings. The Institute on Abernant Road is in the mock Tudor style while the hall is on Bryn Road. Both continue to function.

The village has a primary school, a sports and community centre with playground and playing fields and a selection of shops and takeaways.

Above the village to the south-west is an 86 foot diameter concrete water storage tank belonging to Welsh Water.

Marshfield (Welsh: Maerun)

Marshfield, five and a half miles west of Newport, is another village which has seen dramatic growth as a commuting centre midway between Cardiff and Newport. Like Marshfield in Gloucestershire the name is derived from St Mary's Field.

Away to the east of the main village, the Grade II* Listed St Mary's church was, according to tradition, founded in 1135 by the Countess Mabel, in memory of her father, Robert Fitzhamon, the Norman Lord of Glamorgan and Wentlooge. The west tower and south porch were added in the 15th century. Two accounts around the year 1900 describe the church as having a lofty tower with a spire but the spire has disappeared. There was a restoration begun in 1867 by William Gilbee Habershon which continued into the 1880s when the chancel floor was re-laid. The windows were replaced in 1909 and in 1924 the chancel was re-roofed. A new vestry had been built in 1867 but in 1984 the large new vestry on the north side was added. The church has an immersion baptistery thought to have been added in 1909. The tower contains a ring of six bells. Outside there is the weathered octagonal socket-stone of a churchyard cross.

The Gateway Christian Centre of Castleton Baptist Church on Blacktown Road was built in the late 19th century as a Sunday School.

In 1880 the village had two beer houses, considered to be a lower grade than a public house. By 1901 one had been replaced by the Balaclava Inn on Marshfield Road, now demolished. The other beer house is now the Masons' Arms on Blacktown Road.

There were two major employers in the village, Ansells Brewery Depot and Unigate Dairies. Both have closed and the sites developed for housing, assisting the growth of the village.

Mathern (Welsh: Matharn) Older form: Merthyr Tewdrig

Mathern and Newton Green straddle the M4, two miles south-west of Chepstow.

The old village of Mathern lies south of the M4. It was founded on the burial site of Tewdric, the 6th century King of Gwent and Glywysing. The Mathern Pill reached further inland in the medieval period than it does today, allowing shipping to enter.

Merthyr Tewdrig translates as Tewdrig the Martyr. Baring-Gould gives the following account from the *Liber Landavensis*: "Tewdrig in his old age surrendered the rule over Morganwg to his son Meurig, and retired to live an eremitical life at Dindyrn, now Tintern, on the Wye, where he found a rock suitable for him to make a cell in it. Whilst there, the Saxons burst in on Gwent, and the old king took up arms again to repel them; for it was said of him that he had been ever victorious in all battles. An angel had appeared to him and said, "Go to-morrow to the aid of the people of God against the enemies of the Church of Christ, and the foe will turn to flight as far as Pull Brochuail (now Brockweir above Tintern Parva). And do thou fully armed stand in the front of the battle, and when the foe see thy face they will fly as usual. And thenceforth for thirty years, during the reign of thy son, they will not venture into the land, and its inhabitants will be in peace. But thou wilt receive a wound at Ryt Tindyrn (the ford of Tintern) and wilt die three days after." So Tewdrig, fully harnessed, mounted his horse and stood at the head of the troops to defend the ford over the Wye. The Saxons were put to flight, but one of them hurled a lance across the water and wounded the old King. When it was perceived that the wound was mortal, his men were for removing him, but he forbade them to do so, and said that he would die there, and that he had desired his body to rest in the Isle of Echni, the Flat Holm, in the Severn Sea. On the morrow, however, appeared two stags harnessed to a wagon, and Tewdrig, recognizing that they were sent by the will of God, allowed himself to be lifted into the conveyance. The wagon carried him to the bank of the Severn and there stayed, and on the spot a sparkling spring began to flow. Then suddenly the wagon dissolved, and Tewdrig gave up the ghost. Meurig erected an oratory on the spot, which was blessed by S. Oudoceus. The spot was Mathern, below Chepstow; there the old king was laid, and not conveyed, as he had desired, to Echni. The land around was made over to Oudoceus for the monastery of Llandaff, and in later times the Bishops had a palace there, for about three centuries. In the Church, on the south wall of the chancel, is a tablet set up in memory of Tewdrig, with an inscription in English by Bishop Godwin (1601-18). Godwin in excavating discovered a stone coffin containing the almost perfect skeleton of the saint, and a ghastly fracture in the skull showed plainly the cause of death. At the restoration of the chancel in 1881 the stone coffin with the bones was again found beneath the tablet."

Tewdrig is also referred to by the Latin name of Theodoricus, and he is credited as having founded churches at Bedwas, Llandow, and Merthyr Tydfil. His importance is reflected by Bishop Miles Salley of Llandaff (1500-17) who in his will directed "his heart and bowels to be deposited at the High Altar of the Church at Matherne, before the image of S. Theodorick".

St Tewdrig's Well, where the saints wounds were bathed, is situated 112 yards south of the M4 underpass and has a neat stone wall, with seven stone steps leading down to the water. It is surrounded by a wooden picket fence with plaques and a wooden bench.

The Grade I Listed St Tewdric's church is built on a Celtic site but the present building dates from the 13th century, possibly replacing a smaller Norman church. The nave was rebuilt in the late 15th century when the tower was rebuilt by Bishop John Marshall. There was a refurbishment in 1882 by John Prichard, though the chancel restoration was the work of Ewan Christian in 1890. The vestry is a later addition. Inside there are north and south aisles to the nave with arcades of four columns in the Early English style. There is a squint and a door to the rood stair. The font was replaced in 1882 and the medieval font buried beneath the floor of the porch. This was reinstated in 1943. The tower has a ring of six bells dated 1765, which are rung regularly, apparently causing the tower to 'wobble'. The Revd. Watkin Davies gifted the reredos, east window and choir stalls in 1914. The reredos of the south aisle is a War Memorial of 1921 by W.D. Caroë.

The chancel is slightly out of line, known as a 'weeping chancel', indicating that nave and chancel were built at different times, with builders taking their bearings at sunrise on Easter Day, which of course is a moveable date. Outside the church wall is a modern carving of St Tewdric.

South of the church are the remains of Mathern Palace, dating from the early 15th century when it was built by John de la Zouch, who was Bishop of Llandaff 1408-1423, a monk of the order of Minorites. It was added to by John Marshall at the end of the 15th century, while Miles Salley, who was promoted to the see in 1504, is credited with the chapel, hall, kitchen, and adjoining apartments. The Bishops moved their residence to nearby Moynes Court in 1610, but returned to the Palace with Bishop Bew being the last resident in 1706. The building was then tenanted until it was sold in 1889, though Coxe in 1801 described it as "a quadrangular building, inclosing a court yard, is now converted into a farm house, and is in a sad state of dilapidation; it still, however, preserves some remains of ancient grandeur, and from its irregularities has a picturesque effect. The outside ornaments of the eastern window of the chapel are still visible. The dilapidations have even extended to the library, which was once not inconsiderable: There now remain only a few worm-eaten volumes of the ancient fathers, without covers, and mouldering into dust."

In 1894 it was purchased by Henry Avray Tipping, the French-born British writer, garden designer, and Architectural Editor of *Country Life* magazine. He refurbished the palace with the aid of Eric Francis, architect of Chepstow. He also converted the nearby 17th century barn.

Mathern Ediscopal Palace by Sir Richard Colt Hoare 1800

In 1957 Mathern Palace was purchased by Richard Thomas and Baldwin, owners of the Llanwern steelworks and was subsequently modernized by British Steel for use as a hospitality centre. It is Grade I Listed.

Moynes Court lies some 300 yards west of the church. The medieval Moyns Castle was built by the Bishop of Llandaff and the moat and mound are to the south and west of the house. Coxe records that in ancient deeds the property was known as Monks' Court, suggesting a religious house. Bishop Francis Godwin in 1609-10 built the Court and moved the seat of residence to Moynes Court from Mathern Palace. By 1618 it was the property of Thomas Hughes of Cillwch whose son, Colonel Hughes was later the parliamentary governor of Chepstow Castle. Other residents over the years include the Lewis family of St Pierre. In 1960 the Moynes Court was divided in to three houses. The house is approached through the impressive 17th century gatehouse, now available as holiday accommodation.

East of the church is The Innage, a farm built around 1500 but extended in the 16th and 17th centuries with more modern extensions. Its first tenant was in 1773 so the property was in use by the diocese prior to that.

The main population area is at Newton Green to the north of the M4. There are a number of attractive older cottages, some built by the owners of Wyelands, the family of the Revd. Robert Vaughan-Hughes for their employees and some post First World War mock Tudor houses but housing is mainly modern. The Miller's Arms was described as a beer house in 1901. Mathern Mill stands on Mounton Brook and was in operation as a corn mill until 1968. It retains its machinery. A fishery is now operated on the brook.

The village school began as an endowed school but was taken over as a Board School in 1875. It is now a day nursery.

East of the village is Wyelands, a large 1819 villa designed by Robert Lugar in the style of John Nash, built for George Buckle, Sheriff of Monmouthshire.

Michaelston-y-fedw (Welsh: Llanfihangel-y-fedw)

Michaelstone-y-fedw is a small village five and a half miles south-west of Newport, to the north of the M4. 'Y fedw' means 'the birch tree', but there is a suggestion that the name derives from St Medwy, who according to the Iolo Manuscripts was one of the three messengers said to have been sent by Lleurwg (Lucius) to Pope Eleutherius in 156 AD, and was made a bishop in Rome. He was subsequently bishop at Llanfedwy, in Glamorgan, of which he was patron. (The fact that Iolo Morganwg is the only source of this account casts doubt on its accuracy.) Llanfedw Farm and Coed Llanfedw lie within the old parish boundaries but over a mile to the north-west in the old county of Glamorgan. The original church was burnt down in the wars of Iestyn ab Gwrgant around 1079, and was never rebuilt. The Ordnance Survey map of 1883 gives the village name as Michaelstone Fedwy.

There is a suggestion in the guide to the church that St Michael's has Roman origins in the form of the chancel north wall where there are three filled in round arched doorways, two of which date from the 4th century. The listing text for this Grade II* Listed church dates the origins to the 13th century. The church consists of a chancel, nave, west tower, south porch and the 16th century Kemeys Tynte chapel to the south of the chancel. It was restored in 1897 by John Pollard Seddon and John Coates Carter and again between 1999 and 2005. Inside there is an Early English aumbry, a wall cupboard used for storing chalices and elements of the sacrament. The font is thought to be 17th century Flemish with a depiction of the Tree of Life entwined with the Serpent of Wisdom. The altar slab is of the 13th century, inscribed with five crosses. There is a fragment of late medieval plaster with an early fresco on the north side of the chancel. The Kemeys-Tynte chapel contains the family vault and memorials to the family. The Kemeys, later Kemeys-Tynte lived at Cefn Mably, across the county border, but within the parish. The bells in the tower date from the 18th century and were refurbished in the recent restoration.

In the churchyard is the grave of Elizabeth Mackie Hess, the first wife of Carl Hess, said to be the father by a subsequent marriage of Rudolph Hess. The tomb bears the inscription "Erected by Carl Hess, of Schleswig, Germany, in memory of his wife, Elizabeth Mackie, who died at Exmouth, Devon, June 13th: 1891, aged 35. In life beloved, in death never forgotten". According to Rudolph's son, Wolf Rüdiger Hess, however his grandfather was Fritz H. Hess, not Carl and the family home was in the Fichtelgebirge region of Bavaria not Schleswig. It appears that the story came from Elizabeth Mackie's 77 year old brother who claimed the connection in an article in the *Western Mail* of 26th June 1941, a month after Rudolf Hess flew to Britain.

The Cefn Mably Arms stands next to the church and claims to have its origins as a long house built by Mabel, daughter of Robert Fitzhamon, the

Norman marcher lord who conquered Morgannwg. The building does not appear to be listed and the name is derived from Cefn Mably House, the home of the Kemeys family who are buried in the church. The pub is said to be haunted, while mediums claim to see the children of the witches beneath the oak tree where their mothers were hanged. Witchcraft in Wales was rare and there are only five known trials for the crime before it ceased to be a criminal offence in 1735.

A village school was established in 1826, endowed by the Revd. Dr Tate. It was situated across the road from the village hall which had replaced it as the school by 1900. In that year the village consisted of the church, the Rectory, school, pub, smithy and just one other house. Today Michaelstone has a number of large modern properties. North of the village the River Rhymney forms a wide loop and Michaelston Mill was built using a leat across the loop to power the wheel. It was in use as a corn mill in 1883 but was shown as disused by 1901. Just south of the bridge across the Rhymney there is another small pocket of housing. This was the site of Tirzah Particular Baptist Chapel, built in 1861 but now demolished with only the graveyard remaining.

Mitchel Troy (Welsh: Llanfihangel Troddi)
Church of St Michael on the River Trothy

The village lies two miles south-west of Monmouth and is today by-passed by the A449. The name 'Mitchel' may be derived from St Michael, but might also be derived from 'mickle' meaning much, as in Mitcheldean in the Forest of Dean, while 'Troy' is derived from 'Trothy'.

St Michael and All Angels' church has a nave with north and south aisles, chancel, west tower, north vestry and a south porch. It is largely the work of John Prichard in 1876 when the 8th Duke of Beaufort financed the rebuilding. A church has existed on the site since Norman times, though the only reminder of the early church is the tub font which now stands alongside Prichard's marble font with its with water lilies, passion flowers and fish. The medieval porch, the nave arcades and chancel arch are 14th century. The upper stages of the tower were rebuilt in 1909 by Ernest G. Davies. There was at one time a spire which collapsed in the 18th century. A plaque commemorates the rebuilding, while another is in memory of the Revd. Henry George Talbot, the grandson of the 5th Duke of Beaufort and rector of Mitchel Troy for 42 years. The arcade columns are unusual in being cruciform in cross section. The altar in the Lady Chapel is an ancient stone altar with five incised crosses, discovered under the south aisle during the reconstruction. Set in the south aisle wall is the lid of a child's coffin which had been used as a piscina. At the end of the north aisle is an incised reproduction on black marble of the Last Supper by Leonardo da Vinci. The tower contains three bells. The 14th century churchyard cross is missing its head. The village stocks used to be positioned outside the church wall alongside the lychgate.

The National School, built about 1870, is now a private dwelling. Across the Trothy is Wonaston Mill, a corn mill operating until 1965. The undershot wheel was replaced by a turbine driven disc wheel around 1940. The leat leading from a weir on the Trothy and the mill race have been destroyed. Near the garden centre to the north-east of the village is a leat, the only remnant of a fulling mill which had disappeared by 1880. Further north, at the junction with the B4293 is the 1810 tollgate house which operated until 1870 on the Monmouth to Raglan turnpike road.

There has been some modern development in the village, mainly on Parc Pentre. There is a caravan park on the northern side, while to the south in the area of Mitchel Troy Common there has been further development.

Troy House lies a mile north-east of the village. Coxe, quoting the 15th century William of Worcester, gives the proprietor of Troy House in the 15th century as Thomas Herbert, son of Sir William ap Thomas, squire for the body, who served in the French wars, under Richard Duke of York, and Humphrey Duke of Gloucester, and died at Troy. The estate passed to his brother the Earl of Pembroke and then to the earl's illegitimate son, Sir William Herbert of Troy. By the time of James I, Troy was owned by Sir Charles Somerset following his marriage to Elizabeth Powell, heiress of Sir William Powell of Troy. When Charles I visited Raglan, Troy was owned by Sir Thomas Somerset who took great pride in the gardens, supplying fruit for the royal guest of his brother the Earl of Worcester.

With Raglan Castle lying in ruins after the Civil War, the family bought Badminton House and Troy became the Welsh seat of the Somerset family. Henry Somerset was Lord President of the Council of Wales and was created Duke of Beaufort. He enlarged Troy House as a wedding gift for his son. Some 19th century writers have attributed the design of the enlarged Troy House to Inigo Jones, but as Coxe points out the design would not have reflected much credit on the taste of such a great architect, while the low position of the house is not typical of Jones. Troy House remained in the possession of the Somerset family until 1904, with the remainder of the estate sold by auction in 1901. The house was acquired by the Sisters of the Good Shepherd for use as a convent school, and in 1935 it became an approved school for girls. The house, not accessible to the public stands empty save for a caretaker, subject to planning permission to divide the house into apartments. Attached to the house are a pleasure garden and a four acre walled garden. There is also Troy Farm.

Monkswood (Welsh: Coed y Mynach)
Monkswood is a small village a little over two miles north-west of Usk on either side of the A472. The village was formerly known as Monkswood Chapel and in the 13th and 14th centuries was the site of a grange of Tintern Abbey. The grange together with a chapel was off Estavarney Lane, where the monks also constructed a weir on the River Usk for a fishery. Following the Battle of Pwll Melyn in 1405, many of the defeated Welsh forces were killed in the woodland here as they fled from the English army. The battle, which resulted in the deaths or capture of a number of the leaders of Glyndŵr's rebellion, including his brother and son, saw the tide begin to turn against Glyndŵr.

Monkswood was known as an 'Extra Parochial Liberty', as it was an area previously owned by the monastery and was outside the local ecclesiastical and civil parishes. Such areas were abolished in 1868 and forced to become parishes.

Monkswood did have a church, though it did not have a dedication when it was rebuilt in 1879-84 by Edwin Henry Lingen Barker. The church, which is now dedicated to St Matthew, is situated between the A472 and Cefn Mawr Lane. It has a nave, chancel, south porch, north vestry and a western double bellcote.

Not far from the church was an endowed school which was used as a Sunday School after the formation of the Llanbaddock, Monkswood & Glascoed United School Board in 1879. The building has since been demolished.

The population of the village expanded with the building of houses, south of the A472 to accommodate workers at the nearby Glascoed Royal Ordnance Factory.

There was a pub on the main road, the Beaufort Arms, which is no longer trading. Behind the pub is the local cricket pitch and pavilion.

Near the junction of the A472 and Rumble Street to the west of the village, a furnace and two forges were established in 1565 by Richard Hanbury. The works at Monkswood supplied Osmond iron to the wire works at Tintern. The works closed in the latter part of the 18th century. Rumble Street was cobbled and the sound of the ironstone being carried along it gave the street its name.

Mounton

Mounton is a tiny village two miles west of Chepstow. The name is thought to be a corruption of Monks' Town. It was in the possession of the Priory of St Mary in Chepstow and Lewis suggests that "considerable remains of walls, still traceable in the contiguous woods, manifest that a large town formerly existed here".

The small church is dedicated to St Andoenus, a 6th century Bishop of Rouen. Records show that there were plans to enlarge the church and install a gallery in 1829 which were never implemented, but in 1880-81 Walter Evill of Chepstow supervised the building of a new vestry, new roof, the rebuilding of the chancel arch, reseating and general repairs. There is a west door with bellcote above, nave, chancel and north vestry. In the chancel is a memorial to Capt. Ian Oswald Liddell, VC, 5th Battalion Coldstream Guards, killed in action in April 1945. Liddell's grandfather, Sir Charles Oswald Liddell, was the owner of nearby Shirenewton Hall. Part of the graveyard lies across the road from the church.

There were previously two water powered paper mills in the village, Lady Mill and Linnet Paper Mill, together with the Linnet and Lark Carpet Factory, but these were closed in 1876 after complaints of pollution in the Mounton Brook.

Grade II* Listed Mounton House was built 1910-12 for Henry Avray Tipping of Mathern Palace. Set above a small limestone gorge, the house was designed by Eric Francis in conjunction with Tipping after the latter had inherited a large sum of money. The interior was 17th and 18th century in style. Tipping moved to High Glanau near Mitchel Troy in 1922, passing Mounton House and Mathern Palace to Colonel Holden. In 1950 the property was converted for educational use. The gardens are an important feature and are typical of the Edwardian Arts and Crafts layout, with a mixture of formal and wild garden, set against a wild woodland background.

Mounton sits at the head of the picturesque, wooded valley of the Mounton Brook, which stretches for a mile, with high rocks, crowned with finely-grown yew trees.

Nant-y-derry see Goetre

Nantyglo The Coal Stream

Nantyglo is a former ironworking village a mile south of Beaufort.

The ironworks, consisting of two furnaces together with forges, were established in 1795 by Harford, Hill & Co but within a year were idle. Long Row, the first houses for workers were built on Market Road. The works were purchased in 1802 by Joseph Harrison but their re-opening was short lived and it was not until they were purchased by Joseph Bailey and Matthew Wayne in 1811 that the works started to flourish. Joseph Bailey was the nephew of Richard Crawshay of the Cyfarthfa Ironworks at Merthyr Tydfil. He was left a quarter share of those works by his uncle and sold out to William Crawshay for £20,000. Matthew Wayne was the furnace manager at Cyfarthfa and was bequeathed £800 by Richard Crawshay who died in 1810. Wayne sold out to Joseph's younger brother Crawshay Bailey around 1820 and established the Gadlys ironworks at Aberdare and sank the first deep coal mine at Aberdare. He died in 1853. Joseph retired from the business in 1830 and purchased estates in Brecknockshire, Radnorshire and Glamorgan, making his home at Glanusk Park between Abergavenny and Brecon. He was MP for the City of Worcester 1835-47 and MP for the county of Brecknock 1847 until his death in 1858. He was made a baronet in 1852. His son Joseph died in 1850 and he was succeeded by is grandson Sir Joseph Russell Bailey who was created Baron Glanusk in 1899. The Glanusk estate passed to The Honourable Elizabeth Shân Josephine Bailey, Lord Lieutenant of Powys, who married William Legge-Bourke. Their daughter Tiggy was nanny to Princes William and Harry.

Under Bailey and Wayne and later the Bailey brothers the Nantyglo works flourished. By 1823 five blast furnaces were operating with two more added in 1826-7. In 1833 the Beaufort Ironworks were added.

Progress was interrupted by the end of the Napoleonic wars which saw a slump in the price of iron. While a threatened cut in wages was withdrawn, the Baileys feared for their lives and property in the event of a riot and built two round towers in 1822 with iron used for the roof, floor-joists, window-sills, frames and fireplaces. The iron roof segments were covered with brick. The north tower is well preserved having been used as a dwelling for many years. The south tower is in ruins with the iron removed in the 1940s with the use of explosives. Both are on Roundhouse Farm where the barn roof is supported by iron beams. The Baileys also built Nantyglo House or Tŷ Mawr in 1822 as their residence, but this was demolished prior to 1950. In 1845 Crawshay Bailey switched his attention to the coal industry, leaving his nephew in charge of Nantyglo and Beaufort. He sold the ironworks to the Blaina Iron and Steel Co. Ltd. in 1871 for £300,000, but by 1878 both Beaufort and Nantyglo had closed.

A mile south of the Nantyglo works, George Brewer established the Coalbrook Vale Ironworks in 1820. These were purchased by Levick and Simpson of the Blaina and Cwm Celyn Iron Works in 1855. A cholera epidemic in 1866 saw the works close the following year with the loss of over 3,000 jobs. In 1869 the works were revived under new ownership which also took over the Nantyglo and Beaufort works. A strike in 1873 caused damage to the company finances and it finally closed in 1878. Coalbrook Vale also operated three collieries employing up to 613 men. The collieries continued in operation until 1938.

The village of Nantyglo developed rapidly. The church of St Anne however was built in the 1890s as a mission church to St Peter's, the parish church of Aberystruth. Bethania Calvinistic Methodist Chapel on King Street was built in 1862 but has now been converted to housing. Hermon Welsh Baptist Chapel on Garn Cross was built in 1821 and rebuilt in 1830 and 1920. The cemetery remains but the site of the chapel is now occupied by the Nantyglo Medical Centre. Garnfach Primitive Methodist Chapel also on Garn Cross was built in 1883 but is no longer in use. Bethel Baptist Chapel on Queen Street was built in 1827 and rebuilt in 1867 but is now a residential property.

Much of the industrial heritage has disappeared including early terraces of workers' houses. So too have many of the pubs, with only the Golden Lion remaining in the village. The Royal Oak was run by Zephaniah

Williams who led a column of Chartists from his pub to Newport in 1839. There are some shops and takeaways but the main shopping area is now around the Lakeside development to the north. Parc Nant y Waun and the West Monmouthshire Golf Club lie to the north-west of the village which has seen some new building development.

Nash (Welsh: Trefonnen)

Nash is a small village three miles south-east of Newport city centre on the eastern side of the Usk estuary, and bordering the Bristol Channel. The parish contains Uskmouth Power Station. Built on land reclaimed by the monks of Goldcliff Priory, the surrounding area is flat and fertile. The name is thought to be derived from 'An Ash' and the Welsh Trefonnen translates as Ash Town.

The Grade I Listed church of St Mary dates from the 12th century, though little of the original survives apart from the north wall of the chancel and the squint. There have been a number of restorations over the years, the most recent in 2004-5. The interior has a late 18th, early 19th century gallery, box pews, an 18th century triple decker pulpit, and early 20th century choir stalls. Of particular interest is the medieval tower with its stone spire, positioned at the north corner of the nave and adjoining the chancel. The tower contains a peal of five bells. There are marks on the west wall of the tower indicating that the church once had an additional north aisle. There are drainage ditches or reens across the parish and the 1883 map shows the church partially surrounded and accessed by three footbridges.

Opposite the church is the Waterloo Inn rebuilt in 1838. It is a tenanted free house, owned by the parish council, a gift of the Arney family in the 17th century.

At Pye Corner, north of the church is Nash Baptist Chapel, built in 1822 but no longer in use. Nearby are the RSPB Newport Wetlands Reserve and the 44 ft high steel East Usk lighthouse built in 1893.

Nash has seen some modern housing, but the parish is mainly agricultural with industry along the east bank of the Usk.

Newbridge-on-Usk

Newbridge on Usk is a hamlet four miles north-east of Caerleon. There are two houses and the Newbridge on Usk, a hotel now owned by the

Celtic Manor Resort. It stands on the west bank of the Usk which is crossed by the 1779 three arched red sandstone bridge built by the Edwards family, celebrated for the bridge at Pontypridd.

Newcastle (Welsh: Castell Newydd)
Situated four and a half miles north-west of Monmouth, Newcastle is a hamlet, named after the motte and bailey castle which lies in the grounds of Newcastle Farm. The site has been damaged by building, but the remains of the motte are visible from the road, just past the former Wellington Inn on the road to Llanfaenor.

Newchurch (Welsh: Yr Eglwys Newydd ar y Cefn)
New Church on the Ridge
Five and a half miles north-west of Chepstow is the church of St Peter, the centre of the large rural parish of Newchurch. Formerly divided into Newchurch East and Newchurch West, the parish included Devauden, Kilgwrrwg, Gaer-Lwyd and Wentwood. The area was largely covered by the forest of Wentwood at the time of the Norman invasion, but after being granted by the Lord of Striguil to Tintern Abbey in the 12th century, the monks started assarting (clearing the forest) the area that was to become the parish of Newchurch. In 1291 the area was granted to Roger Bigod, Earl of Norfolk in exchange for land at Woolaston, north-east of Chepstow. Bigod had inherited Chepstow from his father Hugh who had married Maud Marshal, heiress of William Marshal, Earl of Pembroke who in turn had acquired Chepstow from his marriage to Isabel de Clare, the heiress of Richard de Clare, known as Strongbow. It was Bigod who provided the church of St Peter.

As its Welsh name implies, the church stands on a ridge, offering extensive views. The oldest surviving parts of the church are the tower and large porch, dating from the 15th or early 16th century, the remainder of the church having been rebuilt by John Pollard Seddon in 1864. Constructed of coarse red sandstone in the Early English style, it consists of a chancel, nave, south porch and western tower containing a bell dated 1716. There is an early tub font, but the furnishings are Victorian. The east window by Theodora Salusbury depicts the Adoration of the Magi and was installed in 1931. Apart from Church Farm and Pentwyn House and Farm there are no other buildings near the church.

Three quarters of a mile to the south-west is Gaerlwyd, a hamlet with a Neolithic burial chamber consisting of five erect supporting stones, five recumbent megaliths and a displaced capstone, visible from the Llangwm road, north of the crossroads. Gaerllwydd Baptist Chapel started life in 1842 as Mount Zion Calvinistic Methodist Chapel. It was taken over by the Presbyterians and subsequently by the Baptists.

Newton Green see Mathern

New Tredegar (Welsh: Tredegar Newydd)

New Tredegar is a former mining village on the eastern bank of the Rhymney river, three miles south-east of Rhymney. Originally the station on the Brecon and Merthyr Railway was named White Rose after the cottage and colliery of that name, but the village took its name from the Earl of Tredegar who owned much of the land. The Morgan family who owned Tredegar House on the outskirts of Newport traced their history back to Cadifor Fawr, lord of Cil-sant, who died in 1089. The family retained their estates through the Norman Conquest, acquiring more land through marriage over the years. Tredegar means ten acre town.

The White Rose Colliery was open in 1853 when it was owned by Marshall & Knowles, employing 60 men. It had closed by 1901. The New Tredegar Colliery a mile north-west of the village was sunk by Thomas Powell in 1853. It continued in production under Powell Duffryn, employing 1,372 men but was forced to close in 1929 when a mountain slide damaged the shafts. In 1875 22 men died in an explosion at the colliery.

New Tredegar grew to serve the White Rose and New Tredegar collieries and those at nearby Elliots Town and Tir-phil. It was served by the Rhymney Railway as well as the Brecon and Merthyr. The latter has closed but the Valleys Line operates on the Rhymney line with a station across the river at Tir-phil.

Saron Welsh Baptist Chapel on Chapel Street was built in 1858 but has been demolished as has Zion Wesleyan Methodist Chapel on Thomas Street which was built before 1878. Bethel Calvinistic Methodist Chapel on Ruperra Street was built in 1860 and is still in use. Capel-Yr-Uchdir Welsh Independent Chapel on Tredegar Road was built prior to 1878 but has been demolished and a bungalow now stands on the site. New Tredegar Independent Chapel at the northern end of Dyffryn Terrace was built in 1890. It has been demolished and a substantial house built on the site. Carmel Baptist Chapel on Dyffryn Terrace was built in 1899 and is still in use. Also on Dyffryn Terrace is a hall, built for the Independent Order of Rechabites and later used as a synagogue for the New Tredegar Jewish community, but now closed.

St Dingat's Church was built in 1896 on land donated by the 4th Earl of Tredegar in 1894. St Dingat was a 6th century Welsh saint thought to be one of the 36 children of Brychan, himself the son of an Irish chieftain and a Welsh princess, who inherited and controlled much of what is now Brecknockshire through his mother and indeed gave it its Welsh name Brycheiniog. Two firms of architects were involved, Cholton & Morgan and Seddon & Carter. It was enlarged with the addition of a south aisle in 1899, a north aisle having been included in the original plan. Services are still held in the church. The Parish Hall on James Street is now a wedding shop. The War Memorial adjacent to the hall has two life-size figures in white marble, depicting a soldier with gun and his comrade lying wounded, set on a red marble plinth. The work is attributed to Louis Frederick Roslyn, the Lambeth born sculptor. Roslyn was the son of a German sculptor, George Louis Roselieb, who had moved to Britain to work. Roslyn's initial work, including a sculpture of Edward VII, was carried out under the name of Roselieb and it was under this name that he joined the Royal Flying Corps in 1915. He is perhaps best known for his War Memorials which include those at Maesteg, Port Talbot, Kenfig Hill, Pyle and Holyhead. That at Maesteg has a similar portrayal to the New Tredegar memorial.

New Tredegar Workmen's Institute was built in 1878 and enlarged in 1910. A hall was built in 1906, later used as the Empire Cinema. Both hall and institute on Tredegar Road have been demolished with houses built on the site.

The village retains a good selection of local shops and pubs, including the Tredegar Arms Hotel and the Ruperra Arms. Schools are located in Elliots Town and Phillipstown. There are parks and playing fields and the New Tredegar Sports Centre.

Tim Rhys-Evans, founder of Only Men Aloud choir was born in the village.

Oakdale

The hamlet was originally known as Rhiw Syr Dafydd with two pubs and a scattering of houses, a mile and a half east of Blackwood in the Sirhowy valley. Coal mining had been carried on in the vicinity with a number of collieries established in 1815, but in 1907 the Tredegar Iron and Coal Company started the Oakdale Colliery and with it planned a garden village. The village of 660 houses was built between 1910 and 1913, away from the colliery on a hill. Every house had a front and rear garden, hot and cold running water, electric light and bathrooms. Many of the houses were double fronted. By 1914 there was a hospital and the Oakdale Hotel. The Miners' Institute was completed by 1917. The concept was the idea of Alfred Tallis, the managing director of Tredegar Iron and Coal with the layout in the form of a horseshoe running off Central Avenue being designed by Tallis' brother-in-law architect, A. F. Webb of Blackwood, an idea borrowed from Letchworth in Hertfordshire. The new village was called Oakdale and in 1920 was visited by Prince Albert, the future King George VI.

The Waterloo Colliery, named after the battle was started in 1815 by the Tredegar Iron Co. immediately north of the present village. In 1842 it employed 90 with seven under 13, some as young as eight. It closed in 1924. The Woodfield Colliery was opened in 1815 by Evan and Lewis Lewis. Sited to the south west of the village it operated until 1930 employing up to 100 men. Sir Thomas Phillips & Co opened the Cwrt-y-bella Colliery in 1838 north-west of the Waterloo Colliery. It had a chequered history employing up to 150 men before eventually closing in 1962. Oakdale Colliery began production in 1911 and in that year a house coal shaft was sunk to the Brithdir seam at Waterloo (a different colliery to the above). It employed over 2,200 men at its peak and had its own electricity generating plant which also supplied Markham and Wyllie Collieries. It continued in production until 1989, the last deep mine in Gwent, Waterloo having closed in 1970. Remains of the abandoned buildings stand alongside Yard Coal Rise, together with artwork composed of pit wheel segments set on a plinth.

Oakdale Presbyterian Church dates from 1916 and faces Sir Dafydd Avenue. It remains in use. Oakdale Baptist Church on Markham Crescent is of a modern appearance. In 2011 it hit the headlines when Pastor Brian Morris, a former convicted drug dealer, was elected to lead the church. Oakdale Christian Centre, facing up Central Avenue was built as Oakdale Methodist Chapel. St David's Church on Central Avenue is a late 20th century red brick building with a small spire and tower over the porch.

This replaced the corrugated iron mission church of St David which stood on the opposite side of Central Avenue where new houses have been built.

The Miners' Institute had a hall for 300 as well as the usual library and games rooms. It closed in 1987 and has been re-erected at the Museum of Welsh Life, St Fagans. The Oakdale Hotel on Central Avenue is no longer listed with a food hygiene licence. The hospital closed in 2011.

The village is well maintained and the Webb designed part of the village is now a conservation area. Particularly attractive are the gardens in Aberconway Place. Originally the whole of Central Avenue was tree lined but many of the trees have disappeared. Oakdale has expanded in recent years with new housing to the north-east. There is a range of primary and secondary schools, a community centre and local shops. The village is well endowed with sports fields and a bowling green.

There are industrial estates on the site of Oakdale Colliery and on the flattened spoil heaps.

Old Cwmbrân (Welsh: Hen Gwmbrân) Old Valley of the Crow

Cwmbrân as we know it today is a new town created as a result of the New Towns Act 1946 with its first house built in 1952. Prior to 1840 there were just a few scattered hill farms in the vicinity, but by 1865 there were the iron and wire works of Messrs James Charles Hill & Co. as well as the brickworks of Cyrus Hanson, iron works of Messrs. Roper, and The Patent Nut and Bolt Company of James Gibbs which incorporated the Vitriol Works, later owned by the Cwmbran Chemical Co and ICI. Closing in the 1930s. The village quickly grew, known as Cwmbrân but now called Old Cwmbrân or Cwmbrân Village.

St Gabriel's church was built in 1907 to plans by the Cardiff architect F.R. Kempson. It replaced an iron mission church built in 1880. St Gabriel's is a large church with north and south aisles and red brick Memorial Church Hall adjacent. Our Lady of the Angels Roman Catholic church on Wesley Street was built in 1867. Elim Independent Chapel was built in 1844, with a schoolroom added in 1872. It is now the Cwmbran United Reformed Church. The Wesleyan Methodist chapel on Wesley Street is now the Wesley Community Centre but was also used as the Masonic Hall. The Salvation Army Hall is modern. There are the Mount Pleasant and Halfway public houses and a number of small shops and takeaways. The industrial areas have been developed for housing or retail development.

Oldcastle (Welsh: Yr Hencastell)

Oldcastle is a little over six miles north of Abergavenny, signposted off the A465 Abergavenny to Hereford road at the Old Pandy Inn. Oldcastle Court and church are signposted off the Longtown road.

Little remains of the castle which gives the parish its name, and there is scant information about the castle which has largely been obliterated by later building. Dr Gale in an 18th century antiquarian suggested that it was the Roman Blestium, and some Roman finds have been made in the area.

It was in the 15th century however that Oldcastle gained a certain notoriety as the alleged refuge of Sir John Oldcastle, Lord Cobham, the leader of the Lollard revolt against Henry V. Sir John had represented Herefordshire in Parliament in 1404 and became a trusted soldier of Prince Henry. In 1408 he married Joan, heiress of Cobham in Kent. In 1413 he confessed to Lollardy in an ecclesiastical court and was convicted of heresy. King Henry V gave him a stay of 40 days to recant, but Sir John escaped from the Tower of London to the Herefordshire border where he avoided capture until 1417, although he was involved in a number of plots against the King in the intervening period. He was hanged and his body burnt together with the gallows on St Giles' Field in December 1417. Lewis asserts that a portrait of Sir John Oldcastle was retained in Oldcastle Court in 1831.

The church of St John the Baptist was in the diocese of St David's until 1844 when it was transferred to Llandaff. In 1921 it came into the Monmouth diocese and the church was closed in 1987 and converted to residential use. 12th century in origin, it was refurbished by John Pollard Seddon in 1864, though much of the original stonework remains. The 1864 plans reveal that the church was also known as St James. There was further restoration in 1932-33 when the architect was John Merton Jones. Built of the local red and grey sandstone rubble, there is a nave, chancel, south porch and western bellcote with two bells. Set on the side of the hill the churchyard which has the base of a medieval cross is well maintained.

Oldcastle Court Farmhouse dates from the 17th century with a partial rebuilding circa 1760.

Pandy Fulling Mill see Llanvihangel Crucorney

Panteg Fair Hollow

Panteg is a small village two and a quarter miles to the south-east of Pontypool. The old parish of Panteg or as Lewis spells it Panteague, was extensive, containing 3,455 acres and taking in Pont-y-moile and Pen-yr-heol. Lewis in 1848 noted: "Here are iron and coal mines, and quarries of limestone and other stone used for building; several hundred persons are employed at iron-furnaces and forges, and at tin-plate mills". The suburbs of Griffithstown and New Inn now occupy a large part of the old parish and Panteg steel works which closed in 2004 was in Griffithstown, as are Panteg House, the clubhouse for Panteg Cricket Club and Panteg Hospital.

The parish is first mentioned in the *Taxatio* of 1254 when it was too poor to pay taxes. Located at the end of a no through road, the church of St Mary was largely rebuilt in the Victorian era apart from the late medieval tower. It is believed that T.H. Wyatt was the architect of a rebuild in 1849 with Henry Woodyer responsible for adding a new chancel and north aisle in the late 1870s. The chancel is built in the Early English style with lancets and a Tudor style east window while the rest of the church is in the Perpendicular style. There are three arches dividing the nave and chancel. The western tower has a peal of three bells and appears original apart from the possible Victorian addition of the battlemented parapet. There is a nave with north aisle separated by an arcade of octagonal piers, choir and clergy vestries and south porch. The only other buildings in the immediate vicinity are the Rectory and Church Farm, giving the area a very rural feel for somewhere so close to a large urban population.

Pantygasseg The Mare's Hollow

The hamlet of Pantygasseg lies on the ridge road between Pontypool and Oakdale, a little over a mile and a half south-west of Pontypool. The name is said to derive from the shape of the ridge which has a slight dip, resembling in outline that of a mare's back. The position of Pantygasseg offers extensive views to the north and south. Apart from farms, the only building in 1880 was the Masons Arms, now Mountain View House, with old quarries and an old coal level. The first terrace of five houses had been built by 1901, with the remaining small terraces built by 1920, providing housing for the Tirpentwys Colliery in the valley to the north-west. Tirpentwys was sunk by Darby and Norris in 1878 with the first coal produced in 1881. At its height, Tirpentwys employed 1,682 men, eventually closing in 1969. In 1902 eight men were killed when a winding cable snapped.

Parc Seymour

Parc Seymour is a modern development to the north of the A48, six and a half miles north-east of Newport. It takes its name from the Seymour family who owned Penhow Castle. Building started in the late 1960s. The first community village shop in Wales opened here in November 2008.

South of the A48 is the Penhow Baptist Chapel, built in the early years of the 20th century as a Baptist mission hall. The village pound was located to the west of the chapel and beyond that was the smithy. The Groes Wen Inn was converted from a country cottage in 1881 and was shown on old maps as the Cross Wen Inn.

North of the village in Castell-prin Wood are the remnants of the Iron Age Castell-prin defended enclosure.

Penallt Head of the Wooded Slope

Penallt is a scattered village on high ground, two miles south-east of the centre of Monmouth. The main centre of population is Pentwyn.

Set some 400 feet above a bend in the River Wye is the beautiful, Grade I Listed St Mary's Church, known as Penallt Old Church. The first reference to the church is in 1254, but the earliest part of the present building is the 14th century tower with the rest being a late 15th, early 16th century rebuild. The saddleback tower appears to have been heightened in the 17th century to accommodate the four bells. There was a restoration in 1885-7. Penallt was part of the Trellech parish until 1887. A chapel of ease, also dedicated to St Mary, was built in 1869 at Pentwyn and the older church became known as Penallt Old Church. The slope on which the church is built is reflected inside, with the floor sloping down to the chancel. There is a south aisle, separated from the nave by a four bay arcade. The chancel is offset and the chancel arch is almost central to nave and aisle. Windows are set in the east wall of the nave above the arch. Both nave and aisle have fine wagon roofs, while that of the chancel is boarded. There is a medieval wooden chest in the chancel, dug out from a tree trunk. The altar in the south aisle was recovered in 1965 and is thought to have been the medieval altar replaced in 1885. There is a squint from the south aisle and the upper section of the rood stair remains. Outside there is the base of the medieval churchyard cross. The early 20th century lychgate and stile are Grade II Listed, as is the mounting block outside the entrance which is formed of the local sandstone conglomerate and set with three steps. With the church being some distance from the centre of population, the local custom was for funeral processions to stop under an oak tree and the corpse set on a bench while the mourners sang a psalm before continuing.

Pentwyn is a mile south of the church and St Mary's chapel of ease, built in 1869 stands at the southern end, now converted to residential use, as is the old school next door. Almost opposite, Chapel Cottage was built in 1862 as a Primitive Methodist chapel. Penallt Baptist chapel was opened on 10th October 1820 when four sermons were preached in celebration. It has now been converted for residential use.

The Inn at Penallt was formerly known as the Bush Inn and dates from the 17th century. It stands on the village green. The Boat Inn, to the east of the village, stands on the bank of the River Wye near the Redbrook Bridge which was built in 1876 to carry the Wye Valley Railway and is now a footbridge. As the inn name suggests, there was formerly a ferry across the river at this point.

Pelham Hall is a modern village hall to the west of the village with cricket pitch and tennis courts.

South of the village is The Argoed, a house built initially in the 16th century by Christopher Probert of Pant-glas, Llanishen. It was remodelled in the 17th century by Sir George Probert and again in the 19th century by Richard Potter, who bought it in 1865 after retiring as chairman of the Great Western Railway. Potter's daughter, Beatrice married Sidney Webb and together they founded the London School of Economics and Political Science and were influential in forming the Fabian Society. George Bernard Shaw was a visitor to The Argoed during the Potter's ownership and is said to have written a number of plays during his stay. In more recent years it was the home of Robert Plant, lead vocalist for Led Zeppelin.

Pengam Top Step

Pengam is a former mining village in the Rhymney valley, a mile south of Bargoed and a mile and a quarter to the west of Blackwood. Traditionally in Monmouthshire it is now part of Caerphilly. To the south is Fleur-de-lis village, and the two villages merge with Commercial Street, Pengam running into High Street, Fleur-de-lis. Part of Pengam lies across the river in the old county of Glamorgan. This is known as Glan-y-nant and developed with the traditional terraced streets in the early years of the 20th century. It was served by the Rhymney Railway while the Pengam Monmouthshire station was on the Brecon and Merthyr line.

Mining came early to Pengam with the Newplace Colliery opened in the 18th century. Newplace, situated to the north-west of St David's Church was closed by 1900. Plâs Colliery occupied the area of the football field north of St David's Road. In 1853 it was owned by Thomas Prothero and was acquired by Thomas Powell and subsequently becoming part of the Powell Duffryn group. It was shown as closed in 1945.

Pengam Colliery was opened in 1890 by the Rhymney Iron Co. to extract house coal from the Brithdir seam. It was acquired in the 1920s by Powell Duffryn and employed up to 518 men. It was sited between Commercial Street and Pengam Road on what is now an industrial estate. Production ceased in 1956 but the pit was kept open to pump water from the Britannia Colliery. Powell Duffryn sank the Britannia Colliery in 1910 north of High Street. Coal production started in 1912 and continued until 1983 with up to 1780 men employed. Britannia was Britain's first all electric colliery. Siemens generators were used, and a third set was being installed by German engineers at the outbreak of war in 1914. The engineers were interned and installation was completed by English Electric. After closure the colliery was used for training by the School of Mines.

Today Pengam is perhaps best known for the Lewis School. Edward Lewis bequeathed money to set up a school for 15 poor boys of the parish of Gelligaer. Lewis was a grandson of Sir William Lewis of the family known as Lewis of the Van. Edward died in 1728 but the bequest could not be effected until after his mother's death and it was not until 1764 that the school was established, originally close to the Gelligaer Roman fort across the border in Glamorgan. Pengam is the third site for the school which now has a girls section. Among many well known alumni is Lord Kinnock.

Ebenezer English Baptist Chapel on River Terrace was built in 1907 to the design of the Blackwood architect R. Simmons. It is still in use. Nazareth Methodist Chapel on Station Road, Glan-y-nant was built in 1860 and rebuilt in 1899 but is no longer in use. Capel-y-Bont Welsh Baptist Chapel on Commercial Road was built in 1857 and rebuilt in 1865 but has now been converted for residential use.

St David's Church on Commercial Street was built 1895-7 by the architect E.M. Bruce Vaughan. The church is built with the chancel to the north with a Sanctus bellcote containing two bells, west porch, nave and vestry. The church remains in use. The plans give the location as Fleur-de-lis and this is the name of the parish. A mission church was built in 1872 as a precursor to St David's.

Pengam has a range of primary and secondary schools and is blessed with plenty of open space. There is an industrial estate on Pengam Road and modern housing off Pengam Road. The village is served by the old Rhymney Railway with Pengam Station to the west of the village. The Brecon and Merthyr line closed in 1962. Retail is carried on in Fleur-de-lis. The Smiths Arms is the only hostelry.

Penhow (Welsh: Pen-hŵ)

Penhow lies just south of the A48, midway between Newport and Chepstow. The name is thought to be a combination of the Welsh 'Pen' meaning head and the Norse word 'Haugr' meaning hill. The main population is at Parc Seymour.

Penhow Castle was a Pele Tower (a small fortified keep or tower house), built and lived in by Sir Roger de St Maur. He was a signatory to the charter founding the priory at Monmouth in 1129. In 1240, Sir William de Saint Maur entered into an agreement with his brother-in-law, Gilbert Marshal, Earl of Pembroke, to seize the manor of Woundy (Undy) from Morgan ap Howell, last Prince of Gwent, and divide the spoils. By the end of the 14th century the family had adopted the name Seymour and the heiress Isabella Seymour married John Bowles. Their grandson Thomas was knighted after the siege of Berwick upon Tweed and married Maud the daughter of Sir Thomas Morgan of Pencoed Castle. Their granddaughter and heir, Maria, married Sir George Somerset, brother of the 2nd Earl of Worcester. In 1674 Penhow was purchased by Thomas Lewis of St Pierre, whose son was High Sheriff and refurbished the castle. From 1714 the building was tenanted as a farm until purchased by Stephen Weeks in 1973. Weeks was a 25 year old film director and screen writer, who had directed the 1973 film *Gawain and the Green Knight*. He discovered the castle by accident and set about its restoration, opening it to the public in 1979, though when he sold it in 2002, to develop castles in Czechoslovakia, it reverted to being a private home. Weeks described the building as "consisting of a small ward, or courtyard, surrounded by a strong stone curtain wall. On three sides the hill falls away sharply to provide a natural defence. The fourth side remained curiously weak, defencewise, but could perhaps be explained by the lumps and bumps in the field that suggested an outer bailey taking in a greater area including the parish church. The hub of the inner courtyard is a Norman tower, on three floors and with a ramparted top – very much a miniature of the great keep of Chepstow Castle".

The church of St John the Baptist has its origins in the 12th century with a south aisle added 100 years later. The nave and chancel were re-roofed in the 18th century and a further restoration was undertaken in 1914, when the tower was rebuilt, windows replaced and the rood screen restored. This latter work was financed by Lady Perry-Herrick who owned the castle at the time. The church is unusual with the substantial pyramid topped tower centrally placed over the south aisle with the large south porch leading into the tower crossing. There is a 13th century double piscina and stoup, together with squints on each side of the chancel arch. The tower has a peal of six bells.

Penhow Castle and Church by Sir Richard Colt Hoare

Apart from the castle and church, there are a few houses, Penhow Farm and, on the A48, the 17th century Rock and Fountain Inn and the Indian Cottage Restaurant.

Penmaen Head of the Stone
The village, also known as Penmain, lies immediately to the south of Oakdale. Penmaen was created a parish in 1845, though the parish church of St Philip and St James was built to the north and is covered under the entry for Argoed. In 1880 there were a few cottages, the 17th century Penmaen House, Penmain Independent Chapel which was originally built in 1694 and rebuilt in 1828 and the Angel Inn. By 1900 the Angel had been replaced by Angel cottages and the Cross Oak inn had been built. The 1970s saw the building of the bungalows in Christchurch Road, Canberra Close and Vancouver Drive.

Penmaen House still stands, though is now outside the Penmaen boundary. The Independent Chapel is thought to be the second oldest independent chapel in Wales still in use. The Cross Oak and the post office are the only amenities.

Penrhos Head of the Heath
Penrhos is a small village set amongst rich farmland, two and a half miles north of Raglan. Unusually for Monmouthshire the church is dedicated to St Cadog, rather than the local spelling Cattwg.

St Cadoc's church is late 15th century Perpendicular but likely to have Celtic origins. There was a refurbishment in 1848, while the north aisle, arcade and vestry were added in 1878 by John Prichard. The wagon roofs of the nave and chancel date from the 15th century, as does the piscina. The stairs to the rood loft, entered through a Tudor doorway, remain. There was a further restoration of the tower and porch in 1905. The west tower has three bells.

The former National School, opposite the church was built in 1866 and is now a private dwelling. A modern bungalow now occupies the site of the Temple Inn where the Baron of Abergavenny used to hold court. There is a small modern terrace of houses next to the church while The Firs is the former vicarage.

A mile north-west of the church is the ditched motte of Penrhos or Penrose Castle. Now standing some 20 foot high, it was referred to in

1251 when Henry III appointed John de Monmouth keeper of the Castle of Penrose, by patent. A year later another patent pardoned William de Cantalupe, Lord of Abergavenny, for having demolished the Castle of Penrose, belonging to John de Monmouth.

Penterry (Welsh: Penteri)

The scattered community of Penterry lies to the north of St Arvans. The derivation of the name is unclear. While 'pen' means head, 'tiri' may be a corruption of 'tiryf', meaning verdant or fertile.

The church of St Mary stands alone, on sloping ground in a field a mile south-west of Tintern, looking down towards the Wye valley. In the field to the south of the church are the outlines of a former village, whose inhabitants are thought to have been ravaged by the Black Death in the 14th century and the grove of trees near the church has been identified as the site of a 'plague pit'. The church was first mentioned in a charter of 955 and the parish became a grange of Tintern Abbey with a secular firmary or hospital.

The church of St Mary has Norman origins and some 14th century work, but was restored around in 1863 with the porch added in1882. In 2001 the church was under threat of closure, but the community has fought to retain and renovate St Mary's and it remains open with services held once a month. The small single cell church, which has no electricity, has the nave and chancel defined by the altar rail. There is a Norman window in the north wall of the chancel. There is a western porch and bellcote. There are the remains of a medieval churchyard cross.

Half a mile south of the church is Gaer Hill, with its two wireless transmitting aerials, formerly the property of Gwent Police. It is the site of the Gaer Hill Iron Age defended enclosure consisting of two banks and ditches.

Pentre-poeth Burnt Village

Pentre-poeth lies south of the A468 Caerphilly road, to the west of Bassaleg, three miles west of Newport city centre. It has seen considerable expansion since the 1970s, with a primary school and other facilities.

The Wesleyan Methodist chapel was built in 1870 on Caerphilly Road but has now been converted to a private residence. Bethel Particular Baptist chapel lies on a lane between Pen-y-lan Road and Pentre-poeth

Road. It was built in 1825, rebuilt in 1832 and enlarged in 1872. It remains an active chapel.

The Ruperra Arms at the cross roads in the village was shown as a Beer House as opposed to a public house, on the 1883 and 1901 maps. Beer houses were set up under the 1830 Beer Act in an attempt to avoid the evils of gin and strong spirits, and while they were easy to establish, they were restricted to selling beer which was seen at the time as harmless, nutritious and healthy.

Pentwyn see Penallt

Pen-y-cae-mawr End of a Large Field
On the northern edge of Wentwood forest, eight miles north-east of Newport is the scattered hamlet of Pen-y-cae-mawr.

In the middle of a field, are the remains of Castle Troggy, or Cas Troggy, a castle built as a hunting lodge by Roger Bigod, Earl of Norfolk, circa 1300. Antiquarians in the 18th and 19th centuries mistakenly identified it as Striguil Castle, and Coxe in 1801 gave it both names, also suggesting that it was established prior to the Norman conquest of the area. There is a tower with traces of a staircase and part retains a stone roof. The moat is surrounded by trees.

The little Wesleyan Methodist Chapel bears no date plaque and first appears on the 1901 Ordnance Survey map. There used to be a pub, the Fox and Hounds, but this is now a private house.

In the forest to the south of Pen-y-cae-mawr, is a picnic area with two well preserved Bronze Age round barrows just to the east.

Pen-y-clawdd Head of the Dyke
Pen-y-clawdd is a small village two and a half miles east of Raglan.

The Norman church of St Martin was built on an early Welsh defensive earthwork and was largely remodelled in the 15th or 16th century though the round Norman chancel arch is thought to have survived into the 19th century. There was a major refurbishment by Henry Prothero of Cheltenham in 1884-5 which saw the tower raised and a new half timbered porch. The fine 15th century barrel roofs to nave and chancel survive, while the tower has a pyramid roof with red stone tiles, contrasting with the slate used elsewhere topped with red clay ridge tiles.

The medieval churchyard cross base has a modern shaft and crosshead.

Pen-y-clawdd House was formerly known as Upper Pen-y-clawdd and has an impressive arched entrance with arched pedestrian access on either side. In 1349 it was held by Walter de Rymbaud from Lawrence de Hastings, Earl of Pembroke, but was rebuilt in the 17th century and remodelled in the Arts and Crafts style in 1905. There was a school here in 1882, occupying one of the outbuildings, but this closed when the National School was built in 1888. The latter is now the village hall.

There is also a house named Penyclawdd Court covered under Llanvihangel Crucorney.

Peterstone Wentlooge Welsh: Llanbedr Gwynllŵg

Peterstone Wentlooge is located on land reclaimed by the Romans from the Bristol Channel. Some six miles south-west of Newport, the parish is typified by a series of narrow strip fields which is unique and contrasts with the irregular patterns in other parishes along this coast. The name refers to St Peter's church, with Wentlooge derived from the Welsh 'Gwynllŵg', being the name of the ancient cantref.

There is a reference to a monastery in the charter in which the Countess Mabel, daughter of Fitzhamon granted tithes to St Augustine's Priory in Bristol, but in most early documents the church is not linked to a monastery. The 1920 Ordnance Survey map records remains of the monastery on what is now Church Close. The great flood of 1606 destroyed what was at the time a small town with a floating dock, market house and store houses, so that in 1883 there were just a few houses, including Maerdy House, a school, pub, chapel and church. Development began in the 1960s but the village remains small, tucked away behind the ancient sea wall.

The large Grade I Listed church of St Peter is now a private house. The mid 15th century Perpendicular church was restored after the great flood of 1606 (1607 after the change from the Julian to the Gregorian calendar). It was restored again in 1889-91 by Sir George F.R. Walker Bart in memory of his wife, Fanny Henrietta, third daughter of the Baron Tredegar. The work was supervised by Bodley and Garner, architects of London. The church has north and south aisles separated from the nave by four bay arcades, a chancel, west tower containing a peal of six bells, with a carved figure of a saint set within the central crenellation of each face, a vestry and south porch.

Hephzibah Primitive Methodist Chapel stood at the eastern end of Broadstreet Common but had been demolished by the 1960s. The 1875 Board School which was to the west of the Six Bells has also been demolished. The Six Bells dates from the 16th century.

East of the village is the drainage complex and old harbour and beyond the 18 hole Peterstone Lakes Golf Course. South of the sea wall are the remains of four medieval fish traps, the limestone blocks of what was Peterstone Great Wharf as well as the sites of Roman and Bronze Age finds.

Ponthir Long Bridge

Ponthir lies a mile and a half north-west of Caerleon. In 1758 John Griffiths leased land between what was later the railway and the Afon Lwyd to build a tin-plate works. It was near a wooden bridge which gave the village its name. The tin-plate works continued in production into the 20th century, later coming under the control of Richard and Thomas Fothergill. By 1882 the village had hardly developed, with Ponthir House next to the tinplate works, a small terrace near Sion Chapel and a few houses along Caerleon Road including the Star Inn. Ponthir did however have a railway station. The Ponthir House Inn between Stokes Drive and Candwr Road dates from 1710.

Sion Particular Baptist Chapel was founded in 1803 and built in 1836. In 1870 the schoolroom was added in a similar style to the chapel, giving an unusual double fronted appearance. It remains in use.

In 1924 the Star Brickworks Company acquired Penrhos Farm and built the Penrhos Star Brickworks. The site is now part of a trading estate, with the surviving tall chimney a prominent landmark.

Penrhos has grown substantially over the 20th century and has a primary school, community hall, nurseries and local shops, but no longer a station.

Phillip's Town

Phillip's Town was built in the early years of the 20th century to house workers in New Tredegar's collieries. It is named after Nehemiah Phillips, the local manager of White Rose, Elliotts, Coedmoeth & New Tredegar collieries for Powell Duffryn who was also a JP. The village stands to the east of New Tredegar while a massive tip once stood to the east of Phillip's Town. The school was built in the 1920s. There is a football ground, post office, a chip shop and a community house on Penrhyn Terrace. Most of the housing is terraced with some post 1945 council housing.

Cefn Rhychdir farmhouse to the north of the village is 'L' shaped and was the home of Matthew Fothergill, a member of the family of ironmasters of Tredegar, Aberdare and Merthyr.

Pontllanfraith

Pontllanfraith is a large village in the Sirhowy valley, a mile south of Blackwood and a little under two miles south-west of Newbridge. The bridge after which the village is named is in Commercial Street and was in 1880 the centre of a small village. The spelling of the name is a corruption of Tir Penybont Llynfraith meaning land at the end of the bridge near the speckled pool. In 1880 there were two pubs, the Greyhound, now the Bridge Veterinary Centre, and the Plough, St Augustine's Church and Elim Chapel and the New Tir Philkin Colliery, while to the south there was the Tredegar Junction Station and St Mary and St David's Roman Catholic Chapel.

The original Tir Philkin Colliery at Woodfieldside to the north of the village was sunk by Thomas Powell in 1857. The New Tir Philkins Colliery was sunk by Powell Duffryn in 1873. Both collieries closed in 1880. The Penllwyn Colliery to the south of the village had closed by 1862. The Benjamin Hall Tramway ran from the collieries of Manmoel and Waterloo south past Tir Philkins and on through Pontllanfraith to Abercarn. A tunnel survives on Tir Philkins, but much of the route is now used for by-passes. Benjamin Hall was a barrister and through marriage to Charlotte Crawshay, daughter of Richard became a partner in the Cyfarthfa Ironworks. He was an MP, first for Totnes, then for Westbury and finally from 1814 until his death in 1817 for Glamorgan. Hall purchased Hensol Castle in the Vale of Glamorgan. His son, also Benjamin Hall was also an MP, first for Monmouthshire and later for Marylebourne. He campaigned for the use of the Welsh language in the Anglican churches of Wales and for the Truck Acts which outlawed the use of 'truck' or company shops which forced workers to buy from company owned shops by paying wages in tokens which could only be used at these shops. He is best remembered as the Commissioner of Works who oversaw the rebuilding of the Houses of Parliament. It is claimed that Big Ben is named after him. He married Augusta Waddington of Ty Uchaf, Llanover, in 1823 and in 1859 took the

Benjamin Hall Tramway Tunnel, Pontllanfraith

title Baron Llanover of Llanover and Abercarn. Lady Llanover was a champion of Welsh culture and she is credited with the creation of the traditional Welsh costume with the tall hat. She was also a fervent advocate of the temperance movement, closing all the public houses on her estates.

The first rows of terraced houses were built in the early 20th century, but the major expansion of the population occurred after 1945.

Elim Welsh Baptist Chapel has moved over the years. Originally sited at the bottom of what is now Llanarth Road the chapel was completed in 1869. By 1903 it had been decided to hold services in English and the present building on Newbridge Road was built in 1912 and is still in use. Bethany Apostolic Church on Brynglas Avenue was built in the mid 20th century and continues to be used. Siloh Calvinistic Methodist Chapel on Heol Ddu Road in Gelligroes was built in 1813 and is still in use.

There are two Church in Wales churches in the village which is part of the Rectorial Benefice of Mynyddislwyn. St Augustine's church is on Commercial Street and dates from 1870. It was built in a simple form with nave and chancel of equal width and a south-western porch added beneath the bellcote. The original long wall entry porch remains. St Mary the Virgin Church is on St Mary's Road on the Penllwyn housing estate and is a red brick building dating from the second half of the 20th century.

Penllwyn Manor is a 16th century two story house under a stone tiled roof. It was for a number of years used as a restaurant and public house but was sold in November 2013. It is thought to have been the home of a branch of the Morgan family of Tredegar House Newport.

Prior to the coal industry, the village was once celebrated for its sage cheese, a favourite of Lady Llanover. The village has a range of shops, restaurants and takeaways, mainly on Commercial Street and Newbridge Road, including a Sainsbury supermarket. There are a number of public houses including the Crown Inn, the Tredegar Junction Hotel, the White Hart and the Ivor Arms. The village is well served with open spaces and industrial areas.

Pontymister (Welsh: Pont-y-meistr) Master's Bridge

The name is said to derive from the fact that workers were paid from a building near the bridge. The old bridge with its two arches still stands at the end of Fields Road.

Pontymister lies to the east of Risca and now forms a suburb of the town. Much of the housing dates from the inter war period and a number of 19th century streets such as Philanthropic Row, Cardiff Terrace and Club Row have ceased to exist. Even the Forge Hammer pub is now the Tamarind Indian Restaurant.

In 1801 the Pontymister Works opened on the south side of the river, producing bar iron from pig iron that was then sent via a tram road and canal to Newport and later simply by tram. The tram road became the railway in 1850 and the Pontymister Works was joined by the Britannia Foundry in 1854. The Pontymister Works which had switched to steel production finally closed in 1962 and the iron industry came to an end in the village with the closure of Broad's Foundry sited next to the Works in 2004. Local works had a chequered history, with early owners going bankrupt. Bankruptcy also followed a strike in 1896 when the owners tried to reduce wages following protectionist measures in the United States. The village once boasted two corn mills and a 'Blacking' factory, connected with the iron works.

Shops, public houses, churches and chapels followed the influx of workers. The Roman Catholic Chapel dedicated to Saint Anthony of Padua and St Clare was built in 1868 on Lyne Road and remains open. St David's Methodist Church on Elm Drive is a modern building.

There is a good shopping area in Commercial Street which runs into Risca with a number of restaurants and takeaways and there are Tesco, Aldi and Lidl supermarkets. There is the Ty Isaf Junior School and playing fields. Pubs remaining include the Fox and Hounds, The Commercial Inn and the Rolling Mill.

Portskewett (Welsh Porthysgewin) Elder Tree Harbour

Portskewett is an ancient village four miles south of Chepstow, and immediately north of the Second Severn Crossing.

There are the remains of a Neolithic chambered tomb at Heston Brake, north-east of the village. It was excavated by Mary Ellen Bagnall Oakeley, headmistress of Monmouth Haberdashers' School for Girls in 1888, with finds of human and cattle remains as well as pottery. The site is now overgrown. A Roman temple or villa was excavated in 1923 by Sir Mortimer Wheeler on Portskewett Hill. According to tradition, the 6th century Gwent king, Caradog Freichfas, said to have been a Knight of the Round Table, moved his llys or court from Caerwent to Portskewett. The area south of the church was the subject of an excavation in 2007 by Channel 4's *Time Team*, in search of a palace built by Earl Harold of Wessex, at which he entertained King Edward the Confessor, who had been keeping his court at Gloucester, in 1065. They discovered the remains of a Norman tower house, but no evidence of pre-conquest building which was said to have been sacked and burned by Caradoc ap Griffith, who having surprised Harold's followers whilst hunting in the forest of Wentwood, on St. Bartholomew's day 1065 and having put them to the sword, came on to Portskewett and destroyed the palace.

The village declined from the time of the Normans, with the population of the parish falling to 175 in 1861. The need for housing for the workers on the Severn Tunnel saw the population rise to 1190 in 1891 and with new housing the village has continued to expand.

The Grade I Listed church of St Mary occupies a prominent position in the village. The nave is Norman, while the chancel is 14th century and the tower and porch are 16th century. The small west gallery was added in

1818. There was a north and south door, but the northern entrance has been blocked. The church and tower up to the crenellations are cream washed. There is a single bell. There are the remains of a churchyard cross in the form of a five step base and socket stone.

Black Rock Road led to the New Passage Ferry crossing of the Bristol Channel, with the Black Rock Hotel and 258 yard wooden pier which served as the station. On the opposite side of the Channel were an even longer pier and the New Passage Hotel. The steamer service operated from 1863 until the completion of the Severn Tunnel in 1886. It is thought that this was the site of the Roman ferry crossing of the Severn, with finds of coins dating from the time of Claudius. During the English Civil War Charles I pursued by a strong force of Roundheads crossed to Gloucestershire. The ferry returning to Black Rock was met by a force of 60 republicans who, with drawn swords, compelled the boatmen to ferry them across. The boatmen who were Royalists left them on English Stones, an island at low tide, now used by the Second Severn Crossing. The tide having turned, the Roundheads all drowned trying to cross the English Lake. Cromwell in retribution, abolished the ferry which was not resumed until 1718 and then only after a law suit between the Lewis family of St Pierre and the guardians of the Duke of Beaufort, owners of New Passage and Old Passage ferries respectively.

At Black Rock, salmon fishing is still practised using the traditional lave net, with demonstrations near the picnic area which now occupies the site of the Black Rock Hotel which was destroyed by fire.

Princetown

Princetown lies a little over a mile north-east of Rhymney on the northern side of the Heads of the Valleys road. At the boundary of the new Caerphilly County, the Prince of Wales pub is the only property on the north side of Merthyr Road within the county. The village takes its name from Prince Farm, now known as Old Prince Farm. It is a ribbon development with some 19th century and some modern houses. Apart from the Prince of Wales there are no amenities or places of worship.

Pwllmeyric Meurig's Pool

Pwllmeyric is a hamlet on the A48 a mile south-west of Chepstow. There is some confusion over the pool in the name, some attributing it to a pill or creek connecting with the Severn, while the earliest reference is to a pit with a pool described as one of the wonders of Wales. Bradney suggested it was a well on the road to Mathern. Meurig was the son of Tewdrig, associated with Mathern.

The New Inn at the southern end of the village is an early 18th century three storey coaching inn. There was a Wesleyan Methodist Chapel on Chapel Lane, built before 1881 but now a private house known as The Chapel. Pwllmeyric has expanded with new housing in recent years.

Raglan (Welsh: Rhaglan)

The village of Raglan lies to the south of the A40, with its castle to the north, near the junction of the A40 with the A449. The most likely meaning for the name is Rampart. It is first mentioned in 1165 as Ragalan, while in the 16th to 19th centuries the common spelling was Ragland.

Raglan saw a major expansion of housing in the 1960s as new roads provided easy access to Newport, Monmouth and Abergavenny. The old centre of the village had served a large rural area, as well as being a staging point for horse drawn coaches in the days before the railways. Beaufort Square in the centre of the village has the church of St Cadoc to the south with the Beaufort Arms and Castle Hill to the north. In addition to the Beaufort Arms there is the Ship Inn and the Crown Inn on the High Street as well as a small range of shops. By 1587 Raglan was referred to as a town and by 1632 there was a Court House, later the Police Station and now a shop.

The Grade II* Listed St Cadoc's church was probably built by the Bloets in the 12th century, but it was rebuilt in the 15th century and enlarged with the addition of what was to become the Beaufort Chapel by Sir William ap Thomas. A number of tombs of the Somerset family (Earls of Worcester) were damaged during the siege of Raglan Castle in 1646. A family vault beneath contains members of the family who died between 1588 and 1704. There was a restoration in 1868 by Thomas Henry Wyatt, financed by the 8th Duke of Beaufort which included a new north aisle, vestry, windows, roofs, fittings, and stained glass, as well as the rebuilding of the top stage of the tower. The embattled western tower has crocketed pinnacles and contains two bells and a clock, given by Miss A.M. Bosanquet of Dingestow. The north window is in memory of Field Marshal FitzRoy James Henry Somerset, 1st Baron Raglan (1788-1855), with twelve plaques listing his campaigns from Denmark 1807 to the Crimea. It was erected by the subscription of over 600 non-commissioned officers. (See also Llandenny)

Ebenezer, now Raglan Baptist chapel on Usk Road was erected in 1818 and is still in use. Zion Congregational chapel off High Street was built in 1812 but is no longer in use as a chapel.

It is thought a castle was established at Raglan by the Normans as early as 1070, and was in the possession of the de Clare family. In the reign of Henry II it was gifted by Richard de Clare, known as Strongbow, to Walter Bloet and the Bloets held it until the late 14th century when Elizabeth Bloet married successively Sir James Berkeley and Sir William ap Thomas. William ap Thomas was a younger son of Sir Thomas ap Gwyllym of Llansantfraid Court. William fought alongside Henry V at Agincourt in 1415 and was knighted by Henry VI in 1426. After Agincourt William married Gwladys, the daughter of Dafydd Gam (see Llantilio Crossenny). He became known as the Blue Knight of Gwent because of the colour of his armour. William ap Thomas lived at Raglan as the tenant of his stepson, Lord James Berkeley. He purchased the estate in 1432 and then set about transforming the manor into Raglan Castle, a process continued by his son. William achieved considerable influence in Wales, becoming Steward of the Lordship of Abergavenny by 1421, High Sheriff of Cardiganshire and Carmarthenshire in 1435 and High Sheriff of Glamorgan in 1440. In the early 1440s he became Chief Steward of Richard Plantagenet, 3rd Duke of York's estates in Wales. He died in 1443 and was succeeded by his son who adopted the English form of William Herbert, having been commanded to discontinue the Welsh custom of changing the surname at every descent and to assume that of Herbert in honour of his ancestor Herbert Fitzhenry, Chamberlain to Henry I. Known as Black William, Herbert continued his father's support of the Yorkist cause and the building of Raglan Castle. He was made Baron Herbert of Raglan in 1461 and shortly afterwards, Earl of Pembroke, after Jasper Tudor was deprived of that title. He fell out with Lord Warwick, 'the Kingmaker', who led the Lancastrian forces in the Battle of Edgecote Moor in 1469 and William was executed. He was succeeded by his son, the 18 year old William, who surrendered the title Earl of Pembroke in 1479 to be created Earl of Huntingdon. A Yorkist, he married Mary Woodville, sister of Edward IV's queen, Elizabeth Woodville. After Mary's death William married Katherine, an illegitimate daughter of Richard III. William and Mary had one daughter, Elizabeth Herbert, 3rd Baroness Herbert who inherited the Herbert estates on William's death in 1491, but not the Huntingdon title which died with him.

In 1551 Sir William Herbert, grandson of the older William through his illegitimate son, Richard, was created Earl of Pembroke in the 10th creation of that title and that line continues to the present day with the family seat at Wilton House in Wiltshire.

Elizabeth Herbert married Charles Somerset, the legitimised son of Henry Beaufort, 3rd Duke of Somerset, in 1492. Somerset was given the title Lord Herbert and was created Earl of Worcester in 1514. In addition to the Raglan estates, Somerset inherited the estate of his wife's uncle, Sir Walter Herbert which included Caldicot Castle. Somerset was Lord Chamberlain to Henry VIII. Henry Somerset, the 5th Earl of Worcester was created Marquess of Worcester. The second Marquess, Edward, invented what was probably the first working steam engine. He used it to send a spout of water from the moat to the roof of the keep. The noise of the machine apparently frightened away one group of Protestants intent on attacking the castle during the 1640s. He later demonstrated this "water-commanding engine" at Vauxhall, sending a spout of water 40 feet into the air. His efforts were not sufficient to save the castle which was one of the last Royalist fortresses to fall to the Roundheads after the 13 week siege in 1646. In 1682, his son was created Duke of Beaufort, the title reflecting his ancestor, John of Gaunt who had held Beaufort in France and four of whose illegitimate children had adopted the name. Raglan Castle having been made uninhabitable during the English Civil War, the family moved their seat to Badminton House, purchased in 1612 by Edward Somerset, the 4th Earl of Worcester, from Nicholas Boteler. They still have connections with the county and own large tracts of land.

Other Herberts prominent in the county were descendants of William Herbert 1st Earl of Pembroke, while descendants of Herbert Fitz-Herbert after adopting Welsh names, also reverted to the Herbert name. (See Llanarth)

The castle, in ruins following the siege was used as a source of building material, including for Badminton House, until stopped by the 5th Duke after 1756. By this time it had become a tourist attraction. The castle today is one of the most magnificent in Wales and is under the care of

Cadw. Clearly visible from the A40, this castle was built as a statement of the wealth and power of the owner rather than for battle and, even in ruins, still has the ability to impress the visitor with the magnificence of the Gatehouse and Great Tower.

The Great Tower which was five storeys high and surrounded with the moat and six smaller bastion towers was the work of William ap Thomas. It was known as Melyn y Gwent or the Yellow Tower of Gwent. North of the tower is the castle, having the appearance of one of the great chateaux of the Loire, with its angular towers. There were two courtyards divided by the great hall which has the arms of the first marquis of Worcester, sculptured in stone, and surrounded with the garter and the family motto, "Mutare vel timere sperno"; "I scorn either to change or fear".

As an example of the wealth of the family, the First Marquess, a Roman Catholic, gave an estimated £900,000 to the Royalist cause and retained a garrison of 800 men. The castle's dairy farm stretched to Llandenny while the red deer park extended beyond Llantilio Cressenny. Coxe records that "Charles I made several visits to the castle and was entertained with becoming magnificence. The marquis not only declined all offers of remuneration, but also advanced large sums; and when the king thanked him for the loans, replied; "Sir, I had your word for the money, but I never thought I should be so soon repayed; for now you have given me thanks, I have all I looked for." At another time, the king, apprehensive less the stores of the garrison should be consumed by his suite, empowered him to exact from the country such provisions as were necessary for his maintenance, and recruit; "I humbly thank your majesty", he said, "but my castle will not stand long if it leans upon the country; I had rather be brought to a morsel of bread, than any morsels of bread should be brought me to entertain your majesty"." After the surrender of the castle, the First Marquess, aged 70 was taken to London where he died a prisoner in December 1646. He was given a State burial (with Presbyterian rites) in the Beaufort chapel at Windsor.

There is a gift shop at the entrance, a buttery and on the neighbouring farm is the Raglan Castle Café.

Rassau

Rassau was originally part of Beaufort. The name is pronounced Rasa in the local Welsh dialect. The earliest reference is in 1697 as Rhas-y-mwyn and refers to the method of pressurized water mining used locally. The stream is the Rasa Brook and in 1810 there was the Race Mineworks.

By 1880 there were just a few houses along what is now Rassau Road. The Board School was built in 1879 and Rock Independent Chapel, now the Moriah Apostolic Church was built after 1920, but the major building in the village took place after 1945. At first development was to the south of the Heads of the Valleys Road, but later housing was built to the north, together with the Rassau Industrial Estate.

Redwick (Welsh: Y Redwig)

Located some six miles south-east of Newport on the Wentloog Levels, Redwick is an attractive small village. The name derives from Old English and means Farm among the Reeds.

The church of St Thomas the Apostle is Grade I Listed and dates from the 12th century, though the present structure is of the 14th and 15th centuries. It was repaired and new seating installed by the London Architect John Norton in 1875. His plans give the dedication to St Mary and it was only after 1875 that it became St Thomas. There was also an early dedication to St Michael the Archangel, though an inscription on the 1576 chalice is to St Thomas. Even though it was a chapelry to Magor, it is a large church with north and south aisles separated by two hexagonal columns on each side. The tower is positioned at the western end of the chancel with any bell ringers visible from the nave. There is a peal of six bells. Two dating from the 14th century, from the Bristol Foundry, are among the oldest bells still in use in the country. The sixth bell was added in 1994. There is a 13th century font, an immersion baptistery and the remains of a medieval rood screen and loft. There is a mark in the porch indicating the height reached by the great flood of 1606-07. The church was damaged by bomb blast in 1942 which required repairs to the west wall and roof. Outside is the base and socket stone of a medieval wayside cross, thought to have been originally positioned some 200 yards to the west, while outside on the green is a much restored three step based cross. The porch is large and crenellated as is the tower. At the entrance to the church are the village stocks, a mounting block, drinking trough and an interesting building partly formed from old stone serving as a bus shelter and museum, housing a cider press. The side wall has pigeon holes from a dovecot.

Salem Baptist was built in 1832 and rebuilt in 1902.

Opposite the church is the Rose Inn, a relatively modern pub. The old King's Head, further north on Church Row is now a private house. There is a new village hall adjacent to the Rose Inn. Brick House on North Row was the 15th century Whitehall Farm, now a country guest house. It was rebuilt in 1795 by William Phillips MP of Whitson Court, for his son, also William.

William Jones of Redwick was the last man in the county hanged for sheep stealing. He was tried at the Great House before being taken to Monmouth and hanged on 27th April 1819.

Rhiwderin The Bird's Slope
Located three miles west of Newport, Rhiwderin grew to provide housing for workers at the Garth Iron and Tinplate Works east of the Rhiwderin Inn. These works had closed by 1901 and the site is now occupied by the houses on Harlech Drive and Caernarvon Road. In 1883 the village consisted of the terraced houses of Tredegar Street, the school built in 1877, Tabernacle Congregational Chapel, established in 1872 and built in 1880, the Rhiwderin Inn and the railway station. The school is now a community centre and the station a private house but Tabernacle continues in use. Glosch Wen Farm dates to the 16th century but with subsequent enlargement and modernization. To the north-east of the village, beyond the allotment gardens, is the Iron Age Rhiwderin Hillfort which took advantage of the natural scarpment with additional banks, still just traceable on the southern side.

Pentre Tai Road had been built by the 1960s but the rest of the village is more modern. In addition to Tabernacle, there is now the Free Presbyterian Church. There is a post Office and village store on Tredegar Street.

Rockfield (Welsh: Llanoronwy)
Two miles north-west of Monmouth, the scattered village of Rockfield is thought to take its name from Ralph de Rochevilla, a signatory of the Monmouth Charter of the late 11th century. The Welsh version of the name is taken from a reference to 'lann Guoronoi' of 970, but it is not certain that the reference is to Rockfield as the church is dedicated to St Cenedlon. Local residents forced the County Council to withdraw the sign with the Welsh name in 2011. Kelly's Directory of 1901 gave the ancient name as 'Corn-y-Cenhedlon' meaning Cenhedlon's Trumpet.

A number of the houses in the village were built for the Rolls Estate at the Hendre (see Llangattock-vibon-avel). The village has in recent years been celebrated as the home of Rockfield Studio, established in 1963 by Kingsley and Charles Ward at Amberley Farm, now Amberley Court. Recording artists attracted to the studios include Queen, Joan Armatrading, Black Sabbath, Kasabian, KT Tunstall, Manic Street Preachers, Nigel Kennedy, Paolo Nutini, Suede and Super Furry Animals, to name but a few.

St Cenedlon is a somewhat obscure early Welsh saint. Baring-Gould identifies her with the virgin, Cynheiddon, one of the many daughters of St Brychan and as St Keyna who was the founder of Keynsham near Bath and St Keyne in Cornwall. Others suggest she was the daughter of St Briavel. Only the tower survives of the medieval church which was largely rebuilt by John Pollard Seddon in 1860. The Royal Arms of William III were reinstated in the church in 1976 having been used as a notice board at Rockfield School. There is also memorial to John Allan Rolls, 1837-1912, 1st Baron Llangattock. The church consists of a chancel, nave of three bays, north aisle, south porch and a tower with a timber upper dovecote styled belfry containing three bells under a pyramidal roof. Its original listing as a Grade II building was due to the 14th century tower, but the quality of the Victorian Gothic Revival work by Seddon is now also recognized. In the churchyard is a commemorative cross of 1865. The lower step is thought to have been that of a medieval cross, the socket stone of which is now incorporated in the wayside cross at the junction of the B4233 and the B4237 in the village.

The National School was built in 1857 and enlarged in 1890 but is now a private house. Pentwyn, near the church was the home of the Monmouth architect George Vaughan Maddox who enlarged the house. It was later purchased by Rev. Canon John Taylor Harding in 1864, the vicar of Rockfield from 1871. Rockfield House, the other major building in the village was the property of Lord Llangattock in 1900.

Rogerstone (Welsh: Tŷ Du Black House)

Rogerstone today is a large village, three miles north-west of Newport. The naming is a little confusing. Historically, Rogerstone was the south-eastern section of the village, with Tŷ Du a separate hamlet to the north-west and Tregwilym in between. As the communities merged, the English and Welsh names were applied to the whole village. Rogerstone is derived from Roger's Settlement after Roger de Berkerolles, who held Caerphilly

Castle in the 12th century and it is suggested that Tregwilym refers to William de Berkerolles. Tŷ Du is named after the local farm.

Rogerstone Castle is no longer shown on the Ordnance Survey map, but what remains of the motte sits beneath trees and bushes opposite N.J. Criddle's garage on Tregwilym Road.

Rogerstone Ironworks were established on land south of the castle in 1776, later known as the Castle Steel Works after being taken over by Guest Keen and Nettlefolds in 1885. In 1937 the works were transferred to East Moors in Cardiff and the site was purchased by Northern Aluminium and a massive factory employing up to 9,000 opened in 1940. It had, at one time, the longest aluminium rolling mill in Europe. The works closed in 2009 and the plant was demolished in 2011. The wings for the Hurricane fighter were manufactured in a nearby factory using the aluminium produced.

Tin works were established at Tŷ Du, reflected in the name of the local pub, the Rollers' Arms. This became the Castle Nail Works by 1900 but the site was cleared and developed for the Northern Aluminium factory. Meanwhile in the last decades of the 19th century Tregwilym became the site of a major rail marshalling yard. The area still has extensive industrial units, but is now largely residential, the population having expanded from just 2,389 in 1891 to over 8,800 by 2001.

The church of St John the Baptist was designed by Edwin Arthur Johnson of Abergavenny and built in 1886-8 as a chapel of ease to St Basil at Bassaleg. Typically Victorian Gothic, it has a nave, chancel, vestry, south porch and western bellcote. The church room stands alongside. Bethesda Baptist Chapel on Cefn Road was established in 1742 and after several re-buildings, a new octagonal red brick chapel was built in the1990s. Ebenezer Pentecostal Church of the Assemblies of God on Tregwilym Road was built in the 1980s on the site of a former Primitive Methodist Chapel built in the latter decades of the 19th century. A Wesleyan Methodist Chapel was also built on Tregwilym Road but has since been demolished. Cefn Wood Baptist Church is a modern building on Ebenezer Drive. The Roman Catholic Church of St Basil and St Gwladys on Tregwilym Road was constructed in the late 19th century in the simple Gothic style. Ebenezer Independent Chapel was built on Western Valley Road in 1832 and rebuilt in the late 19th century. The site is now occupied by the Chapelwood Surgery.

Rogerston Public Library on Tregwilym Road was opened in 1905 from a design by Swash & Bain. It is a Grade II Listed building.

The Crumlin branch of the Monmouthshire and Brecon Canal passes through the village with a number of bridges. Near the M4 there are 14 locks which raised/lowered the canal by 268 feet in half a mile. A restoration project is now underway and a visitor centre has been opened on Cwm Lane.

Rogerstone has a range of schools, services and shops including a Morrison's supermarket.

Rogiet

The triple villages of Rogiet, Ifton and Llanvihangel near Rogiet now lie between the M4 and the M48, less than a mile west of Caldicot. The local railway station is Severn Tunnel Junction. The name Rogiet is thought to derive from Old English, meaning 'Gate for Roe Deer'. On old maps it was spelt Roggiet, reflecting the local pronunciation of 'Rogg-yet'.

There are two rectangular enclosures visible to the east of Ifton Manor Farm, thought to be Iron Age or Roman in origin. In 1998 a find of 3,778 Roman coins was found at Rogiet, dating from 253 to 296, now held at the National Museum of Wales. West of the village is a standing stone now dwarfed by the M4 embankment.

In the 13th century the Manor of Rogiet was held by the Gamage family. Sir Pain de Gamage, Lord of Rogiad married Margaret, daughter of Roger de St Pierre. Their grandson William who was sheriff of Gloucester in 1325 married the daughter and heir of Pain de Turberville of Coity Castle in Glamorgan.

In 1891 the combined populations of the three parishes was just 188, mainly engaged in agriculture with a twice monthly fair held as late as 1900 for the sale of cattle, sheep and pigs. St James Church Ifton which stood on what is now Chestnut Drive was demolished around 1755. The church of St Michael at Llanvihangel has now closed for worship and is in a deteriorating condition. It is a small building dating from the 13th century, though an earlier church mentioned in the Domesday Book stood on the site. It consists of a chancel, nave, north aisle which was apparently taken down before 1830 to be restored in 1904 by Henry Prothero of Cheltenham and a lofty embattled western tower containing a pre-Reformation bell. The church contains the 13th century effigies of John

Martel, dressed in chain mail with shield and sword, legs crossed, head on cushion and Anne Martel with hands in prayer and feet resting on a lapdog, both in shallow relief with Norman French surrounding inscription. The font is 12th century. Outside is the three step base and socket of the medieval churchyard cross. St Michael's is visible from the B4245 and is surrounded by the buildings of Old Court.

The church of St Mary was previously dedicated to St Hilary. It sits in the heart of the old village with the Manor House, now Manor House Farm. There were few other houses, with The Old School House now being one of the few buildings to survive. It was the school prior to the National School being built in 1887, though this latter school, like the smithy has disappeared. St Mary's dates from the 14th century and was restored in 1903-4 by John Coates Carter and John Pollard Seddon, when the north aisle was built as well as the vestry. There is an unusually large chancel, nave, south porch and a western tower containing one bell with an attached stairtower with pyramidal roof. The font is Norman while set in the tower wall are painted the Ten Commandments.

The Rogiet Methodist Church is a 20th century building on Ifton Road, replacing the Mission Room formerly on Station Road.

Rogiet has grown substantially as a commuter village and had a population of 1,813 in 2011. There is a new school, service station, village shop and post office and the Severn Tunnel Non Political Club. The Roggiett Hotel has closed. There are some industrial units next to the railway.

St. Arvans (Welsh: Llanarfan)

St Arvans lies two miles north of Chepstow on the road to Tintern, at the northern end of Chepstow Racecourse. It takes its name from the church thought to have been established in the 9th century by Arvan, a Celtic hermit who lived on salmon from the nearby Wye. The church is built on a traditional Celtic llan, almost circular in shape.

Baring-Gould identifies the church with that of Ecclesia Sanctorum Jarmen et Febric, where in 955, a deacon sought sanctuary after an argument in a field between the deacon and a reaper. In the course of the argument, the reaper sliced off a finger of the deacon who appealed for aid, but while being tended, stabbed the reaper to death and escaped to the church. The relatives of the murdered man broke into the church and killed the deacon before the altar. Bishop Peter was furious. He summoned a Council, and threatened the King with excommunication, unless the culprits were delivered up. King Nogui surrendered the six men, and the bishop confined them in prison at Llandaff, fast chained for six months, and then only released them on condition that they paid a heavy fine in money and surrendered their possessions to the church.

The church has been enlarged over the years with the octagonal tower built in 1820 at the expense of Nathaniel Wells of Piercefield (see below). Further renovations in 1882-4 were by John Prichard and amounted to a rebuild of the nave, with its side aisles and dormer windows. The chancel with its wagon roof is 13th century. The east window and oak screen in the tower arch date from 1931. At the entrance is the remnant of a 10th century Celtic cross.

St Arvans Independent Chapel was built in 1849 on Devauden Road but has been converted for residential use. Further along Devauden Road are the remains of the village pound.

At the entrance to Fordwich Close is the ornate cast iron village fountain, constructed in 1893. It takes the form of a bowl with two figures and a central pillar. Close by is Turnpike Cottage, built in 1829 as part of the Chepstow to Monmouth Turnpike road. The Piercefield Hotel is an old coaching inn on the main road and the village has its Memorial Hall dating from 1924. The centre of the village is a conservation area but there has been considerable select development on the outskirts.

Wyndcliffe Court and Gardens, an Arts and Crafts Listed house and gardens on Penterry Lane date from the 1920s. The gardens were designed by H. Avray Tipping in conjunction with Eric Francis, architect of the house, and Charles Clay, the owner. The gardens are open at weekends during the summer as a sculpture garden. Nearby is the site of the Wyndcliffe Roman Villa and Temple enclosure. Wyndcliffe Wood lies to the east on the Tintern road, with a viewpoint and picnic area. Moss Cottage was a thatched building built as a tea room by the Duke of Beaufort with walks up the 365 steps to the top of Wyndcliffe or down through the Piercefield Estate. The cottage was demolished in the 20th century, but the steep path with its rock cut steps has been restored. Thomas Roscoe described the impact of the scene after making the climb: "On gaining the open space, one of the most extensive and beautiful views that can be imagined bursts upon the eye. In the valley, the eye follows for several miles the course of the Wye; which issues from a wooded glen on the left hand, curves round a green garden-like peninsula, rising into a hill studded with beautiful clumps of trees, then forces its foaming way to the right, along a huge wall of rock, nearly as high as the point where you stand, and at length, beyond Chepstow Castle, which looks like a ruined city, empties itself into the Bristol Channel, where ocean closes the dim and misty distance. On the other side of the river, immediately in front, the peaked tops of a long ridge of hills extend nearly the whole district which the eye commands. It is thickly clothed with wood, out of which a continuous wall of rock, festooned with ivy, picturesquely rears its head. Over this ridge (Llaucaut Cliffs, or Bannagor Crags) you again discern water, the Severn five miles broad, thronged with white sails, on either side of which are seen blue ridges of hills, full of fertility and cultivation. The grouping of the landscape is perfect I know of no picture more beautiful. Inexhaustible in details, of boundless extent, and yet marked by such grand and prominent features, that confusion and monotony, the usual defects of a very wide prospect, are completely avoided."

The *Tourist in Wales* published in 1851 adds "It is an expanse of vision over which the eager eye, in the rapidity of its flight, seems to rejoice like a bird at the vastness and magnificence of its glance over the outspread glories of creation. Such is the wide scope, and such the principal objects of the landscape; but, on a clear day, and furnished with a map, the tourist may make out, on either side the Channel, and beyond the isolated Holmes Rock, the hazy coast and highlands of Devon and Glamorgan, the nearer hills of Somerset, the conspicuous Dundry Tower, above Bristol, the mouth of the Avon, and as the eye ranges up the Severn, Thornbury church, Berkeley Castle, and the vale of Gloucester to the distant Cotswold, while, more near at hand, the undulating variety of hill and dale of Monmouthshire are unrolled beneath the eye, from Caldicot level to the majestic mountains of its interior."

Piercefield House today lies in ruins three quarters of a mile south-east of the village, overlooking Chepstow Racecourse. The first reference to Piercefield was in the 15th century when it was owned by John Walter. Some references imply that the family connection goes back to the time of the Norman Conquest. The family Coat of Arms was described as "Azure a squirrel sejant Or". The Walter family were leaders of the puritan movement in the county and they remained in possession until 1727 when it was purchased by Thomas Rouse. In 1736 it was acquired by Colonel Valentine Morris. Morris was a descendant of John Morris of Tintern who as Captain John Morris sailed with Sir George Ayscough and the Parliamentary Army to take Barbados in 1651. Morris married a wealthy Barbados woman and had four sons, two of whom settled in Antigua. The Antiguan line descended to Valentine Morris born in 1678. At the age of 16 he was commissioned into the army as a colonel and fought in the attack on Guadeloupe. He was befriended by General Codrington and then made Governor of the Leeward Islands. Through inheritance and marriage he acquired sugar plantations in Antigua. He died in 1743 when his son, also Valentine, was just 16 and at school in England.

Valentine Morris set about creating one of the finest landscaped estates in Britain. He was renowned for his generosity as *The Times* Obituary reads, an "inconsiderate desire to make others happy". "In improving the natural beauties of his Monmouthshire estate he refused no expense, and in rendering it universally acceptable to the numerous friends and crowds of strangers by whom it was visited he employed an hospitality which was bounteous beyond example. Persons of every rank were conducted with all

St Arvans Piercefield House by George Eyre Brooks (1800-1877)

Piercefield by Sir Richard Colt Hoare

possible convenience and the most respectful accomodation, through the long circuit of his terrestrial paradise, and had nothing to pay when they came to the end of it. Mr M. was, we believe, the first who abolished the odious tax which, some years ago were levied by servants on the visitors of their masters. Thus he lived for many years in a place which was more visited than any spot in the kingdom, and was visited by none who did not bear away with them a most respectful esteem for the owner of it."

Valentine Morris was a magistrate who imposed standard weights and measures on the county and was also responsible for the building of some 300 miles of turnpike roads in Monmouthshire. He married Mary Mordaunt, a niece of the third Earl of Peterborough in 1748 and in 1771 stood for Parliament in a by-election against John Morgan of the Morgan family of Tredegar House but lost.

The expense of Piercefield, coupled with gambling and political expenses, exceeded his not inconsiderable income. In 1772 he left for the West Indies, becoming Governor of the island of St Vincent's. His role however went unpaid and when the French forced his surrender in 1779 he returned to Britain, and was forced into prison by his creditors. He surrendered his estates in the West Indies and sold Piercefield for £26,000, half the price which Lord Clive of India had agreed to pay before his abrupt return to India. Morris spent four years in Debtors' prison but was released when the government agreed to pay him for his time in St Vincent. He died in 1789. *The Times* offered this tribute in his obituary: "The leading feature of his character was a zeal which approached to Quixotism, whether it was employed in the service of his country, his friend, or the distressed. He has, indeed been represented as too much under the influence of a vain ostentation; and the generosity, the urbanity, and the charities of his life, have been imputed to that principle; but, by whom? by those who envied his prosperity; and fought to frame an excuse for their ingratitude in his adversity: what other vanity governed his character, than that which is the main spring of human excellence, we know not; but this we know and repeat, that he was a most faithful servant of his country, that he possessed an eminent capacity for friendship, that he never failed to assist distress when he could, and that he did assist it when he ought not. He shared his good things in the days of his fortune, with the friends of his prosperity, and he divided the pittance that remained in the hour of his distress with the companions of his adversity. He had his failings, which disasters might encrease, and the insolent rigour of affected virtue may condemn. That his passions might sometimes overcome his morality, and that the benevolence of his heart might too often extinguish his prudence, and circumstances which it is the duty of friendship to lament; but the best of us are the children of infirmity, and the virtues of Valentine Morris were sufficient, in the opinion of those who knew him best, to counterbalance all his errors."

Piercefield was purchased by the Durham banker George Smith who set about building a new house, designed by John Soane. He also altered some of the paths created by Morris. Work on the new house started in 1792 and had reached roof level when Smith got into financial difficulties after joining with John Curre of Itton in the Monmouthshire Bank. He mortgaged Piercefield in 1792 but went bankrupt the following year and the estate was sold to Colonel Mark Wood of the East India Company. Wood, who had been Surveyor General of Bengal, returned home with a fortune of £200,000. He purchased a seat in Parliament and properties in

Monmouthshire and Glamorgan. He completed Piercefield, though not strictly to Soane's designs, using the architect Joseph Bonomi who incorporated a Doric portico and wings. He sold Piercefield in 1802 to the 23 year old Nathaniel Wells.

Nathaniel was the son of William Wells of Llandough, a slave trader and wealthy plantation owner on the island of St Kitts. William was the son of Revd. Nathaniel Wells, Rector of St Andrews and Llandough, and brother of the Revd. Robert Wells, Rector of the parish of Penmaen and Ilston in the Gower. After the death of his wife, William Wells fathered a number of children by his house slaves. He died in 1794. In his will he gave the mothers an annual income and their freedom and the daughters a cash sum and an income. His son Nathaniel was by a slave known as Juggy. In his will William bequeathed "the remainder of my Estate both real and personal whatsoever and wheresoever I give unto my Natural and Dear Son Nathaniel Wells whose mother is my woman Juggy and who is now in England for his Education and at School at Newington near London and under the care of his Uncle my Brother Nathaniel Wells Esquire of London". The young Nathaniel remained in Britain and was accepted in society, which ignored his colour (Mark Wood described him as "a West Indian of large fortune, a man of very gentlemanly manners, but so much a man of colour as to be little removed from a Negro") and his illegitimacy. He married Harriet, the only daughter of Charles Este former chaplain to George II. Nathaniel played an important role in local Monmouthshire Society, becoming Britain's first black High Sheriff in 1818 and Deputy Lieutenant of the county. He also became only the second coloured man to hold an army commission, when in 1820 he became a Lieutenant in the Chepstow Troop of the Yeomanry Cavalry of Gloucestershire and Monmouth. He was appointed a Justice of the Peace in 1806 and was a churchwarden at St Arvans and a member of the Chepstow Hunt. After the death of Harriet he married Esther Owen at St George's Hanover Square in 1823. In total he had 22 children, a number of whom entered the clergy. He retained his estates in St Kitts though these were controlled by local managers.

Wells continued the practice of allowing visitors access to the grounds of Piercefield, a practice not followed by subsequent tenants. Lewis described the estate: "From Piercefield Park, a splendid seat, the views are remarkably magnificent, and embrace numerous reaches of the Wye, the Severn, and a great range of the surrounding country. The mansion, situated on an eminence, in the midst of fine plantations, is a superb elevation of freestone, consisting of a centre and two wings, and much admired for its tasteful architecture: on the spacious staircase are four beautiful pieces of Gobelin tapestry which belonged to Louis XVI, representing subjects in the natural history of Africa".

Wells died in 1852 at Bath, leaving an estate of £100,000. He had sold Piercefield in 1850 to John Russell, a prominent coal owner in Monmouthshire with collieries at Risca and Cwmtillery, who sold it in 1861, using the proceeds to set up a trust for the families of miners killed in the Blackvein Colliery disaster at Cross Keys. The purchaser was Henry Clay, a brewer and banker from Burton on Trent. The family bank was merged with the Burton Bank in 1839 becoming the Burton, Uttoxeter, and Ashbourne Union Bank, which was subsequently taken over by Lloyds Bank. After his death in 1871 Piercefield passed to his son also Henry Clay who was JP for Monmouthshire. On his death in 1921 at the age of 95, the property passed to his son Henry Hastings Clay who sold the house and park to the Chepstow Racecourse Company. The racecourse opened in 1926 but sadly Piercefield House was neglected. During World War II it was used for target practice by American soldiers and now stands as a roofless shell.

The house is now a Grade II Listed ruin and the Park is a Grade I Historic Park, deemed as important as Hafod in Ceredigion as an outstanding example of the 'picturesque'. Four of its viewpoints are scheduled ancient monuments, the Platform is a viewpoint built out over a natural rock outcrop, the Giant's Cave which once had a statue of a giant above one of its entrances, the Grotto and Standing Stone, set in the middle of an Iron Age enclosure and the Alcove. All four feature in the Piercefield Walk for which Monmouthshire County Council have produced a guide, available online entitled Picturesque Piercefield. The impressive Lions Gate entrance to the park still stands with its twin lodges and lion topped pillars. It now forms the horsebox entrance to the racecourse. The wall around the estate was built by Colonel Wood in 1790.

St Brides Netherwent (Welsh: Sant-y-brid)

Two miles north of Magor, and three miles west of Caerwent is the isolated church of St Bridget on the site of the deserted medieval village of St Bride Netherwent. In the valley of St Bride's Brook, the village, said to have been founded by Brochwael, the son of Meurig of Gwent, in the 10th century once had a Manor, mill, bakehouse, smithy and vicarage. The mill was operating into the 20th century. St Brides Netherwent was abandoned in the 18th century. The church, which dates from the 13th century, once had north and south aisles, but both had fallen by 1812. In a dilapidated condition the church, apart from the tower, was demolished and rebuilt in 1848. It was re-roofed in 1956-7. There is a Norman font and in the tower which is topped by a steep saddleback roof are two bells, the oldest of which, the Angelus, dates from 1290 making it the second oldest in Wales. The medieval churchyard preaching cross was restored to commemorate the Diamond Jubilee of Queen Victoria in 1897.

On the wooded hill to the north-east of the church was an Iron Age enclosure and in the field to the north of this was a Bronze Age Round Barrow, excavated in 1860. The site is still visible as a low mound despite ploughing and clearly visible as a crop mark from the air.

St Brides Wentlooge (Welsh) Llansanffraid Gwynllŵg)

Three and a half miles south-west of Newport city centre St Brides Wentlooge was an agricultural community. Still an attractive small village, there has been new building with the 1970s Neville Park estate.

The parish is mentioned in 1254 but the Grade II* church, was rebuilt in the 15th century when the tower, north chapel and south porch were added. It was refurbished in 2008. Of particular note are the pre-reformation carvings on the tower and the wagon roofs. The tower contains a peal of six bells, four of which are dated 1734. A plaque records the high water mark of "The Great Flud, 20 Januarie, 10 in the, morning, 1606". (Under the Gregorian Calendar the year is 1607.) There are the remains of a churchyard cross in the form of a single step base and socket stone. Rehoboth Baptist Chapel was built in 1837 but has been converted for residential use. Providence Welsh Independent Chapel on Beach Road was built in 1826 and rebuilt in 1899. It is now a private home. A Board school was built in 1850 and has now been converted to a house.

The Church House Inn has closed and the Inn at the Elm Tree closed in January 2014. The Lighthouse Inn on the sea wall to the south of the village was formerly the Tŷ'n-y-pwll public house. The Lighthouse Holiday Park is close by.

St Illtyd See Llanhilleth

St. Maughans (Welsh: Llanfocha)

Three miles north-north-west from Monmouth is the scattered parish of St Maughans. The earliest reference is in the *Liber Landavensis* as Lann Mocha but it is generally accepted that Maughan is derived from Machlou, born to Caradog and Derwela of Gwent. He is better known as St Malo who was educated at Llancarfan and left for Brittany at the time of the Yellow Plague around 547.

St Maughans is a rural parish with the main centre of population at St Maughan's Green half a mile to the east of the church. Described in 1868 as a small rustic place, the River Monnow marks the boundary with Herefordshire. Coedanghred Hill offers views to the Wrekin, the Malvern Hills, Fairford, and the hills of Hereford, Gloucester, Monmouth, Glamorgan, and Brecknockshire.

The *Liber Landavensis* relates that during the time of Joseph as Bishop of Llandaff (1022-1059) "Rhiwallon son of Tudfwlch came one day, accompanied by his household, to Lannmocha, excited by anger and fury, and plundered the people of that church; and proceeding with his prey, the relics of the church following him, with great outcry and groaning, he fell down at Ffynnon Oer, [Cold Well,] being exceedingly amazed at seeing a great fish leap out of the well, on account of which his horse started, and threw his rider to the ground; and having broken his arm, and being half-dead, he called his household to him, and gave up the prey. And in that place he gave to St. Dubricius, St. Teilo, and St. Oudoccus, and to Bishop Joseph, and all Bishops of Llandaff, his hereditary estate of Cecin Penicelli, without any payment to any mortal man, except to the Church of Llandaff, and its Pastors for ever."

Found on a no through road signposted from St Maughan's Green, St Maughans church dates from the 13th-14th century, with a rebuilding at the turn of the 16th. It was restored in 1865-6 by John Pollard Seddon, architect for Mr J.E.W. Rolls of The Hendre, who financed the work. The most striking feature of this lovely church is the arcade to the north aisle, which consists of three octagonally-shaped oak tree-trunks. The circular font may date from the 9th century. There is a memorial to General Sir Robert Brownrigg of Hilston House, Governor of Languard Fort and Colonel of the 9th Regiment of Foot, who died in 1833. (For Hilston House see Crossway.) The west tower, containing a single bell, is topped by a low pyramidal two stage timber-framed 'dovecote' belfry.

St Maughan's Green is a hamlet of no more than twelve houses.

The layer of old red sandstone from the Devonian period is known as the St. Maughans Formation after the village.

St Mellons (Welsh: Llaneirwg)

St Mellons lies four miles north-east of Cardiff city centre, and is today a suburb of the city. Its Welsh name is Llaneirwg, Eurwg being King of Gwent in the Romano British period. The village was on the old A48 trunk road between Cardiff and Newport and until 1974 was in the county of Monmouthshire. An ancient village, in Norman times St Mellons was a small manor held for the service of a half knight's fee to the lordship of Wentloog. St Mellons church was granted to St Augustine's Abbey Bristol in the early 12th century. The village remained small until the late 1960s since when it has expanded dramatically. The centre of the old village however remains and this entry is confined to that area.

The church is dedicated to St Mellon who according to legend was born 229AD in Cardiola (Cardiff), and was sent to Rome where he was converted to Christianity by Pope Stephen I, and ordained a priest and became the first Bishop of Rouen. It is claimed he performed many miracles before his death in 314. The present church dates to the 14th century though there was a refurbishment in 1868. The four storey tower is 15th century while the north chapel dates to the early 17th century. The tower, which contains a set of six bells, is set alongside the porch with the Lady Chapel leading off it. The nave which has a wooden barrel roof leads to a narrow chancel with an unusual double arch. The hexagonal font is early. The north chapel is known as the Llanrumney Chapel, because it was used by the local owner of Llanrumney Hall. (Llanrumney Hall is now a public house, three quarters of a mile west of the church.) In 1665 this was Edward Morgan whose daughter Elizabeth married Captain Henry Morgan. In the graveyard is a monument to Joseph Benjamin Hemingway who built Quarry Hill House. The column is deliberately cut off. There is also the stump of a churchyard cross. The lychgate on Ty'r Winch Road is large with a central pair of gates to allow traffic into Church Lane and two side gates for pedestrians.

Caersalem Baptist Chapel on Mill Lane was built in 1830 and rebuilt in

1842 and 1880. It remains in use. Bethania Calvinistic Methodist Chapel on Bethania Row was built in 1820 and rebuilt in 1869 and is also still in use. Soar Congregational Chapel on Newport Road was built in around 1840. Today it is the Kingdom Hall of the Jehovah's Witnesses.

A poor house was built on The Ton in around 1650. This became a school in the 19th century but was damaged y fire in 1989 and has been replaced by private housing.

Ty-to-maen was built in 1885-89 to a design by the Llandaff diocesan architect, E.M. Bruce Vaughan for Richard Allen of the Spillers Company. It was donated to the Cardiff Royal Infirmary along with its estate as a convalescent home by Sir William Edgar Nicholls, manager of Spillers in memory of Richard Allen. Since 1987 it has been home to St John's College, a mixed independent school.

There are two inns in the old village, the Coach House, formerly known as The White Hart and the Bluebell Inn which once had the village pump outside.

St Pierre (Welsh: Sain Pŷr)

There is some confusion as to the origin of the name. It is generally accepted that it derives from the dedication of the church to St Peter but Bradney claimed that it was a Norman family of St Pierre, while others hold that a Welsh family adopted the name from the church. In 1764 two sepulchral stones were discovered, one bearing the name Urien St Pierre, identified by Dugdale as having died in 1239. By 1395 St Pierre was held by Robert ap Ieuan ap David, in right of his wife and then by Sir David ap Philip (1387-1423). Sir David had fought alongside Henry V in France and his son Lewis's name was adopted as the family surname. According to Burke, the Lewis family of St Pierre descended from Cadivor ap Collwyn Lord of Blaencuch and Cilsant (995-1089). Cadivor's great-great-grandson, Llewellen Lord of St Clare married the heiress of Sir Morgan Meredith, Lord of Tredegar. They had two sons, Morgan, Lord of St Clare and Tredegar, from whom descended the Morgans of Tredegar and Philip Llewelin ap Ivor who went on to found the line which became the Lewis family of St Pierre. The family continued to hold St Pierre until 1910, though they moved to Moynes Court in 1893 (see Mathern). The Lewis family played an important role in the life of the county for 500 years, with a number serving as High Sheriff and MP. The family took over the New Passage Ferry (see

Portskewett) in competition with the Duke of Beaufort's Old Passage Service from Beachley. In the 16th century Henry Lewis enhanced the family fortunes by marrying Bridget, daughter and heir of Thomas Kemeys of Caldicot, and widow of Thomas Herbert, while in the 19th century the family acquired the 1400 acres of the Abbey Dore estate, Herefordshire.

In the 1960s St Pierre became a hotel and the deer park a golf course, now the Marriott St Pierre Hotel & Country Club.

The church of St Peter has Norman origins. The chancel was added in the 14th century and after a restoration in the 16th century, there was work by the Gloucester architect Alfred William Maberly in 1873-5 when the altar slab, font and screen, removed at the time of Cromwell were restored, and by Eric Francis in the early 20th century. The rood screen has been much restored while the two sepulchral stones mentioned above have been removed from the porch, where they were seen by Coxe and are now part of the chancel floor. The lion's head carving on the south wall represents the coat of arms of the Lewis family. Nave and chancel are the same width. The herringbone work in the north wall of the nave

St Pierre House by Sir Richard Colt Hoare

and the east wall of the porch are thought to be Norman. There is a north porch with a priest's door in the south wall and a western bellcote.

The house was built by William Lewis and his son George around 1500 but was largely rebuilt in the 17th century and remodelled in 1765 by Morgan Lewis and in the 19th century by Charles Lewis. After 1960 there were further extensions for the conversion to a hotel. After the sale by the Lewis estate, St Pierre was purchased by Daniel Lysaght of the Newport based Lysaght Steelworks. It was used by Bristol Corporation in World War II and later became a training centre for the National Association of Boys Clubs before its conversion to a hotel in 1960. Extensions have obscured much of the original appearance of the building but the gatehouse remains prominent.

A mile north-west of St Pierre was the medieval village of Runston, which at one time contained some 25 cottages around a village green, a chapel and a fortified manor house. The walls of the Norman St Ceina's Chapel remain, showing that there was a nave and chancel though the tower had been replaced by a bell turret. The chapel was in use until the early 18th century. St Ceina has been identified as St Cenedlon (see Rockfield).

On the coast, south-east of St Pierre is St Pierre Pill, once an important harbour now silted up, but still the home of Chepstow and District Yacht Club's moorings.

Shirenewton (Welsh: Drenewydd Gelli-farch)

The quiet, attractive village of Shirenewton enjoys an elevated position, two miles north of Caerwent. The name Shirenewton was derived from Sheriff's New Settlement whereas the Welsh name translates as New Settlement at the Stallion's Grove. Around 1100 Sheriff Walter de Gloucester cleared the surrounding forest to create a settlement. Over the years it was variously known as Caldecot cum Newton and Newton Netherwent.

Shirenewton Court was the home of the Blethin family, descendants of Hywel Dda. William Blethin was born in 1530 and became Bishop of Llandaff in 1575. Whilst Bishop, he retained his other church appointments, including that as rector of Rogiet, because of the impoverishments of the diocese. He died in 1590 and is buried at Mathern church. The Blethin family owned the Court until 1785. In 1830, William Hollis, the owner of the paper mills at Mounton, rebuilt the Court which was renamed Shirenewton Hall by Edward Joseph Lowe in 1880. Lowe was a noted botanist and meteorologist. In 1900 he sold the Hall to the Scot, Charles Oswald Lidell a shipping agent in the Far East trade, who extended the house and designed the Japanese/Chinese Garden with an impressive one and a half tonne Temple Bell under a pagoda style roof, no doubt using his experiences in the Far East. Lidell was High Sheriff of Monmouthshire in 1918. In 1988 Shirenewton Hall was the setting for the film *The Woman He Loved*, the story of Edward VIII's abdication. The house in Tudorbethan style enjoys views across to the Severn Estuary.

The church is dedicated to St Thomas a Becket and is first mentioned in 1254. It was founded by Humphrey de Bohun, Earl of Hereford, about the middle of the 13th century but the oldest surviving part of the church is the early 14th century tower. There was a major rebuilding in 1854 by John Norton, funded by the Revd. Edward Inward Jones, the Rector of Shirenewton. The organ was donated by Edward Lidell in 1908 while the reredos was formerly at St Woolo's Cathedral. There was a peal of five bells installed in 1746 with a sixth added as a War Memorial by Charles Lidell in 1918. Two bells were replaced in 1997 when a new frame was installed. The tower clock is a War Memorial. There is a three bay arcade separating the nave and north aisle. The central tower and chancel are out of alignment with the nave, pointing to a later construction date. The castellated tower has a square projecting stair turret on the north side.

The old chapel on the Chepstow road was built as the Shirenewton Friends Meeting House in 1724. It changed denomination to Wesleyan Methodist in 1823 but closed in 1925 and has been converted for residential use.

The Tredegar Arms had a license between 1861 and 1880 but was not shown as being a public house between 1882 and 1921, while the Tan House only had a beer license as late as 1921 and closed in 2011. There were other public houses, the Upper House on Earlswood Road but this had closed by 1920, The King's Head is now the Old Rectory while the Engineer's Arms and the Five Bells are now private houses and the Butcher's Arms has disappeared. At Mynydd Bach to the north of the village is the Carpenters Arms and the Huntsman Hotel, formerly the Cross Hands whose most famous landlord, Bill Benjamin, was a prize-fighter who lost to Tom Sayers, champion of England in three rounds in 1858. There has been some modern development in the village, but

Mynydd Bach is the main centre for modern housing, including the school. The 1876 Board School was located at Earlwood.

There were a number of paper mills around the village, including White Mill, while Tuck Mill was a woollen mill, both closed and in ruins by 1882. On the road to Mounton is The Gondra, a three storey 18th century house enlarged in 1840 with walled garden and ice house. In 2008 the owner was fined for carrying out work at the Grade II Listed property without planning permission and forced to reinstate the property.

Skenfrith (Welsh: Ynysgynwraidd)
Cynwraidd's Water Meadow Island

Skenfrith is a lovely, quiet old village though described by Coxe in 1800 as "a miserable village containing a church, a few cottages and two public houses". It lies on the banks of the Monnow, five miles north-west of Monmouth.

Skenfrith Castle predates the Norman Conquest, but Henry II ordered its strengthening by Ralph Grosmont in 1187 but abandoned this in 1188. Skenfrith, along with Grosmont and White Castle were granted by King John to William de Braose in return for 800 marks, three steeds and ten greyhounds in 1205. The castles were seized by Henry III and granted to Hubert de Burgh who is thought to have been responsible for much of the stone building, though in 1220 it was flooded by the Monnow and river gravel was used to raise the ground level and a new set of buildings was erected inside. Excavations have revealed the original great hall buried beneath the gravel. The castles were surrendered in 1239, Hubert having incurred the King's displeasure, and granted to Henry III's younger son, Edmund Crouchback, Duke of Lancaster (see Grosmont). The King's tower was roofed in lead in 1244. The castle is trapezoidal with five towers around the walls and a juliet or circular keep-tower in the inner ward. Leland described the castle as "yet standeth" around 1538, but stonework has been used in local building and the north-west wall has been breached around the old entrance. The only other entrance appears to have been the water gate at the centre of the long north-east wall. The castle was surrounded by a 20 foot moat fed by the Monnow. The castle is now in the care of the National Trust.

The Grade I Listed church of St Bridget dates from the time of King John with north and south aisles added by the 15th century. The roofs were

Skenfrith Bridge and Castle by Sir Richard Colt Hoare

renewed in 1896 by E.G. Davies while there was a sympathetic refurbishment by William Weir of London in 1909-10 under guidance of the Society for the Protection of Ancient Buildings. There is a 13th century moulded semi-circular arched piscina, a 15th century cope, Morgan family box pew and a reading desk made from the former rood screen. The 1587 chest tomb is of John Morgan Esquire and his wife Ann. Morgan was MP for Monmouthshire and Steward of the Duchy of Lancaster. He died in 1557 and his wife in 1564. The most prominent feature of the church is the thick squat western tower with its massive buttress. The tower which contains six bells is topped by a two stage timber-framed 'dovecote' belfry.

Associated with the church is St Bride's Well, a spring between the road and the river to the east of the Bell Inn. Skenfrith Bridge opposite the Bell was rebuilt in 1824. The Bell Inn, much extended dates from the 18th century. The other public house mentioned by Coxe was the New Inn. It is now Sarn private house opposite the castle. The War Memorial stands prominently at the entrance to the village and doubles as a horse trough. As well as listing the nine men who lost their lives in the First World War, it lists the 42 men who 'served and returned'. Behind the memorial is the three storey Skenfrith Corn Mill, with its large iron-framed undershot waterwheel which operated into the 1990s. The leet providing the water formed part of the castle moat. A National School was opened in 1843, later becoming a Sunday School and now the Church Hall. A new Board school was opened at Norton in 1877, to the west of the village, but this closed in 1991. Norton was the home of Graig Wesleyan Methodist Chapel built in 1883 but now a private house. Norton Baptist Chapel was built in 1830 and still in use. There was the Bridge Inn at Norton, now opposite the Three Castles Campsite. In 1843 the Roman Catholic chapel of the Immaculate Conception was built at Coedangred on land originally gifted to Abbey Dore by Hubert de Burgh.

Striguil (Entry for clarity)
Striguil is the old name for Chepstow Castle and Lordship. Antiquarians in the 17th and 18th centuries, from William Camden on assumed it was Castle Troggy at Pen-y-cae-mawr. The Marcher Lordship of Striguil was established by William fitz Osbern, who was created Earl of Hereford in 1067 and by 1069 had started the building of Chepstow Castle. The name is thought to derive from the Welsh 'ystraigyl' meaning a bend in the river. Confusion arose as the town was known from around 1300 as Cêapstöw from Old English meaning Market Place and over the years this name was applied to the castle. The Lordship of Striguil, which also contained lands in Gloucestershire, continued in the hands of the de Clares and subsequently William Marshal until 1245 when it was divided.

Sudbrook
Sudbrook, half a mile south of Portskewett, was a model village built between 1873 and 1886 by Thomas Walker for the tunnellers on the Severn Tunnel and subsequently railway employees. Some of the houses were built of concrete, possibly the first in Britain. The village included a mission hall, school and infirmary. The name is derived from the old English Suthebroc and was also known as Southbrook in the 19th century.

During the Iron Age there was an Iron Age fort on the low cliffs along the coast. This appears to have been used by the Romans and there is a ditched rampart forming a triangular camp. Later there was a medieval village with Holy Trinity church built in the 12th century but abandoned by 1720. The ruined nave, south porch and 14th century chancel with belfry over the chancel arch are visible, but much of the churchyard has been eroded and the socket stone of the churchyard cross has been moved inside the church.

The village is dominated by the massive tunnel pumping house which housed six steam engines. These were replaced by electric pumps in 1962 and the associated chimneys demolished in 1968. 50 million litres of water a day is pumped out of the Severn Tunnel. In the late 19th early 20th century there was a small shipbuilding industry associated with the jetty to the east of the village, while to the west was the St Regis Paper Mill, opened in 1958 and closed in 2005.

Talywain (Welsh: Tal-y-waun) End of the Moor

Talywain lies to the west of Abersychan and to the south of Garndiffaith. Ironworks were built to the west of the village in 1826 by Shears Small and Taylor which were taken over by the British Ironworks Company in 1829. A substantial operation with six blast furnaces, refineries, rolling mills and collieries and mines, it covered a large area, including small terraces of houses to form a settlement known as British. In 1852 the company was bought for just £8,500 by the Ebbw Vale Company. An incline plane was constructed to meet the new railway completed in 1853, later replaced by a branch line from Talywain to Pontypool. The works closed in 1876 though the collieries continued in operation.

Only Elizabeth Row now stands at the end of British Road. Edgehill Row, Long Row, John's Row, Dublin Row, York Place, King's Parade, Queen's Parade and Monmouth Row have all disappeared, as has Abersychan House although there are some modern bungalows near Elizabeth Row and a modern Kingdom Hall of the Jehovah's Witnesses. The area is still littered with the ruins of the iron and mining era, with a colliery chimney, a Cornish beam pumping engine-house and the offices of the British Iron Company prominent in a still unreclaimed landscape. The area can be accessed through the Big Arch road tunnel off the B4246.

The upper Talywain or Cwmsychan Colliery was sunk in 1860 and later leased to the Abersychan Elled Company before closing in 1934. A small mine employing just 40 men in 1929, it experienced no less than 17 fatalities over its life. The Lower Navigation Colliery was sunk in 1880 by Abersychan Elled Co. It employed up to 739 men but by the time of Nationalization it was used for pumping.

The church of St Thomas was built in 1832 by Edward Haycock of Shrewsbury and apparently paid for by the British Ironworks Company. It consists of a chancel, nave with gallery, aisles and vestry, west porch and western belfry containing one bell. Originally a chapel of ease to Pontypool it became a parish church in 1844. There was a reseating in 1869 and a refurbishment in 1974 but it closed in 1995. While the windows are covered, this Grade II Listed church is suffering signs of decay and vandalism but plans have been put forward to create a community centre. The first vicar, the Reverend Bluett served the parish for 28 years and Bluett's Bridge and Bluett's Road are named after him.

There has been a large amount of building in Talywain, using the land previously taken up by railway sidings. The railways have gone, but the impressive Talywain Viaduct still towers over Viaduct Road. Consisting of nine arches it was opened in 1876 and carried the London and North Western Railway connecting Abersychan and Talywain to Brynmawr. There is a small shopping area on Commercial Road where are also found the British Constitution and The Globe Inn.

The Bryn See Llangattock Nigh Usk

The Narth
The Narth is first mentioned as Y Narth, meaning waste land, in 1630. Situated four and a half miles south-east of Monmouth, it is an unplanned settlement of mainly 20th century properties on the summit of a hill overlooking both the Wye and Whitebrook Valleys. An agricultural area, with medieval farms and scattered 19th century cottages, its nature changed following a land sale in 1920. Popular with commuters, the only amenity is the village hall.

Tintern (Welsh: Tyndyrn)
Tintern was originally two villages, Chapel Hill, which contains the Abbey, and Tintern Parva to the north. Tintern Abbey was founded on the banks of the River Wye, four miles north of Chepstow, by Walter fitz Richard de Clare, Lord of Striguil, in 1131. The name is thought to derive from din dyrn meaning Dyrn's fort and there is a defended enclosure on the hill south of the village.

Tintern was the second Cistercian foundation in Britain. The monks came from the Abbaye Notre-Dame de l'Aumône, north of Blois. Cistercians were celebrated for their agriculture and Tintern was gifted lands on both sides of the Wye which were farmed through a series of granges. By 1291 the Abbey estates amounted to more than 3,000 acres, including land in Norfolk gifted by Roger Bigod, Earl of Norfolk and Lord of Chepstow. Its wealth at this time saw a rebuilding with the great abbey church consecrated in 1301 and finally completed around 1320. The Abbey suffered financially following the Black Death in the latter part of the 14th century, when it became difficult to recruit new monks, and in the 15th century following attacks by the Welsh under Glyndŵr. In 1536 the Abbey, with its monks then numbering just 13, was surrendered to the King and its treasures were removed to the Royal Treasury. The lead from the roof was sold and the building and estates were given to Henry Somerset, Earl of Worcester, the Lord of Chepstow and Raglan. The roofless building fell victim to the elements. Many of the buildings were used for industry or destroyed but the church remained largely untouched and protected by the Somerset family. In 1750 the 4th Duke of Beaufort carried out some repairs and it became a tourist destination, especially for those seeking the 'picturesque'. The Revd. William Gilpin in 1770 said "the noble ruin of Tintern-abbey is esteemed, with its appendages, the most beautiful and picturesque view on the river. It occupies a great eminence in the middle of a circular valley, beautifully screened on all sides by woody hills, through which the river winds its course; and the hills, closing on its entrance and on its exit, leave no room for inclement blasts to enter. A more pleasing retreat could not easily be found. The woods and glades intermixed; the winding of the river; the variety of the ground; the splendid ruin, contrasted with the objects of nature; and the elegant line formed by the summits of the hills which include the whole, make all together a very enchanting piece of scenery. Every thing around breathes an air so calm and tranquil, so sequestered from the commerce of life, that it is easy to conceive a man of warm imagination, in monkish times, might have been allured by such a scene to become an inhabitant of it." William Wordsworth described it in poetry and J.W.M. Turner and Thomas Gainsborough painted it. During the 19th century Tintern became more accessible with the opening of the Turnpike road in 1829 and the railway in 1876 although as late as 1900 there were boats transporting visitors on the nine mile river journey from Chepstow.

In 1901 the Abbey was purchased by the government and renovations under F.W. Waller and Sir Harold Brakspear continued until 1928. In 1984 the site came under the control of Cadw and is Grade I Listed. The cruciform building built of the local red sandstone is in remarkably good condition and complete save for the north nave arcade and the vaults. The south nave aisle and porch are roofed. In addition to the church there are extensive ruins of the cloisters, working and living quarters.

Following the closure of the monastery, Tintern became the centre of an iron industry. In 1565 the Mineral and Battery Company was established, by Royal Charter, to exploit the iron resources of the country. Eager to establish a wireworks near Bristol, William Humfrey and the German engineer Christopher Schutz found the ideal site at Tintern and the foundations were laid in 1566. Osmond iron was supplied by Richard Hanbury from his iron works at Pontypool. The industry developed quickly and by 1572 between 120 and 160 men were employed at the Tintern wireworks. The wire was used for cages, curtain rings, hooks, woolcards, dog chains, mouse traps, knitting needles and other consumer goods. It is estimated that some 5,000 people were employed across the country in manufacturing from the wire supplied by Tintern. By the end of the 16th century employment at the works had risen to 600 and wire was exported to France, Turkey and the Barbary States. The workers were well treated,

Tintern Abbey by Sir Richard Colt Hoare

with provision for a schoolteacher, priest, pensions for older workers and compensation for widows. The industry continued until 1826, with a blast furnace and ironworks built in 1671 in the Angiddy Valley. The wireworks site is now a car park next to the bridge but the excavated and restored remains of the iron works in the Angiddy Valley were opened to the public as a national heritage site in 1982.

The Abbey Mill was originally a corn mill but after 1536 gained a new life as a wire-drawing mill reverting to its original use in the 1820s before becoming a saw mill. It is now the Wye Valley Centre, with shops, a cafe and restaurant.

Tintern is a tourist village with the Abbey Hotel, Anchor Inn, Royal George Hotel, and Wye Valley Hotel. There are also guest houses, tea rooms, restaurants, the Rose and Crown, Cherry Tree and the Moon and Sixpence pubs, the latter renamed from the Mason's Arms following Somerset Maugham's stay in 1948. There are antiques and book shops. The Abbey Hotel was known as the Beaufort Arms and the building was originally part of the abbey complex with parts dating back to 1206. It has been a hotel since 1835 when the landlord was the keyholder and official guide to the abbey. The Anchor Inn was a cider mill with the miller's house attached. The miller was also the ferryman. It has been a licensed premises since 1806.

The ruined St Mary's church on the hill south-west of the abbey dates from the 14th century. It was restored by John Prichard in 1866 but was declared redundant in 1972 and destroyed by fire in 1977. It is roofless apart from the saddle back roof of the tower. The graveyard is still in use and contains a number of interesting tombstones. Of particular note is the recently restored sarcophagus tomb of Richard White who operated the wireworks for 30 years before his death in 1765. The inscription describes him as "inoffensive and benevolent, he lived without an enemy and died, beloved by all".

St Anne's House next to the Abbey Hotel is mainly 19th century, but contains part of the old Abbey Gatehouse and chapel dedicated to St Anne. The house was the home of John Loraine Baldwin, who founded the I Zingari Cricket Club in 1845. Tintern Wesleyan Methodist Chapel on the lane leading down from Tintern Surgery was built in 1861 and is now a private dwelling. There was also a Bible Christian Chapel on Chapel Hill. The church of St Michael at Tintern Parva lies on the banks of the Wye. First mentioned in 1348 it was rebuilt in 1846 and little of the original remains.

The font bowl is medieval but other furnishings are Victorian. There is a western bellcote with a single bell. On Trelleck Road there is the modern Bethel Pentecostal church. Parva Farm has a well established vineyard.

Tredunnock (Welsh: Tredynog)

Tredunnock is a small village four miles south of Usk. The name derives from 'Tref redinauc' meaning Fern farm. At the centre of a parish of 1,366 acres the village in 1882 contained the church, rectory, Ton Farm and some cottages. Newbridge on Usk is within the parish.

St Andrew's church dates from the 12th century though it is first recorded in 1254. The building is mainly 15th and 16th century. Of the peal of six bells five are dated 1662 as is the font. There was a restoration in 1910 by Arthur Grove and the seating dates from this time. A tablet recording the 1910 restoration is by Eric Gill. The churchyard contains the tomb of Isabella Gill, wife of Revd. John Philip Gill. On the north wall of the nave is a Roman memorial stone to Julius Julianus of 2nd Augustan Legion stationed at Caerleon. The church consists of a nave, weeping chancel, south porch, north vestry and west tower with a pyramid roof topped by a weathervane. Outside is the restored churchyard cross while the lychgate, which leads through a hedged avenue to the church, was erected as a War Memorial. Opposite is the well preserved village well. Ty Coets next to the church was the coach house to Ton Farm and later the Rectory Room. Ton Farmhouse dates from the 17th century with later additions.

Tredunnock has seen new housing in the latter part of the 20th century but remains a small, attractive, rural village.

Tregare (Welsh: Tre'r-gaer) Fortress Settlement

Two miles north of Raglan the tiny village of Tregare sits on the site of an Iron Age defended enclosure with the church of St Mary at its centre. Traces of the enclosure ditch and banks are visible.

St Mary's dates from the 14th century with the tower a later addition. It was restored in 1850-51 by Charles Lawrence and in 1900 by G.E. Halliday. There is a spiral staircase which led to the rood loft and a 15th century octagonal font. The arch to the tower is formed by the 14th century west window. The tower which has a peal of five bells has a pyramidal roof with a prominent cock weathervane. There is a priest door in the chancel and a south porch. The head and shaft of the churchyard cross are modern, set on the three stepped medieval base.

White Lion Cottage dates from the 17th century and was the White Lion Inn. Externally it was remodelled in the Victorian era.

Trellech (Welsh: Tryleg) Three Stones

Trellech which is also spelt Trelech, Treleck or Trelleck lies five miles south of Monmouth. It takes its name from the the three Bronze Age standing stones known as Harold's Stones which still stand in a field south of the Chepstow Road and are accessible by a footpath. The three stones are aligned 72 degrees east of due north and their significance is not known. The largest stone is 15 feet tall but angled in the direction of the other two. There were a number of stories about the origin of these stones. Lady Maud Probert in the 17th century attributed them as commemorating a victory of King Harold over the Welsh, hence the name Harold's Stones. A local legend suggested they were the result of a competition between John of Kent (see Grosmont) and the Devil throwing stones from the Skirrid. It has

Trelech Stones by Sir Richard Colt Hoare

been surmised that this was a Druidic site and a small hillfort to the south is known as Cae'r Higga or the enclosure of the gownsmen.

After the Conquest Trellech became an important town with its own charter. There was a small castle mentioned in 1231 but abandoned by 1301 and the motte which is in the grounds of Court Farm is now known as Tump Terret. There were additional buildings to the south of the village and the town had 388 burgages in 1288. Trellech was hit hard by the Welsh rebellions of 1295-6 and 1400-10 and the plagues of the 14th century, as evidenced by a large number of skeletons discovered beneath the church. The last of the de Clares who had controlled the area had died at Bannockburn in 1314 and unlike other towns Trellech never recovered from this catalogue of disasters and changed from being an important town to a sleepy village, losing its status in the 17th century.

The village which stands in a slight indentation on top of an 800 foot hill is dominated by the Grade I Listed church of St Nicholas with its lofty spire visible for miles. Although a church existed here from the 7th or 8th century, the present building dates from the early 14th century and appears to be of a single build. The tower was damaged in a storm around 1792 and was rebuilt with the spire added at that time. There have been a number of restorations over the years, including in 1830, by Edwin Henry Lingen Barker in 1893 and in 1992 when it was re-roofed, re-floored and redecorated. The nave has two aisles with five bays. There is a clerestory or set of windows in the nave above the aisles. The three storey west tower has a peal of six bells and is topped with an octagonal stone spire with the 1792 weathercock at 180 feet. In the church is a sundial, originally positioned at the school. It was presented by Lady Maud Probert in 1689 and depicts Harold's Stones on one side, the motte described as "Magna Mole" on another and the Virtuous Well on a third. There is a concrete replica outside. The preaching cross in the churchyard dates from the 15th century but the upper part is a restoration. There is the two step base and socket stone of a wayside cross at Trellech Cross three quarters of a mile south of the village.

Ebenezer was built in 1838 as a Bible Christian chapel and is now Trellech Methodist Church.

In a field east of the Llandogo Road is the Virtuous Well, also known as St Anne's Well. This medieval well has a stone surround and was known for its healing properties, said to have been particularly beneficial for eye and women's conditions, the water being rich in iron.

Trelech Church by Sir Richard Colt Hoare

The old village school opposite the church was built in 1820 and is now the village hall. The Croft south of the church is said to have been the village school from 1691 to 1820. The building next door was the Crown Inn, later the village Green Inn and Restaurant but closed at the time of writing. Some suggest that it dates from 1684, but the appearance is early 19th century. Opposite the church is the early 18th century Lion Inn. Court Farm was originally known as Court House. Built in the early 17th century it was purchased by John Rumsey from the Seymour family in 1697, becoming a farmhouse in 1846 when the Rumseys left.

Trellech is a conservation area with new building restricted to the north and east of the old village.

Trelleck Grange

The hamlet of Trelleck Grange is situated two and a half miles south of Trellech. Ecclesia mainuon id est villa guicon, identified as Trelleck Grange was mentioned in 960 and was granted by Gilbert de Clare to Tintern Abbey in 1138. It became a grange supplying food to the abbey with a corn mill, smithy farm and chapel. The chapel of ease has no known dedication and while medieval in origin was subject to a major refurbishment in 1860-62 by John Prichard and John Pollard Seddon. It is a single cell structure with a south door and a western bellcote. It is surrounded by Chapel Farm. Three quarters of a mile to the south-east is the Fountain Inn.

Trethomas

Situated to the east of Bedwas, Trethomas is a 20th century village built by William James Thomas, one of the owners of the Bedwas Navigation Colliery to accommodate miners at that colliery which started production in 1912 (see Bedwas). The original name was the English form Thomastown. In addition to the colliery there was the British Benzol and Coal Distillation Ltd coke and by-products plant opened in 1929. Up to 53 coke ovens produced gas which supplied Newport. By-products included ammonia, naphtha, benzol, pitch, sulphuric acid, tar, creosote, benzene and toluene. The plant closed in 1986 but the site is heavily polluted. Prior to the building of the village Cwmyglo Colliery had opened in 1873 and closed in 1893, south of Newport Road.

The oldest building in the village is the Ty'n y Pwll public house which was formerly a toll gate house and the locals still refer to it as the 'Pike' after the Turnpike road.

The village follows the usual pattern of terraced streets, many named after Thomas family members.

Peniel Welsh Independent Chapel on Newport Road was built around 1900. It is now a day nursery. Trinity Calvinistic Methodist Chapel on Standard Street has been rebuilt as Trethomas Christian Fellowship Church. Salem Welsh Calvinistic Methodist Chapel was built before 1911 on the corner of Standard and Navigation Streets. It has been demolished and a bungalow now occupies the site. The site of Tabernacle Baptist Chapel on Newport Road is now occupied by a fish bar. There was a cluster of churches and chapels on Navigation Street near the school. This included a Roman Catholic Church, a Primitive Methodist Church which became a Pentecostal church known as Bethany Chapel Assembly of God and Trethomas Church of the Church in Wales. All have been demolished making way for car parks and new houses with the exception of Trethomas Church which has been rebuilt as St Thomas Community Church.

The village has an array of shops including a Tesco Express, a junior school and a health centre. There has been some new building in Trethomas but major expansion has taken place to the east with the Graig y Rhacca estates which have their own school.

Underwood
Five miles north-east of Newport and just south of the M4, Underwood is a modern housing development built on the site of a World War II Prisoner of War camp. There was a sports and leisure centre which closed in 2013. Llanmartin Primary School is located in the village where there is a community centre, church and other amenities on Birch Grove.

Undy (Welsh: Gwndy)
Undy, eight miles east of Newport, lies to the east of Magor with the two villages expanding to meet. The origin of the name is unclear, it was first recorded as Wundi in the 13th century.

Undy is divided by the main London to Cardiff railway, with the older part south of the track.

St Mary's church dates from the 12th century and contains a 13th century chancel arch. A central tower was replaced in 1880 with a heavy bell turret by John Prichard. The bell dates from the 14th century and is inscribed 'Virgini Marie Laudes'. The font is 12th century. A small church with just 84 sittings, there is a nave, chancel, south porch and north vestry. Outside are the remains of a medieval churchyard cross. The graveyard has been extended and includes the area of the former village pound. The National School of 1871 stands to the west of the church while to the east was the smithy. Vinegar Hill was a separate hamlet, said to have been named after the Battle of Vinegar Hill in the Irish Rebellion of 1798.

In the field alongside Pembroke Court there is the clearly defined moat of a medieval house.

The village has seen a major expansion along with Magor and is now a commuter village enjoying good links to the M4.

Upper Redbrook
The hamlet of Upper Redbrook, two and a half miles south-east of Monmouth, straddles the border between Monmouthshire and

Gloucestershire, with the brook leading down to the Wye forming the boundary.

Redbrook was an important industrial centre with corn mills, iron, tin and copper works. Above the valley on the Monmouthshire side was the Redbrook Old Forge with an incline railway, the bridge for which still crosses the road. There were two pubs, the Queen's Head and the Founder's Arms together with the Redbrook Brewery, though Brewery Terrace lies on the Gloucestershire side.

Varteg (Welsh: Farteg or Y Farteg)

Varteg lies between Abersychan and Blaenavon and was established following the opening of an iron furnace in 1802 by Knight and Company. By 1839 there were five blast furnaces in operation which from 1854 were operated by the Golynos Iron Co. in conjunction with works at Golynos and Pentwyn. The ironworks occupied a site to the west of the post war council estate. The ironworks closed in 1868 and employment in the village relied on the mining industry.

In 1860 the Varteg Hill Colliery was opened by John Vipond, producing coal and iron ore linked to mine and calcinating kilns and by an incline to the Monmouthshire Railway at Cwmavon with a later branch line replacing the incline. Up to 970 men were employed and the mine continued in operation until 1957.

Little of the old village of Varteg remains. Streets with imaginative names such as Twenty Houses, Ten Houses and Four Houses as well as Teetotal Row, Incline Row, Slate Row, Cross Row and The Square have all disappeared. Of the pre-1880 housing only Pembroke Place, Kear's Row and Gladstone Terrace remain, together with the Crown Hotel, (formerly the Varteg Brewery) and the Wesleyan Methodist Chapel. Salisbury Terrace was built by 1901. Varteg Wesleyan Methodist Chapel was built in 1824 and rebuilt in 1868. It is now the Varteg Community Centre. Varteg Primitive Methodist Chapel was built in 1875 but has since been demolished. Zion Pentecostal Chapel is a modern prefabricated building now Sardis Congregational Chapel. The village had a school in 1882 to the north of the Wesleyan Methodist Chapel, the foundations of which are still visible. An Infants' school was built by 1900 on the site of what is now the Welsh Medium Ysgol Bryn Onnen.

In 2013 attempts by the Welsh Language Commissioner to change the official spelling to the Welsh form Y Farteg were dropped after being met with local opposition fearing that an Anglicized pronunciation would open the village to ridicule. It is thought that the name is a corruption of Y Farch Teg meaning Fair Steed.

Wattsville
Wattsville is a former mining village in the Sirhowy valley a little over a mile west of Cross Keys.

The village was built to accommodate miners at the New Risca and Nine Mile Point Collieries covered under Crosskeys and Cwmfelinfach. The name derives from the Watts of Watts, Ward & Co. who sunk the New Risca Colliery before merging with the London and South Wales Colliery Company.

By 1900 there were two terraces along the south side of what is now Islwyn Road. The rest of the village followed over the next 14 years.

Wattsville Methodist Chapel was built on Islwyn Road in the early 20th century and demolished by 2000. The site. next to the bus stop, is undeveloped. Zion Congregationalist Chapel on Hafod Tudor Terrace was built in the early years of the 20th century but has been replaced by a private house. Bethel Church in the Community at the end of Duffryn Terrace was built as Wattsville Baptist Church in 1905.

There has been little development in Wattsville which enjoys woodland on both sides of the valley with the Sirhowy Country Park to the south. Colliery sites to the east and west are now industrial estates. There is just one shop and no public houses.

Whitebrook (Welsh: Gwenffrewd)
Whitebrook is named after the stream which flows through the wooded valley down to the Wye, four and a half miles south-east of Monmouth.

The village which is a ribbon development owes its existence to the stream which powered a number of mills and factories.

In 1606 the Whitebrook Wireworks were established, an offshoot of the Tintern Wireworks. These were situated above the valley in woodland at the end of Pool Lane, accessible from The Narth. The water power was provided by a leat of over a mile in length. The works operated until 1720 and some of the buildings can be found in the woods. Paper mills developed in the valley from 1760. The Glynn Mill operated between 1800 and 1850 at the lower end of the valley. The mill pond, dam and mill-race survive at what is now Whitebrook Farm with the manager's house now the farmhouse. Next up the valley were Bridget's Mills, later Wye Valley Mills. These were small hand mills producing paper. The manager's house is now a private dwelling with the leat forming a garden feature. The Clearwater Mill was the first paper mill in the valley established in 1760. From 1863 there was a steam powered paper making machine in addition to a water turbine and the undershot wheel. The mill collapsed in 1875 leading to closure. Farther up the valley were the Sunnyside and Fernside paper mills and the New Mills corn mill. There was also a grist mill on the Manor Brook.

Holy Trinity church was built as a chapel of ease to Llandogo after 1840. A Church of England school was attached. It is now a private dwelling. A Particular Baptist chapel was built in 1829 on the hillside south of the church. The three storey Bell public house next to the church is now a private house but the village has the Michelin starred Crown at Whitebrook restaurant with its accommodation.

The cast-iron Bigsweir Bridge over the Wye, south of the village, dates from 1825. It was built at Merthyr Tydfil and has a span of 160 feet. The bridge takes its name from Bigsweir House on the English side of the river, the home of the Rooke family whose members included Admiral Sir George Rooke, who captured Gibraltar in 1704 and General Sir Henry Willoughby Rooke who fought at Waterloo. Florence, an Anglo-Swiss cottage residence, now a guest house, was built as the shooting seat of Captain George Rooke, the General's son. The dilapidated toll house still stands on the Welsh side of the bridge.

Whitson

On the Caldicot Levels seven miles south-east of Newport is the little village of Whitson. The name is thought to derive from Old English meaning Wid's settlement. It stands on land reclaimed from the sea by the monks and is below the high tide level. The fields are characteristically small with drainage ditches.

The now closed medieval parish church, known locally as St Mary's, has its origins in the 12th century and was refurbished in the 19th century. The most unusual feature is the tower with its polygonal stair turret with conical stone roof. Bethesda Independent Chapel was built in 1840 and rebuilt in 1900 but is now a private dwelling. The 1870 National School now forms two houses.

Whitson Court, formerly Whitson House, is thought to have been designed by John Nash for William Phillips of Whitson who had been High Sheriff in 1761. The family were prominent in Newport with another William Phillips of Whitson a magistrate at the time of the Chartist riot in 1839. The Phillips family resided at the house until the death of St. John Knox Rickards Phillips in 1901. The house was then used as a convent and training school for African missionaries until 1917 when the estate was sold. The Court remained empty until 1933 when Mr Garroway Smith took up residence together with his brother-in-law Mr William Maybury and his family. It remained in the Maybury family until the death of Olive Maybury at the age of 99 in 1998. During this time the grounds became a zoo with a number of bears, a lion, monkeys and exotic birds. The zoo closed in 1980 and the animals which were regarded as family pets were sent to zoos or safari parks or allowed to live out their remaining lives on the estate. Whitson Court lay empty for some time but was sold in 2008 and renovation carried out under the guidance of Cadw.

A small airfield operated at Upfield Farm between 1995 and 2009.

Wilcrick (Welsh: Chwilgrug)

Wilcrick is a deserted medieval village with just three farms, a church, one cottage and a single new house, a mile west of Magor below Wilcrick Hill. The name is thought to mean a mound infested with beetles, though other interpretation offer Bare Hill or Willow Rock. Roger de Wilcrick is mentioned in 1297. The earthworks of the village are in the field south of Church Farm. The wooded Willcrick Hill is the site of a double banked and ditched Iron Age hillfort. The little church of St Mary the Virgin was rebuilt in 1860 and is still in use. It has a nave, chancel, western bellcote and south porch. The font is 12th century and there is a pedestal sundial. John Wesley visited the church in 1741.

Wolvesnewton (Welsh: Llanwynnell)

Wolvesnewton is small scattered village five miles west of Usk. The earliest reference to it was in 1160 when it was known as Nova Villa. It was later known as Nous villa lupi in 1348 after Radulfi Lupi or Ralph le Wolf, the lord of the manor in 1193 with the family still holding the manor in 1398. The Welsh Llanwynell would indicate a dedication of the church to St Gwynnell though it is to St Thomas á Becket though St Gwynell's Well is mentioned in 1425.

The church which is to the north of the Devauden to Llangwm road dates from the 13th century. It had opposing north and south nave doors though the north door has been blocked. Some windows date from the 15th -16th century and there was a refurbishment by John Norton in 1855 when the vestry was added. The interior furnishings are Victorian while the tower contains a peal of three bells dated 1607, 1680 and 1682, recast in 1914. The west tower has a saddleback roof and in addition to the south porch there is a priest's door. There is a restored four step churchyard cross and a spring to the east of the church.

Cwrt y Gaer Farm to the west of the church is built on an ancient fortified position and was the home of the le Wolf family. The moat still remains to the south and west. A little under a mile south-west of the church is the Model Farm built around 1840 for the Duke of Beaufort. The complex consists of the farmhouse, corn mill now converted to housing and the unique barn and stable of cruciform shape extending from a central octagonal building, also converted for housing. The Model Farm was for a time the site of a folk museum and craft centre. To the west of the farm in the parish of Llangwm is Gaer Fawr, a ten acre Iron Age hillfort with multiple ramparts.

Wonastow (Welsh: Llanwarw)

Wonastow is a scattered parish with the church of St Wonnow two miles south-west of Monmouth just off the old Raglan road.

St Wonnow is identified by Baring-Gould as St Winwaloe, a 5th century saint the son of Fracan, cousin of Cado Duke of Cornwall and Gwen of the three breasts who emigrated to Brittany. Winwaloe's name is spelt in at least 50 different ways. According to one story, a gander flew at Winwaloe's little sister, Creirwe, and actually swallowed the eyeball, but Winwaloe replaced it in its socket, and the girl suffered no ill effects. The church, located behind Wonastow Court, is screened from the road by trees. A small building, medieval in origin but restored in 1860-63 in memory of Sir William 8th Baronet of Chevet and Dame Mary Milborne Swinnerton-Pilkington. It contains a 1913 rood screen and chancel reredos by G.E. Halliday. The tower is of three storeys plus a wooden belfry containing two bells under a pyramidal roof. The porch is in the Arts and Crafts style of 1909 funded by Sir John and Lady Adela Searle. The churchyard cross has a restored shaft and crosshead. Court Farm lies south of the church.

Wonastow Court was built by Sir William Herbert of Troy (died 1557), the illegitimate son of William, first Earl of Pembroke. In 1552 Wonastow Court was bought by his brother Sir Thomas Herbert and remained in the family until passing by marriage to George Milborne of Milborne Port in Somerset in the early 17th century. Again through marriage it passed to Sir William Pilkington, Bart. The house was rebuilt around 1803 though by 1952 it was derelict but has since been renovated. Wonastow House to the north of the Court was built in 1800 as St Wonnow's Vicarage. To the east of the house is the site of a small Roman fort.

A mile and a half west of the church is Tre-owen, according to Pevsner the most important early 17th century house in Monmouthshire. The Manor of Tre-owen was awarded to Sir Peter Huntley after the Norman conquest of Gwent and remained in the family until the 15th century when Sir Thomas Huntley died without male issue and Margaret Huntley, one of five daughters, inherited the manors of Tre-owen and Llanarth. Margaret married David ap Jenkins ap Howel, Lord of Cefn-dwy-glwyd and their great-grandson William Jones was Standard Bearer to Henry VIII, adopting the English form of surname. (See Llanarth for further details of lineage.) William's great-grandson, also William Jones inherited a large fortune from his uncle Philip Jones, a member of the Grocer's Guild and a Merchant Adventurer as well as MP for Monmouth Borough from 1588 to 1593, and built the present building 1615-27. William's son was Sir Phillip Jones, whose wife was a member of the Marquess of Worcester's family. Sir Phillip was Sheriff of Monmouthshire in 1642 and a defender of Raglan Castle during the siege after which his estates were confiscated and only returned after payment of a fine. Sir Phillip died in 1659 and his widow Elizabeth remained at Tre-owen and it became a centre for Roman Catholicism. Meanwhile the heir to Tre-owen, William Jones had established the family seat at Llanarth Court. After Lady Jones' death Tre-owen was let to a series of tenant farmers. In 1848 the owner of Llanarth Court and Tre-owen, John Arthur Edward Jones changed the family name to Herbert and his son, Ivor John Caradoc Herbert was raised to the peerage as Lord Treowen in 1917. He spent considerable sums renovating Tre-owen before his death in 1933. The estate passed to his nephew, Sir John Arthur Herbert, Governor General of Bengal who died in Calcutta in 1943 and Tre-owen was sold to the sitting tenant Mr Davies in 1945. In 1954 it was bought by a stockbroker, Harry Wheelock for his son, Richard Hugh Wheelock and remains in the Wheelock family, now run as a wedding and conference venue offering accommodation to large parties. The top floor and attic of the front range were removed in the 18th century but the building otherwise remains in its original form. It is Grade I Listed.

Wyesham

Wyesham stands on the eastern side of the River Wye, across the bridge from Monmouth and is in effect a suburb of the town, but the area stretches up the hill known as the Kymin and south along the bank of the Wye which is the site of the Monmouth Showground. Mayhill, Wyesham and Upper Redbrook were hamlets in the parish of Dixton until the church of St James was built at Wyesham in 1875. Mayhill was the industrial area of Monmouth, with railway station, gas works, brick and lime works, water works and steam saw mills. Wyesham in the 1890s was a small hamlet. The main expansion in housing came after 1945 and into the 1960s and 70s. Mayhill is still a commercial area, but with sports and recreation facilities as well as industrial units. The Mayhill Hotel was Mayhill House.

St James Church was designed by John Pollard Seddon and was a chapel of ease to St Peter's at Dixton. Built in the Early English style, it consists of a chancel, nave, and a north western tower containing one bell. The saddleback roof had a wooden spire but this has disappeared. The former school and teacher's house next to the church was also designed by Seddon and built at the same time as the church. It is now the St James Community Hall. The village has a modern primary school.

The Duke of Beaufort Bridge was one of two railway bridges crossing the Wye here. It carried a single track of the Hereford Ross and Gloucester Railway with three spans of steel lattice girders on paired steel tubular piers. It is now a footbridge. 140 yards away are the approach viaducts of the 1861 Wye Viaduct of the Coleford, Monmouth, Usk and Pontypool Railway which closed in 1964. The central span has been removed.

Above Wyesham is the Kymin, an 800 foot hill which has been popular with tourists since the 18th century. Originally part of the Duke of Beaufort's estate it is now a National Trust property. In 1794 the Kymin Tower or Belvedere was built affording extensive views over nine counties. Nearby is the Naval Temple, erected in 1800 to celebrate the 2nd anniversary of the Battle of the Nile. It is a small building topped by an arch surmounted by a statue of Britannia on her rock. On the walls are the names of sixteen admirals. Nelson visited in 1802 and breakfasted at the tower. He commented "it was the only monument of its kind erected to the Royal Navy in the Kingdom". There is also the bowling green, used as a recreation ground.

Wyllie

Wyllie is a former mining village in the Sirhowy valley a little over a mile south of Pontllanfraith. It takes its name from Colonel Alexander Wyllie a director of the Tredegar Iron and Coal Company which started the mine in 1924. Wyllie Colliery was situated to the south of the village which was built to accommodate the miners. It was the company's last pit and employed up to 830 men, closing in 1968. The village had a halt on the London and North Western Railway which also served the colliery but has now closed.

A Methodist Church was built on The Avenue, but has been replaced by a block of flats called Marion Jones Court. Opposite the church was the Miners' Institute and Library, now the Islwyn Inn.

The major part of the village was built by the colliery but there has been modern development partly on the site of the colliery, taking advantage of a quiet village with views across the valley. Caerphilly Council Social Services has offices in the village in a modern building shaped like a boomerang.

Ynysddu Black River Meadow

The village which lies between Wyllie and Cwmfelinfach was founded in the early 19th century by a local landowner John Hodder Moggridge, a Unitarian from Bradford on Avon in Wiltshire. He also founded Blackwood and was known for his enlightened views in providing houses with gardens. The houses built in Ynysddu were around the Black Prince but have long disappeared. Moggridge married the daughter of Lewis Weston Dillwyn the Swansea industrialist.

The village was still small and described as a hamlet in 1901 though it did have a board school built in 1877 and the Black Prince Inn. It was after 1901 that the village expanded with its rows of terraced houses, built to accommodate the miners of nearby Cwmfelinfach. Ynys-Ddu Methodist Chapel was built in 1895 on the old tramroad, now the B4251 next to the Black Prince. By 2001 it had been demolished and the site was used for car sales. Twyn Gwyn Baptist Chapel was built in 1829, above the village on Twyn Gwyn Road. It is now a private dwelling. Sardis Congregational Chapel off High Street was built in 1909 and is still in use. St Theodore's Church was built in 1925 in the Gothic style between Ynysddu and Cwmfelinfach on a north-west south-east axis. There is a nave, chancel, vestry and a north-west porch under a bellcote and window. It is still in use.

The village expanded across the Sirhowy where there was a station on the London and North Western Railway, now dismantled. The Ynysddu Hotel is on this side of the river. There has been some building in the village which has a primary school and playing fields, the two pubs, the Ynysddu Progressive Workingmen's Club and a number of takeaways. There is woodland to the west and farmland to the east on the gently sloping valley sides.

Bibliography

Barber, J.T. 1803. *A Tour Throughout South Wales And Monmouthshire.*
Baring-Gould, Sabine. 1905. *A Book of South Wales.*
Baring-Gould, Sabine and Fisher, John. 1913, 2005 reprint. *The Lives of the British Saints: The Saints of Wales, Cornwall and Irish Saints.* Kessinger Publishing 2005.
Bradney, Sir Joseph Alfred. 1907. *The History of Monmouthshire from the Coming of the Normans Into Wales Down to the Present Time.* Mitchell, Hughes and Clarke.
Burke's Genealogical and Heraldic Dictionary of the Peerage and Baronetage of the British Empire, 1869.
Burke's Genealogical and Heraldic History of the Landed Gentry, 1879.
Cliffe, Charles Frederick. 1848. *The Book of South Wales, the Bristol Channel, Monmouthshire, and the Wye.*
Coxe, William. 1801. *An Historical Tour in Monmouthshire.*
Davies, Canon E.T. 1977. *A Guide to the Ancient Churches of Gwent.* Hughes & Son.
Davies, John Reuben. 2003.*The Book of Llandaf and the Norman Church in Wales.* Boydell Press.
Evans, C.J.O. 1953. *Monmouthshire, Its History and Topography.* W Lewis.
Hall, Mrs. S.C. 1861. *The book of South Wales, the Wye, and the Coast.*
Knight, Jeremy. 2013. *South Wales: From the Romans to the Normans.* Amberley Publishing.
Lewis, Samuel. 1848. *A Topographical Dictionary of England.*
Morgan, Richard. 2005. *Place-names of Gwent.* Gwasg Carreg Gwalch.
Newman, John. 2000. *Gwent/Monmouthshire - Pevsner Architectural Guides Pevsner buildings of Wales series The buildings of Wales.* Yale University Press.
Roscoe, Thomas and Meredith, Mrs. Charles. 1844. *Wanderings and excursions in South Wales: with the scenery of the river Wye.*
Williams, David. 1796. *The History of Monmouthshire.*
Wyndham, Henry Penruddocke. *A gentleman's Tour Through Monmouthshire and Wales in 1774.*

Online Resources
www.genuki.org.uk/big/wa
National Library of Wales Dictionary of Welsh Biography
http://welshjournals.llgc.org.uk/.
http://www.celticchristianity.infinitesoulutions.com/Book_of_Llandaff_source.html
www.map.coflein.gov.uk
www.britishlistedbuildings.co.uk
Kelly's Directory of Monmouthshire 1901
 (http://freepages.genealogy.rootsweb.ancestry.com/)